VIRTUE, VICE, AND VALUE

VIRTUE, VICE, AND VALUE

Thomas Hurka

OXFORD
UNIVERSITY PRESS

OXFORD

UNIVERSITY PRESS

Oxford   New York

Auckland   Bangkok   Buenos Aires   Cape Town   Chennai
Dar es Salaam   Delhi   Hong Kong   Istanbul   Karachi   Kolkata
Kuala Lumpur   Madrid   Melbourne   Mexico City   Mumbai   Nairobi
São Paulo   Shanghai   Singapore   Taipei   Tokyo   Toronto

Published by Oxford University Press, Inc.
198 Madison Avenue, New York, New York 10016

www.oup.com

First issued as an Oxford University Press paperback, 2003

Oxford is a registered trademark of Oxford University Press.

Library of Congress Cataloging-in-Publication Data
Hurka, Thomas, 1952–
Virtue, vice, and value / by Thomas Hurka.
p. cm.
Includes bibliographical references and index.
ISBN 0-19-513716-7 (cloth); 0-19-515865-2 (paper)
1. Virtue. I. Title.
BJ171.V55H87   2000
179'.9—dc21   00-022588

1 3 5 7 9 8 6 4 2

Printed in the United States of America
on acid-free paper

FOR TERRY AND ALEX

Preface

Few philosophical ideas are new, and that is certainly true of the ideas in this book. As I point out near its start, the main elements of the account of virtue it defends were widely accepted in what I think was a golden age for moral theory, the period from Sidgwick to Ross and including, as defenders of the account, Brentano, Moore, Rashdall, and Ross himself. The book's ideas also had to be urged on me by two people. One was my wife, Terry Teskey, whose unfortunately never written Ph.D. thesis on the morality of fantasy would have argued that it is wrong to take pleasure in the thought of what it would be wrong to do. The other was Donald Regan, who was familiar with similar ideas from Moore. Only after numerous conversations with them did I realize how worth developing these ideas were.

The book is in one way a continuation of my earlier book *Perfectionism* and in another way a departure from it. The book still discusses perfectionist value theory: now the view that virtue is good and vice evil regardless of a person's attitude to them. But this particular view was excluded from *Perfectionism,* for two reasons. That book discussed versions of perfectionism that ground the human good in human nature, and I still think the constraints implicit in that project preclude any intrinsic preference for virtue over vice. But for most of the time I was writing *Perfectionism* I also thought, more generally, that no version of perfectionism, given its consequentialist structure, can value virtue more than instrumentally. The recursive account of virtue in the present book shows that that more general thought was mistaken.

While writing this book I have been helped by many people. I have discussed its ideas over many years with my colleague Dennis McKerlie, whose influence is present throughout and especially in chapter 8. I have also benefited from numerous conversations with Don LePan, not an academic philosopher but, perhaps more useful, a sound intelligence from outside the discipline. My wife, Terry, has patiently helped me edit the book's successive drafts.

Donald Regan and Shelly Kagan pointed out inadequacies in my initial treatment of the mathematics of virtue in chapter 3; Peter Gibson, then a Ph.D. student in mathematics at the University of Calgary, showed me how to correct them and also prepared the book's graphs. I am grateful to all three for their help with material I could not have handled on my own.

I was able to hire Peter as a research assistant using the second of two Standard Research Grants I was awarded for this project by the Social Sciences and Humanities Research Council of Canada. I am grateful to the council for its support, and to the Killam Foundation for a Killam Resident Fellowship at the University of Calgary in 1996.

The book's penultimate version benefited from the comments, especially about its structure, of Peter Vallentyne and another, anonymous, referee for Oxford University Press. And Peter Ohlin of the Press had the good sense to give me a deadline and make it sound serious.

The book has been improved at many particular points by suggestions from individual students, colleagues, and audience members at talks I have given. I have not recorded these particular debts within the text of the book, since as a reader I find that practice distracting. But I would like to express my thanks to Donald Ainslie, Miri Albahari, Julia Annas, Gustaf Arrhenius, Brenda Baker, Lawrence Becker, Samantha Brennan, Todd Calder, Ruth Chang, Brian Chellas, Thomas Christiano, Roger Crisp, Stephen Darwall, Julia Driver, Jill Gatfield, Allan Gibbard, Philip Hanson, Brad Hooker, Vicki Igneski, Frances Kamm, Ali Kazmi, Samuel Kerstein, Robert McKim, David Mellow, Cheryl Misak, Sean O'Riordan, Derek Parfit, Karen Pilkington, Peter Railton, Arthur Ripstein, Michael Slote, Wayne Sumner, Christine Swanton, Mark Thornton, John Thorp, Scott Woodcock, Robert Woodrow, and Michael Zimmerman. To those others whose help I have forgotten, I apologize for my vice of indifference.

Articles based on earlier versions of the book's chapters have appeared previously in journals and anthologies. I would like to thank the relevant editors and presses for permission to reproduce material from the following: "Virtue as Loving the Good," *Social Philosophy and Policy* 9, no. 2 (1992); "Monism, Pluralism, and Rational Regret," *Ethics* 106 (1996); "The Justification of National Partiality," in

The Morality of Nationalism, ed. Robert McKim and Jeff McMahan (Oxford University Press, 1997); "Self-Interest, Altruism, and Virtue," *Social Philosophy and Policy* 14, no. 1 (1997); "How Great a Good Is Virtue?" *Journal of Philosophy* 95 (1998); and "The Three Faces of Flourishing," *Social Philosophy and Policy* 16, no. 1 (1999).

Contents

VIRTUE, VICE, AND VALUE

They smiled at the good
and frowned at the bad

Ludwig Bemelmans,
Madeline

1

The Recursive Account

One task of moral theory is to explore the relationships between the fundamental moral properties of goodness, rightness, and virtue. Different substantive theories understand these relationships in different ways. For example, consequentialist theories take goodness to be explanatorily prior to rightness, which they always characterize in terms of goodness, whereas deontological theories treat rightness as at least partly independent of goodness. And this difference has profound implications for many further claims these theories make.

In recent philosophy the third moral property, virtue, has mostly been understood in either of two extreme ways. One view defines virtue as a disposition to produce what is otherwise good or to do what is otherwise right, thereby giving it only derivative and instrumental significance. Virtue may be crucial practically, if inculcating it is the best means of ensuring that people fulfill their moral responsibilities. But theoretically it has no intrinsic importance. The contrary view makes virtue the central property in a distinctive moral theory called virtue ethics, which is proposed as a fundamental alternative to consequentialism and deontology. Far from defining virtue as a means to goodness or rightness, this view treats it as primary, so that what is right and even what is good are identified by some relation to virtue. Virtue has sufficient importance to generate a comprehensive approach to ethics, one where it plays the foundational role.

The aim of this book is to develop an account of virtue intermediate between these extremes. The account treats virtue as intrinsically good, or good apart from its consequences, and it likewise treats vice as intrinsically evil. A person's having virtuous desires, motives, and feelings by itself makes her life better, and her having vicious attitudes makes it worse. But the account does not call for any new theory such as virtue ethics. It can be accommodated within a more familiar theory and, more specifically, within a theory that many think excludes it, namely consequentialism. The account is not confined to consequentialism, and in a later chapter I will show how it can be extended in a deontological setting. But its central claims are consistent with consequentialism, so it gives a consequentialist account of the intrinsic values of virtue and vice. Virtue and vice are good and evil in themselves, but in a way that satisfies consequentialist assumptions.

As I have said, many philosophers think this kind of account is impossible. Before developing it, I need to determine whether, given what consequentialism is, it can indeed value virtue intrinsically.

1. *Consequentialism and Virtue?*

Consequentialist moral theories are distinguished by the central role they give the properties of intrinsic goodness and evil. They take these properties, as had by states of affairs, to be the primary moral properties, and they characterize all other moral properties in terms of goodness and evil. Thus, standard consequentialist theories identify right actions by the quantity of good and evil in their outcome, so that, for example, right actions are always those with the best outcomes, or whose outcomes contain the greatest surplus of good over evil. In the bulk of this book I will assume that consequentialism identifies rightness in this way. But the more general definition of this position says it characterizes all other moral properties by some relation to intrinsic goodness and evil.

Despite agreeing that goodness and evil are primary, different consequentialists understand these properties in slightly different ways. Some, such as G. E. Moore, take goodness to be a simple, unanalyzable property had by some states of affairs.[1] Others, notably Franz Brentano, analyze goodness in terms of the correctness or appropriateness of certain emotions, so "we call a thing *good* when the love relating to it is correct."[2] Yet others analyze goodness in terms of reasons or oughts, so the good is what people have reason or ought to desire or pursue. Henry Sidgwick says the good is what one would desire if one's desires "were in harmony with reason," where

---

1. Moore, *Principia Ethica*, chap. 1.
2. Brentano, *The Origin of Our Knowledge of Right and Wrong*, p. 18.

reason is a faculty that apprehends "oughts."[3] Similarly, Shelly Kagan writes, "to say that from the moral standpoint one outcome is objectively better than another, is to say that *everyone* has a reason to choose the better outcome."[4]

Despite their differences, these three views about goodness are closely connected. Those who, like Moore, understand goodness as an unanalyzable property usually agree with Brentano that loving what is good is correct. They merely deny that a state's goodness is reducible to this correctness; it is something separate and more fundamental that explains the correctness. Similarly, both Moore and Brentano agree that agents have reason to desire or pursue what is good, but they deny that a state's goodness is reducible to the existence of this reason. The goodness is again something more fundamental that explains the reason. Most consequentialists, in short, accept Sidgwick's and Kagan's claims about the good. It is just that some, such as Brentano, add one and others, such as Moore, add two more foundational claims that explain them.

Given these connections, we can for the most part abstract from the differences between the three views when discussing the goodness of virtue. More specifically, we can assume those claims about goodness that are shared by all consequentialists while remaining agnostic about any further claims. We can assume that to call a state good is to say at least that agents have reason to desire or pursue it; it may also be to say that love of the state is correct or that the state has an unanalyzable property, but we can ignore these further possibilities. To say that virtue is intrinsically good, we can assume, is to give it the same status, whatever exactly that is, as any other good in a consequentialist theory.[5]

---

3. Sidgwick, *The Methods of Ethics,* p. 112; see also my *Perfectionism,* pp. 57–58.

4. Kagan, *The Limits of Morality,* p. 161. Note that Kagan's definition is of what I later call "agent-neutral" goodness.

5. In abstracting from these issues we can also abstract from issues about moral realism and anti-realism, issues about whether judgments ascribing moral properties such as goodness can be objectively true or, on the contrary, express only sentiments or feelings. All three views about goodness are compatible with moral realism, but they are also compatible with anti-realism. On an anti-realist interpretation, the last two views take judgments ascribing goodness to have a distinctive subject matter: they express sentiments about emotions, actions, or desires rather than about other possible objects. On an anti-realist interpretation, the first view takes judgments ascribing goodness to express a qualitatively distinct sentiment, one that grounds other moral sentiments. Here the claim that goodness is a simple, unanalyzable property is read as the claim that it expresses a simple, unanalyzable sentiment. But all three views are compatible with both realism and anti-realism and can therefore be discussed independently of them.

Consequentialists can also disagree about what makes goodness "intrinsic." A strict view, defended by Moore, says that a state's intrinsic goodness can depend only on its intrinsic properties, that is, properties it has independently of any relations to other states. When value is "intrinsic," Moore writes, "the question whether a thing possesses it, and in what degree it possesses it, depends solely on the intrinsic nature of the thing in question."[6] A looser view equates intrinsic goodness just with non-instrumental goodness, or with that portion of the overall goodness of the world that is located in or assignable to a particular state. It is the state's own goodness, whatever its basis, rather than some other's.[7] Unlike the strict view, this looser one allows a state's intrinsic goodness to be affected by its relational properties. For example, it allows the view that a state such as knowledge is intrinsically good only when accompanied by desire for or pleasure in it for itself.[8] But again, we need not choose between these views when developing an account of virtue. On the few occasions when the difference between them is relevant to the account, this fact can be noted.

Many consequentialisms start from claims about the good that are agent-neutral, with the same force for all moral agents. They make certain states good from all persons' points of view, or good simply, so all persons have reason to pursue the same moral goals. But some consequentialists say their theory can equally well be agent-relative. It can make what is good from different persons' points of view different, so they are directed to different goals. For example, it can say that what is good from each person's point of view is just some state of himself, so he has reason to pursue only that state and no comparable states of others.[9] Whether such agent-relativity is possible depends on our choice among the three views of goodness distinguished above. If goodness is a simple, unanalyzable property, it is hard to see how it can be agent-relative. How can a state have such a property "from one point of view" but not "from" another? Surely it either has the property or not. For this reason, those who accept

6. Moore, "The Conception of Intrinsic Value," p. 260; see also *Principia Ethica*, pp. 93, 95, 187; and *Ethics*, pp. 24, 68. A similar view is defended in Korsgaard, "Two Distinctions in Goodness"; Chisholm, *Brentano and Intrinsic Value*, pp. 52–53; and Lemos, *Intrinsic Value*, pp. 8–11.

7. For discussion of this looser view, see Kagan, "Rethinking Intrinsic Value," and my "Two Kinds of Organic Unity."

8. See Frankena, *Ethics*, pp. 89–92; and Parfit, *Reasons and Persons*, pp. 501–2.

9. See, e.g., Sidgwick, *The Methods of Ethics*, pp. 420–21, 497–98; and Sen, "Rights and Agency."

this view of goodness usually deny the coherence of agent-relative consequentialism.[10] But there is no such difficulty given either of the other two views. If goodness is analyzed in terms of reasons or of the correctness of emotions, a theory can say that each person has reason to desire and pursue only states of himself, or that only his loving states of himself is correct. Since we are assuming only what is common to the three views of goodness, we are free to consider agent-relative consequentialism. That said, I will develop the account of virtue initially in an agent-neutral setting. A later chapter will extend the account to include agent-relative values and, with them, agent-relative virtues. But the initial formulation will be agent-neutral.

A final distinction concerns the content of a consequentialist theory. Subjective or welfarist theories make each person's good depend on certain of her subjective mental states, such as her pleasures or desires. Hedonism, which holds that only pleasure is good and pain evil, is a version of subjectivism, as are theories that equate the good with the fulfillment of desires. Objective or perfectionist theories, by contrast, hold that certain states are good independently of pleasures or desires. Knowledge and achievement, for example, make a person's life better regardless of how much she enjoys or wants them, and their absence impoverishes her life even if it does not cause her regret.

Given this general account of consequentialism, it may seem easy for this type of theory to treat virtue as intrinsically good. It simply adds virtue, or a set of individual virtues such as benevolence, courage, and so on, to its list of basic intrinsic goods, and it likewise adds vice or a set of vices to its list of basic evils. Assuming that we know independently what virtue and vice consist in, it treats them as underivative intrinsic values. Virtue and vice are perfectionist rather than welfarist values, since they make a person's life better or worse regardless of his attitude to them. But in this they are like knowledge, achievement, and other perfectionist values, and they play a standard role in the evaluation of actions. If an action will embody or lead to virtue, this counts in favour of its being right; if to vice, this counts against it.

But this approach—simply adding virtue and vice to a list of underivative values—is not fully or properly consequentialist. If conse-

10. See Moore, *Principia Ethica*, pp. 97–102; and Regan, "Against Evaluator Relativity."

quentialism characterizes *all* other moral properties in terms of goodness and evil, it must characterize virtue and vice in terms of goodness and evil. These, too, are moral properties and require a consequentialist treatment. A fully consequentialist approach cannot assume that we know from elsewhere what virtue and vice consist in but must somehow identify them, as it identifies right actions, by reference to the intrinsic values of states of affairs.

It is this requirement that leads many philosophers to conclude that consequentialism cannot treat virtue as intrinsically good. If it characterizes virtue in terms of goodness and evil, they argue, it must characterize virtue as a disposition to promote good and prevent evil. But this makes virtue in essence instrumentally good, or good because of its consequences. And if virtue is in essence instrumentally good, it cannot at the same time be intrinsically good.

The most careful presentation of this argument is in Sidgwick's *Methods of Ethics.* Sidgwick is defending hedonistic consequentialism against rival versions, including one that says virtue is intrinsically good. He considers both a strong version of this view, that virtue is the only intrinsic good, and a weaker version, that it is one intrinsic good among others.

Against the strong version Sidgwick argues as follows. Virtue, he says, is a disposition to perform morally right actions, where right actions are identified by the quantity of good in their outcome. (He takes himself to have justified this second, consequentialist premise earlier in *The Methods of Ethics.*) Virtue is therefore a disposition to perform actions that promote what is good. And this implies that treating virtue as the only intrinsic good involves a "logical circle": virtue is a disposition that promotes what is good, where what is good is itself just a disposition that promotes what is good.[11]

We may dispute Sidgwick's first premise—his definition of virtue as a disposition to perform right actions. This definition is on the one hand too narrow, because it restricts the expression of virtue to the sphere of action. Though a person can certainly act virtuously, she can also have virtuous desires and feelings that never issue in action—for example, compassion for someone whose pain she is unable to relieve. So the definition excludes some important forms of virtue. On the other hand, Sidgwick's definition is also too broad. It counts as virtuous any disposition that reliably produces right actions, whatever motives that disposition involves.[12] This, too, is

---

11. Sidgwick, *The Methods of Ethics,* p. 392.
12. See Sidgwick, *The Methods of Ethics,* pp. 223–24.

counterintuitive. Imagine that a store owner reliably gives his customers accurate change, but only because he believes that doing so is in his economic self-interest. If his motive is in this way selfish, his disposition, however reliably it produces right actions, does not on most views count as virtuous.

These flaws in his definition of virtue do not substantially affect Sidgwick's first argument, which can be generalized to avoid them. Within consequentialism virtue must be characterized, if not as a disposition that promotes what is good, then in some way by reference to the good. And this means that treating virtue as the only intrinsic good does involve a logical circle. If virtue consists in a relation to other goods, it cannot be the only such good.

As Hastings Rashdall notes in a commentary on Sidgwick, one can accept something close to the premises of this argument yet reject its conclusion, agreeing that virtue must be characterized by reference to some other states yet still holding that it is the only intrinsic good. One can do this if one denies that the other states are good.[13] This is the Stoic view: certain states are "preferred" and provide the criterion for right action but are not themselves intrinsically good. What is good is only a virtuous attitude or relation to these states. But Rashdall agrees that this Stoic view is "in a high degree paradoxical." How can it be right to promote certain states, he asks, and how can they be the defining objects of virtue, if they are not themselves intrinsically good? If states playing these roles must be good, as consequentialism assumes, Sidgwick's first conclusion follows and virtue cannot be the only intrinsic good.

Against the weaker view that virtue is just one intrinsic good among others, Sidgwick's argument is by his own lights less conclusive, but it starts from similar premises. If virtue is a disposition that promotes what is good, it is by definition something instrumentally good. And "it seems difficult to conceive any kind of activity or process as both means and end, from precisely the same point of view and in respect of precisely the same quality."[14] Sidgwick acknowledges that a state can be at once intrinsically and instrumentally good. But he argues that in normal circumstances, different properties give it the two kinds of goodness. If a pleasure is both intrinsically and instrumentally good, its being pleasant is what makes it intrinsically good, while its promoting other pleasures makes it in-

13. Rashdall, "Professor Sidgwick's Utilitarianism," p. 207.
14. Sidgwick, *The Methods of Ethics*, p. 396; see also p. 393.

strumentally good. What Sidgwick finds "difficult to conceive" is that the same property—promoting something good—should give a state at once instrumental and intrinsic value. Yet precisely this would be the case if virtue, defined as a disposition that promotes what is good, were as such intrinsically good.

What Sidgwick finds "difficult to conceive" is impossible given the strict view of intrinsic value, according to which such value must rest on a state's intrinsic properties. But it is not impossible given the looser view. If a state's intrinsic value can depend on its relational properties, it is in principle possible for the instrumentally good to be as such intrinsically good. And in a certain restricted context this view is attractive. Several philosophers argue that when a person pursues a worthwhile goal, his successfully achieving that goal makes his activity intrinsically better than if it had ended in failure. Imagine that someone spends many years working for the preservation of Venice.[15] If after his death Venice is in fact preserved, and in a way that depends on his efforts, this outcome, it is said, makes his labours intrinsically better than if, through no fault of his, Venice had ended in ruins.[16] Here an activity's goodness is enhanced by a causal relation to another good. Nonetheless, even given the looser view, Sidgwick's second argument remains persuasive against its intended target. What is plausible given this view is only the restricted claim that an activity that is already intrinsically good, because it is aimed at a worthwhile goal, will be intrinsically better if its goal is achieved. What Sidgwick challenges is the more radical claim that a disposition's being instrumentally good can be a complete source of intrinsic goodness, or by itself make it intrinsically good. Sidgwick is surely right that this view is "difficult to conceive" in the sense of not being intuitively plausible. If virtue is defined as any disposition that promotes what is good, the view that it is as such an intrinsic good is not credible.

15. Parfit, *Reasons and Persons*, p. 151; there is a related discussed in my *Perfectionism*, pp. 108–12.

16. A claim somewhat similar to this one is allowed by the strict view of intrinsic goodness. Given this view, we cannot say that the preservation of Venice makes the person's activity in pursuit of that goal intrinsically better, but we can say that it makes a whole consisting of his activity plus its outcome plus the causal relation between them intrinsically better. (This claim relies on Moore's "principle of organic unities"; see *Principia Ethica*, pp. 27–36, 92–96, 183–225.) But this latter claim does not seem intuitively right. Surely success in pursuit of a worthwhile goal makes one's pursuit itself, and not just some whole containing it, intrinsically better. See my "Two Kinds of Organic Unity," p. 306.

Given his definition of virtue, then, Sidgwick is right that virtue is not plausibly even one intrinsic good among others. But we have seen that this definition is at once too narrow and too broad. And when his second argument is generalized to assume only that virtue involves some relation to goodness and evil, its persuasiveness disappears. Given only a general consequentialist definition of virtue, the argument can no longer exclude virtue from the list of intrinsic goods. As Rashdall points out, there is an account of the intrinsic goodness of virtue that satisfies consequentialist assumptions, is logically possible, and is intuitively attractive as well. If it incorporates this account, consequentialism can treat virtue as intrinsically good. The account agrees with Sidgwick that virtue must be defined somehow by relation to goodness and evil; it therefore accepts his first conclusion, that virtue cannot be the only intrinsic value. But it maintains against his second conclusion that virtue is one intrinsic value among others. The account takes virtue to consist in a noncausal, and more specifically an intentional, relation to goodness and evil and holds that as this relation, virtue is a further intrinsic good. The account has two principal components: a *recursive characterization of good and evil* and a *definition of virtue and vice* that fits this characterization. Together these components comprise a *recursive account* of the intrinsic goodness of virtue and intrinsic evil of vice. I will now present this recursive account, starting with its first component, the recursive characterization of good and evil.

2. *The Recursive Characterization of Good and Evil*

The idea of a recursive characterization should be familiar to philosophers from the characterization given in elementary logic of a well-formed formula. This characterization starts with a base-clause stating that certain atomic sentences, for example, *a*, *b*, *c*, and *d*, are well-formed formulas. It then adds a recursion-clause, one whose application iterates or recurs, for each logical operator. Thus, the recursion-clause for "or" says that if *X* and *Y* are well-formed formulas, then *X or Y* is a well-formed formula. This makes *a or b* a well-formed formula, and also *(a or b) or c*, *((a or b) or c) or d*, and so on.

The recursive characterization of good and evil has a similar structure. It starts with a base-clause stating that certain states of affairs other than virtue are intrinsically good. For our purposes it is not crucial what these states are, but let us assume the characterization starts with the following *base-clause about goods*, (BG):

(BG) Pleasure, knowledge, and achievement are intrinsically good.

This clause, which combines the welfarist good of pleasure with the perfectionist goods of knowledge and achievement, is agent-neutral. It says that each person's pleasure is good not just from his point of view, but from that of all persons; this means they all have the same reason to pursue his pleasure, as he has a parallel reason to pursue theirs.

Though the specific goods in (BG) could be replaced by others, it will be useful to describe them briefly. The first good, pleasure, is a sensation or feeling distinguished by an introspectible quality of pleasantness.[17] This quality can vary in intensity, with more intense pleasures having more intrinsic value. The quality of pleasantness can never be experienced on its own; it is always accompanied by other introspectible qualities that vary among pleasure sensations and make, say, the pleasure of suntanning introspectively very different from that of eating ice cream. In this it is like the loudness of sounds.[18] Loudness is an introspectible quality of sounds and can be used to rank them, but it cannot be experienced apart from other qualities of pitch, timbre, and so on. Among pleasures as so defined, there is an important division between the simple and the intentional. Simple pleasures, such as that of suntanning, are unstructured sensations with the quality of pleasantness and other introspectible qualities that distinguish them from each other. Intentional pleasures have the internal structure of directedness to an intentional object. One is pleased *by* some object or *that* something is the case—for example, that one's friend got a promotion. These intentional pleasures are more complex than unstructured pleasure sensations and, as we will see, raise more complex issues in the theory of value. But they share with simple pleasures the defining element of introspectible pleasantness.

(BG)'s remaining goods, knowledge and achievement, are parallel goods of theory and practice.[19] Both involve a relation of corre-

---

17. For this general view of pleasure, see, e.g., Bentham, *Introduction to the Principles of Morals and Legislation;* and Sidgwick, *The Methods of Ethics,* p. 94.

18. See Kagan, "The Limits of Well-Being," pp. 172–73. My account of pleasure in this paragraph is based on Kagan's, which he in turn says is influenced by work by Leonard Katz.

19. For a fuller account of knowledge and achievement see my *Perfectionism,* chaps. 8–10.

spondence between a mind and the world, either of true belief or of the successful realization of a goal. Both require this relation not to be a matter of luck: a person's true belief must be justified, and his goal must have been pursued in a way that made its attainment likely in advance. Finally, for both goods the degree of value of an instance of them is determined by formal rather than substantive criteria. The best knowledge is not that of any particular subject matter but that whose content extends farthest across times and objects—think of scientific laws—and which has the most other knowledge subordinate to it in an explanatory hierarchy. Similarly, the best achievements are not those with any particular goals— hence the independence of achievement from virtue—but those whose goals extend most across times and objects and organize the most other goals in a means-end hierarchy. There is therefore high achievement value in complex, difficult activities such as chess, novel writing, and political leadership.

The recursive characterization, then, starts with a base-clause such as (BG) affirming a set of intrinsic goods other than virtue. It then adds a recursion-clause about the intrinsic goodness of a certain attitude to what is good, namely, loving it, or, more specifically, *loving for itself what is good*, (LG):

(LG) If *x* is intrinsically good, loving *x* (desiring, pursuing, or taking pleasure in *x*) for itself is also intrinsically good.

This recursion-clause does not follow from the base-clause (BG); it is an independent principle requiring independent justification. The recursion-clause (LG) is like (BG) in being agent-neutral, making any person's loving what is good intrinsically good not just from her point of view, but from that of all persons. But what does it mean to "love" a state *x*, and what does it mean to love *x* "for itself"?

To "love" *x* is to be positively oriented toward *x* in one's desires, actions, or feelings, or, more generally, in one's attitudes. This positive orientation has three main forms. One can love *x* by desiring or wishing for it when it does not obtain, by actively pursuing it to make it obtain, or by taking pleasure in it when it does obtain. In the first case, one believes that *x* does not exist and desires or wishes that it did. Given the requisite further beliefs, this desire can lead to action aimed at producing *x*, but the desire can also exist before any action is performed, or even when, because circumstances will never be appropriate, no action will be possible. Thus, one can desire or wish that *x* will obtain in the future, but one can also wish that it did obtain now or had obtained in the past, and these latter desires can never issue in action. The second form of loving *x* does involve action, aimed either at producing *x* or at preserving it into the future. Regardless of whether this action succeeds in its aim, its origin in a desire for *x* makes it a form of loving *x*. The third form of loving *x* involves no desire or action: one takes *x*'s existence as given and feels pleasure that it does, did, or will obtain. Instead of a conative orientation toward *x*, there is here an affective one, involving feeling. Despite these differences, the three forms of loving *x* all involve a positive attitude to *x* and are therefore variant forms of a single orientation toward *x*. Which particular form of love one can have for a given state *x* depends on facts about *x* (does it obtain or not?) and about oneself (can one effectively promote *x* or not?). But for any state *x*, some form of loving *x* is possible.

To love a state *x* "for itself" is to love *x* apart from its consequences or for its own sake—that is, to love instances of *x* because they are instances of *x*. Thus, one loves pleasure for itself if one loves instances of pleasure because they are pleasures or because of their pleasantness. Similarly, one loves knowledge for itself if one loves instances of knowledge because they are knowledge. One does not love knowledge in this way if one cares about its instances only for some other reason. There are two more specific ways of loving a state such as pleasure for itself. One can believe that pleasure is intrinsically good and love it as something good or because of its goodness; here one's love derives from a prior judgment of intrinsic value. Alternatively, without relying on any belief about goodness, one can just be directly emotionally inclined toward pleasure for its own sake, desiring, pursuing, and taking pleasure in pleasure just because it is pleasure. Here one's love does not derive from any evaluative judgment, but is purely emotional or unreflective. These two forms of loving a state are importantly different, and their respective merits will be discussed in chapter 6. But in both forms one loves a state such as pleasure for itself rather than as a means to something beyond it, or loves particular pleasures for their pleasantness rather than for some other property.

Understood in this way, "loving for itself" is a morally appropriate response to intrinsic goodness. If an intrinsic good does not obtain, it is fitting or appropriate to desire it for its own sake and, if possible, to try to make it obtain. If an intrinsic good does obtain, it is appropriate to be pleased by this fact. What the recursion-clause (LG) affirms is the intrinsic goodness of a fitting or appropriate response to intrinsic goods, where loving for itself is that fitting response.

To see more concretely what this involves, let us combine the implications of base-clause (BG) and recursion-clause (LG). (BG) says that a pleasure felt by a person *A* is intrinsically good. (LG) adds that if another person *B* loves *A*'s pleasure for itself—if, for example, *B* desires or pursues *A*'s pleasure as an end in itself—his doing so is also intrinsically good. Since (LG)'s application iterates or recurs, (LG) also says that if a third person *C* loves *B*'s love of *A*'s pleasure for itself—if, for example, *C* is pleased by *B*'s desire for *A*'s pleasure—this too is intrinsically good. To take another example, (BG) says that knowledge is intrinsically good. (LG) adds that pursuing knowledge for its own sake is intrinsically good, as is being pleased by the pursuit of knowledge. Loving the good of knowledge is intrinsically good, as is loving the love of that good. And it is likewise good to love achievement and the love of achievement.

In some cases, a person's loving a good for itself will lead to action that produces that good, in which case her love is instrumentally good. But this need not be so. In the first example above, *B* may desire *A*'s pleasure for itself but be unable to pursue it; she may try to produce *A*'s pleasure but fail to do so; or encountering *A* already experiencing pleasure, she may simply take pleasure in this fact. In each of these cases, *B*'s love, though it does not have good consequences, is still by (LG)'s lights intrinsically good. And even when *B*'s love does have good consequences and is therefore instrumentally good, it is not only instrumentally good. As an instance of loving for itself what is good, it is also good in itself.

The recursive characterization that starts with (BG) and (LG) can extend itself if it adds a second base-clause stating that certain states other than vice are intrinsically evil, as in the following *base-clause about evils*, (BE):

> (BE) Pain, false belief, and failure in the pursuit of
>   achievement are intrinsically evil.

As with the earlier base-clause (BG), (BE)'s specific contents are not crucial for our purposes, though its agent-neutrality is. But (BE) fits well with (BG), making intrinsically evil states that are the exact contraries of the goods affirmed in (BG). Thus, pain is a sensation with an introspectible quality contrary to that of pleasantness, namely painfulness. Similarly, false belief and failure to achieve a pursued end involve not just a lack of correspondence between a mind and the world—as when one has no beliefs about a subject or pursues no end at all—but a positive mismatch between them. Since each of

(BE)'s evils is in this way the contrary of a good affirmed by (BG), the second base-clause is a natural complement to the first.[20]

Given (BE), the characterization can then add another independent recursion-clause about the intrinsic evil of *loving for itself what is evil*, (LE):

> (LE) If x is intrinsically evil, loving x for itself is also intrinsically evil.

Whereas loving for itself is an appropriate response to intrinsic goods, it is a positively inappropriate response to intrinsic evils, and (LE) makes this second kind of loving intrinsically evil. Together with (BE), it says that a person B's desiring or pursuing another person A's pain for itself is intrinsically evil, as is B's taking malicious pleasure in A's pain. And if a third person C loves B's love of A's pain for itself—for example, by taking pleasure in B's malicious pleasure as malicious—that too is intrinsically evil, as is loving another's false belief or failure or loving someone's love of false belief or failure.

There can be further recursion-clauses about hating what is good or evil, that is, about desiring or pursuing its not obtaining or being pained by its obtaining. One such clause concerns the intrinsic evil of *hating for itself what is good*, (HG):

> (HG) If x is intrinsically good, hating x (desiring or pursuing x's not obtaining or being pained by x's obtaining) for itself is intrinsically evil.

Since hating is an inappropriate response to intrinsic goods, (HG) makes it intrinsically evil. Thus, (HG) makes it intrinsically evil for person B to desire or seek for itself the destruction of A's pleasure or to be pained by A's pleasure. A parallel clause concerns the intrinsic goodness of *hating for itself what is evil*, (HE):

> (HE) If x is intrinsically evil, hating x for itself is intrinsically good.

---

20. It is not clear that failure belongs on a list of intrinsic evils. It is plausible that pain is intrinsically evil and also plausible that false belief is intrinsically worse than ignorance, or than having no belief at all about a subject. But is failure in pursuit of a highly general end worse than no pursuit at all? May it not be "better to have sought and failed than never to have sought at all"? Despite this worry, I have included failure as an evil in (BE) for the sake of symmetry with (BG).

(HE) makes it intrinsically good for *B* to be sympathetically pained by *A*'s pain—to feel compassion for *A*'s pain—or to desire or try to relieve it. Even if *B*'s compassion has no further effects, it is something good in itself. So are *B*'s wanting to remove or being pained by *A*'s false belief and her hating for itself *A*'s love of evil or hatred of good—for example, being pained by *A*'s malicious love of another's pain.

Behind these four recursion-clauses (LG), (LE), (HG), and (HE) is a simple idea: that it is intrinsically good to be oriented positively toward good and negatively toward evil, and intrinsically evil to be oriented negatively toward good and positively toward evil. In each case, a morally appropriate response to good or evil is intrinsically good and a morally inappropriate response is evil. It is intrinsically good if one's desires, actions, and feelings are oriented fittingly and intrinsically evil if they are oriented unfittingly.

The recursive characterization can be extended further by some non-recursive clauses about attitudes to instrumental goods and evils. Imagine that *x* is instrumentally good because it promotes intrinsic good *y*. One can love *x* as a means to *y*, or because it promotes *y*. A first instrumental clause about *loving as a means what promotes good* says that doing so is intrinsically good:

If *x* is instrumentally good because it promotes intrinsic good *y*, loving *x* because it promotes *y* is intrinsically good.

Combined with (BG), this clause says that loving a cause of pleasure because it causes pleasure is intrinsically good, as is loving a cause of knowledge because it causes knowledge. The clause does not say that the love of instrumental goods as means is good instrumentally, though this is often the case. If *x* is instrumental to intrinsic good *y*, a desire for *x* as a means can lead one to produce *x* and thereby to produce intrinsic good *y*. But the instrumental goodness of this desire does not need to be affirmed by a separate evaluative principle. It already follows from the intrinsic goodness of *y* plus empirical facts about the effects of one's desire for *x*, namely, its helping to produce *y*. What the clause says, rather, is that loving the means to goods as means is *intrinsically* good; it is another appropriate response to a kind of good and therefore good in itself. The love of good means presupposes a love of good ends and can only be an addition to it: one can love *x* for promoting *y* only if one already loves *y*. But the clause says this is a morally appropriate addition: responding fully to what is good requires loving intrinsic goods intrinsically and instrumental goods as means.

There are further clauses about attitudes to instrumental goods and evils. A state *x* can also be instrumentally good if it prevents intrinsic evil *z*; a second instrumental clause says that loving what prevents evil because it prevents evil is intrinsically good. And further clauses make it intrinsically evil to love as a means what is instrumentally evil in either of the two possible ways, intrinsically evil to hate as a means what is instrumentally good, and intrinsically good to hate as a means what is instrumentally evil.

There can also be clauses about attitudes to states non-instrumentally related to intrinsic goods and evils. For example, *x* can be a standard effect of intrinsic good *y* or, without being an effect, can be a reliable indicator of *y*, perhaps because *x* and *y* are joint effects of a common cause.[21] One can then love *x* because it is an indicator of *y*. For example, one can desire, pursue, and take pleasure in a person's smile because it indicates that she is experiencing pleasure. In general, our attitudes to states for themselves tend to spread themselves. When we care about one state for itself, we naturally care about other states related to it because of that relation. A series of further relational clauses says that those attitudes can be intrinsically good and evil.

If it includes the instrumental and other relational clauses, the recursive characterization implies that a single state can be the object of more than one intrinsically good attitude. Imagine that person *B* tries to promote *A*'s pleasure for itself and does so successfully. It is intrinsically good for a third person *C* to love *B*'s action for itself, as involving the active pursuit of pleasure. But it is also good for *C* to love *B*'s action as a cause of pleasure, that is, for its instrumental as well as its intrinsic properties. In some cases, contrary attitudes can be appropriate to the same state. Imagine that *B* tries to promote *A*'s pleasure but ends up through no fault of his causing *A* pain. Here it is intrinsically good for person *C* to love *B*'s action for its intrinsic character but to hate or regret it for its effects. The best balance of attitudes for *C* to take to *B*'s action depends on which response should be stronger, the love or the hatred, which in turn depends on the magnitude of the values at which they are directed. If the intrinsic value of *B*'s action is greater than its instrumental disvalue, *C*'s best overall attitude to *B*'s action is positive, though with

21. For this concept of "indicating" goodness, see Feldman, *Doing the Best We Can*, p. 26; and Thomson, "On Some Ways in Which a Thing Can Be Good," pp. 100–101.

an element of regret for the action's bad effects. If the action's instrumental disvalue is greater, *C*'s best overall attitude is negative.

Multiple attitudes can also be appropriate to a state because of its intrinsic properties. Imagine that *B* takes pleasure in *A*'s knowledge. His pleasure is good as an instance of love of what is good, but it is also good as an instance of pleasure, or as involving the quality of pleasantness that (BG) makes a base-level good. It is therefore good for *C* to love *B*'s pleasure both for its directedness to a good object and for its pleasantness, that is, for two intrinsic properties. Once again, contrary attitudes can be appropriate to the same state. If *B* takes pleasure in something evil such as *A*'s pain or false belief, his pleasure is intrinsically evil as a love of what is evil, but also intrinsically good as a pleasure. It should therefore be hated for itself for the one quality and loved for itself for the other, with the best overall attitude to it depending on which is greater: the evil *B*'s pleasure involves as a love of evil or the good it involves as a pleasure. (On this issue see chapter 5.) Or, if *B* is pained by *A*'s pain, his attitude is intrinsically good as a hatred of evil and intrinsically evil as pain, with contrary attitudes again appropriate. A similar conflict is possible for another base-level good, achievement. Imagine that *B* has the goal of causing *A* pain and achieves it. If this goal organizes a great many others in a means-end hierarchy, *B*'s realizing it has positive value as an achievement. But his pursuing this goal also has negative value as an instance of the active pursuit of evil. Here, the best overall attitude to *B*'s activity depends on the relative magnitudes of its intrinsic goodness as an achievement, its intrinsic evil as a form of loving evil, and its instrumental evil as causing *A*'s pain.

These multiple attitudes are possible because the elements of the recursive characterization—the two base-clauses, the four recursion-clauses, and all the relational clauses—are stated in terms of universals. They say it is good or evil to have attitudes to certain universal properties, or, more precisely, to have attitudes to particular states as instantiating these properties. If a state instantiates several relevant properties, either intrinsic or instrumental, it will be intrinsically good to have several (perhaps conflicting) attitudes to it. But each of these attitudes will be in some way appropriate to it.

3. *The Definition of Virtue and Vice*

Even as fully assembled, the recursive characterization makes no mention of virtue or vice. It says that certain attitudes to goods and evils are intrinsically good and evil, but not that they are virtuous or vicious. This lack is easily remedied by adopting a *definition of virtue and vice* that fits the characterization:

> The moral virtues are those attitudes to goods and evils that are intrinsically good, and the moral vices are those attitudes to goods and evils that are intrinsically evil.

If this definition is combined only with the recursion-clauses (LG)–(HE), it equates the virtues with appropriate attitudes to intrinsic goods and evils, namely, loving the former and hating the latter for themselves. It likewise equates the vices with inappropriate attitudes to intrinsic goods and evils. If the recursion-clauses are supplemented by the eight instrumental clauses, the definition finds further forms of virtue in appropriate attitudes to instrumental goods and evils and of vice in inappropriate attitudes to them, with a similar extension following from the other relational clauses. And when the recursive characterization is elaborated in greater detail, as it will be in chapter 3, the definition yields yet further forms of virtue and, especially, of vice. On its own the definition has no determinate content. To identify any particular states as virtuous or vicious, it must be combined with independent claims to the effect that some attitudes to goods and evils are intrinsically good and others intrinsically evil. Since these are just the claims we find in the recursive characterization of good and evil, that characterization gives the definition content. In its present form, it makes the definition equate virtue more specifically with loving what is good for the properties that make it good and hating on a similar basis what is evil. In return, the definition connects the recursive characterization to the concepts of virtue and vice, so that the latter's clauses identify forms of virtue and vice. Given their close mutual fit, the recursive characterization and the definition together comprise a recursive account of the intrinsic goodness of virtue and the intrinsic evil of vice, one claiming that certain attitudes to good and evil are intrinsically good and virtuous and others intrinsically evil and vicious.

More specifically, the recursive characterization and definition together equate the virtues and vices with subsets of the intrinsic goods and evils in a multilevel theory of good and evil. The recursive characterization starts by affirming certain base-level goods and evils, those identified by (BG) and (BE). It then adds to its base-level goods an infinite series of higher-level intrinsic goods, with the goods at each higher level consisting in appropriate attitudes to intrinsic goods or evils at the immediately lower level or to relational goods or evils defined in terms of them. The characterization likewise adds to its base-level evils an infinite series of higher-level evils consisting in inappropriate attitudes to lower-level goods or evils. The definition then identifies the moral virtues with all the higher-level goods in this multilevel theory and the moral vices with all the higher-level evils, so any intrinsic good above the base level is a virtue and any intrinsic evil above it a vice. We have already seen what some of these individual virtues and vices are. (For further discussion see chapter 4.) Combined with the recursive characterization, the definition implies that benevolence—that is, desiring, pursuing, or taking pleasure in another's pleasure for itself—is a virtue, as are desiring, pursuing, and taking pleasure in one's own or another's benevolence. Pursuing knowledge for its own sake is virtuous, as is feeling compassion for or trying compassionately to relieve another's pain. It is vicious to maliciously desire, pursue, or take pleasure in another's pain or maliciously desire or seek to destroy his pleasure. But it is virtuous to be pained by malice, in oneself or others, and to try to eliminate it.

To some extent this definition of virtue and vice is stipulative and could be replaced by some other definition. The attitudes the recursive characterization makes intrinsically good and evil can also have instrumental qualities and on that basis be all things considered good or evil. Consider again the case where *B* tries benevolently to promote *A*'s pleasure but through no fault of his causes *A* pain. *B*'s benevolent action, though intrinsically good, is instrumentally evil, and if the pain it causes *A* is sufficiently great, it can be all things considered evil. Similarly, if a malicious attempt to cause *A* pain in fact gives *A* pleasure, it can be instrumentally and even all things considered good. An alternative definition of virtue and vice focuses on these judgments of all-things-considered rather than just intrinsic goodness and evil. It equates the moral virtues with those attitudes to good and evil that are good all things considered, or good counting both their intrinsic and instrumental qualities, and the moral vices with those that are evil all things considered. Like Sidgwick's definition, this one counts an attitude's instrumental qualities as relevant to its status as virtuous or vicious, though it also counts its intrinsic qualities. It can even be seen as lying behind Sidgwick's definition. If one assumes that attitudes cannot be intrinsically good or evil, as Sidgwick appears to, the all-things-considered definition collapses into a simpler one defining the virtues and vices just as instrumentally good and evil.

This alternative definition cannot be dismissed as utterly false to our everyday understanding of virtue and vice. That understanding sees the virtues as states that are in some way desirable, and the all-things-considered definition interprets this desirability in one intelligible way. Nonetheless, and though the issue to some extent calls for stipulation, I think there are several reasons to prefer our initial definition's focus on intrinsic rather than all-things-considered goodness and evil.[22]

First, this definition has what I find more attractive implications than the all-things-considered definition. The latter implies that intense malice with sufficiently good consequences can be a virtue, while benevolence with sufficiently bad consequences, as when *B*'s attempt to give *A* pleasure causes *A* pain, can be a vice. But surely it is counterintuitive to say that malice can ever be a virtue or benevolence a vice. The alternative definition could try to avoid this implication by equating the virtues with attitudes that are normally, or in standard conditions, good all things considered.[23] This would allow that in an exceptional case like that of *B* above, a particular instance of benevolence can be all things considered evil yet still virtuous. But this proposal does not entirely remove the difficulty, since we can imagine a possible world where benevolence regularly has bad effects and malice good ones, and it still seems counterintuitive to say that in this world benevolence is a vice and malice a virtue. Our definition has what some may see as its own odd implication, namely that in a situation like the one just described, a virtue can be all things considered evil and a vice all things considered good. But this implication does not seem to me unacceptable; on the contrary, it seems correct. What we think on balance about the value of a virtue can depend on its effects, so that what remains a virtue can be all things considered unfortunate. And as we will see more fully in chapter 4, our definition has many other attractive implications about particular virtues and vices. Though the all-things-considered definition is not entirely false to our everyday understanding of

---

22. A third alternative is a definition that equates the virtues with attitudes that are both intrinsically *and* all things considered good. But my arguments against the simpler all-things-considered definition tell for the most part also against this more complex alternative.

23. This version of the instrumental view is suggested in Driver, "The Virtues and Human Nature," pp. 122–25.

virtue and vice, our initial definition, I think, fits that understanding better.

Second, our initial definition fits far better with the main aim of this book: to give a consequentialist account of the intrinsic goodness of virtue and evil of vice. This kind of account is certainly possible given the all-things-considered definition. Assuming the recursive characterization of good and evil, the latter implies that many virtues are intrinsically good and many intrinsically good attitudes are virtues. But the overlap between the two categories is not perfect. Some virtues are not intrinsically good—for example, malice that has sufficiently good consequences—and some intrinsically good attitudes are not virtues. This lack of overlap is avoided by our definition, which makes virtue always intrinsically good and vice always intrinsically evil. In fact, this definition allows a simple, rhetorically effective statement of the recursive account of the intrinsic goodness of virtue and evil of vice. If this account includes the definition, it treats the virtues as intrinsically good because it identifies them with a subset of the intrinsic goods, namely, all those above the base level in a multilevel theory of good and evil. Given the definition, it is not just that some intrinsically good attitudes are virtues and some virtues are intrinsically good. All the virtues are intrinsically good because they are defined as a kind of intrinsic good, one consisting in appropriate attitudes to other, lower-level goods and evils.

4. *Antecedents*

The recursive account outlined above is by no means original to this book. It or parts of it have been defended by several philosophers from Aristotle to the present day. Consider Aristotle's view of the value of pleasure:

> Now since activities differ in respect of goodness and badness, and some are worthy to be chosen, others to be avoided, and others neutral, so, too, are the pleasures, for to each activity there is a proper pleasure. The pleasure proper to a worthy activity is good and that proper to an unworthy activity bad; just as the appetites for noble objects are laudable, those for base objects culpable.[24]

---

24. Aristotle, *Nicomachean Ethics*, 1175b24–30.

Aristotle here affirms the core idea of the recursive characterization: that the value of an attitude, in this case pleasure, depends on the value of its object. For him, pleasure as such has no intrinsic value. (If pleasure in the neutral has neutral value, pleasure is not a base-level good.) But pleasure in a good activity is intrinsically good and pleasure in an evil activity intrinsically evil. Thus, if contemplation is good, pleasure in contemplation is also good, and contemplation plus pleasure in it is better than contemplation alone. If gluttony is evil, pleasure in gluttony is evil, and its presence makes gluttonous action worse. This core idea explains how for Aristotle pleasure "completes" a good activity "as the bloom of youth does . . . those in the flower of their age."[25] It completes the activity's value by adding an extra, though intimately connected, intrinsic good.

At the end of the quoted passage, Aristotle extends this core idea from pleasures to "appetites" or desires and from there implicitly to actions springing from desires. The idea is also connected for him with moral virtue, which he says involves at least partly having correct feelings and, in particular, being pleased and pained by the correct objects.[26] But Aristotle does not state the core idea of the recursive account in its most general form. There is, first, no hint in his main discussions of pleasure of an agent-neutral account of base-level values. He seems concerned only with a person's virtuous pleasure in his own activity and does not suggest that being pleased by another's good activity is good. Second, his restriction of the objects of good pleasures to *activities* prevents him from giving the core idea a recursive formulation. Since pleasure in a good activity is not itself an activity, there is no way that a further pleasure in that pleasure can by Aristotle's lights be good.[27] Aristotle has the core idea that the value of an attitude depends on the value of its object, but

---

25. Aristotle, *Nicomachean Ethics*, 1174b23–33. In the part of the *Ethics* containing this and the previously quoted passage, Aristotle assumes that an activity can be good when no pleasure is taken in it; see especially 1174a4–9. Elsewhere, however, he claims that pleasure in an activity is a necessary condition of its being good (1099a16–20). For a discussion of the difference between these views, see chapter 6.

26. Aristotle, *Nicomachean Ethics*, 1099a7–21, 1104b3–1105a17, 1106b16–23, 1152b5–6, 1172a19–27.

27. In *Nicomachean Ethics*, 1164a13–b13, Aristotle argues that pleasure is an activity rather than a "movement," but there is no suggestion that its being an activity in this sense makes it an activity of the kind that can be the object of a virtuous pleasure.

he applies that idea only once, and without iteration, to a person's pleasure in his own activities.

This core idea is formulated recursively by several consequentialists of the late nineteenth and early twentieth centuries, though usually about only one kind of attitude. As we have seen, Rashdall argues against Sidgwick that while virtue cannot be the only intrinsic good, it can be one intrinsic good among others. This is because virtue involves pursuing a "good of the whole," and it is reasonable to call "the pursuit of this good of the whole a good to the individual."[28] Or, as Rashdall puts it in *The Theory of Good and Evil*, the intrinsic goodness of virtue can be grounded on the "idea of the intrinsic worth of promoting what has worth."[29] These remarks apply the core idea of the recursive characterization to only one form of loving the good, actively pursuing it, and not to desiring or taking pleasure in it. But they do so agent-neutrally and with iteration.

In *The Origin of Our Knowledge of Right and Wrong*, Brentano analyzes the good as that the love of which is correct. After claiming that insight and joy are two states that are good in this sense, he continues:

> A third example may be found in those very feelings that are correct and are experienced as being correct. The correctness and higher character of these feelings . . . is itself to be counted as something that is good. And love of the bad is something that is itself bad.[30]

Like Rashdall's, Brentano's formulation of the core idea is both agent-neutral and recursive: any person's insight or joy is good to love, as is any person's love of what is good to love.

Recursive ideas are also prominent in Moore's *Principia Ethica*. Moore claims that among the intrinsic goods are "the appreciation of what has great intrinsic value" and the "hatred of what is evil." His intrinsic evils include, alongside pain, the "enjoyment of admiring contemplation of things which are themselves . . . evil," as in cruelty, and the "hatred of what is good."[31] These are all recursive values, though primarily involving feelings rather than desires or actions. Moore also defends other, rather different values. He believes that the admiring contemplation of beauty is intrinsically good and

28. Rashdall, "Professor Sidgwick's Utilitarianism," p. 219.
29. Rashdall, *The Theory of Good and Evil*, vol. 1, p. 59; see also vol. 2, pp. 41–42.
30. Brentano, *The Origin of Our Knowledge of Right and Wrong*, pp. 22–23.
31. Moore, *Principia Ethica*, pp. 204, 217, 208–9, 211; see also pp. 177–78.

in fact defines beauty as that the appreciation of which is good.[32] But despite arguing in *Principia Ethica* that the existence of beauty apart from any appreciation of it is good, he does not insist on this view, allowing that beauty on its own at best has slight intrinsic value and may have none.[33] And in his later work *Ethics,* he denies that beauty has intrinsic value.[34] But none of these qualifications shakes his belief that the appreciation of beauty has value. If he retains this belief, Moore envisages a case where the love of *x* is good but *x* itself—in this case beauty—is not. Here, as on the Stoic view, an attitude's value depends on its object but not on that object's having value. And the love of beauty has another role in Moore's theory. Moore believes that once there is a conscious appreciation of beauty, the real existence of that beauty makes a great difference to the overall goodness of the situation, much greater than any goodness the beauty has in itself. Here the love of *x* is a necessary condition of *x*'s having or making for significant intrinsic value. I will discuss this second view of Moore's—that the love of *x* can be a condition of *x*'s making for intrinsic value—in chapter 6. Here we need only note that once Moore has established the intrinsic goodness of the contemplation of beauty, his recursive principles govern attitudes to it. Thus, the appreciation of another's good qualities that constitutes the intrinsic good of "personal affection" consists largely, in Moore's view, in appreciating her appreciation of beauty, and one's appreciation of her aesthetic taste is then itself an object of proper appreciation by others.[35]

Related claims are made by W. D. Ross, though he is of course no consequentialist. According to Ross, there are three human goods: pleasure, knowledge, and virtue. Virtue itself has three principal forms, of which two are "action springing from the desire to bring into being something good" and "action springing from the desire to produce some pleasure, or prevent some pain, for another being."[36] These two desires must be understood intentionally, as the desire to produce something because it is good or because it is a

---

32. Moore, *Principia Ethica,* p. 201.
33. Moore, *Principia Ethica,* pp. 189, 202, 203.
34. Moore, *Ethics,* p. 107.
35. Moore, *Principia Ethica,* p. 204. Moore does not connect his recursive claims to claims about virtue. Instead, he defines virtue as any disposition to act that is instrumentally good and then denies that virtue is intrinsically good (pp. 170–78).
36. Ross, *The Right and the Good,* p. 160. The third form of virtue is action springing from the desire to do one's duty.

pleasure. Otherwise, since pleasure is a good, the second desire would be subsumed under the first. And Ross explicitly claims that a virtuous desire for another's pleasure need not involve the thought that this pleasure is good.[37] But this claim points to a puzzling omission in Ross's account. If it is intrinsically good and a form of virtue to pursue another's pleasure just as a pleasure, without the thought that it is good, why is it not equally good to pursue knowledge or virtue without the thought that it is good? Why are there not two virtuous ways of pursuing knowledge and virtue, as there are of pursuing pleasure? This omission prevents Ross's account from being fully recursive. There can be iteration of his first form of virtue, the love of what is good because it is good. But his second form of virtue, like good pleasure as Aristotle characterizes it, is restricted to just one base-level object. It can be virtuous to pursue another's pleasure without the thought that it is good, but not to pursue in the same way his virtuous pursuit of pleasure for others.

Finally, there are several presentations of parts of the recursive view by contemporary philosophers. There are elaborate accounts, inspired by Brentano, of the intrinsic value of pleasures and pains in work by Roderick M. Chisholm and others influenced by him.[38] There are also less formal allusions to the core idea of the recursive characterization in some work on virtue ethics or the "ethics of care."[39] But the most striking contemporary discussion of the recursive account is in Robert Nozick's *Philosophical Explanations*.[40]

Nozick does not use the traditional language of loving and hating goods and evils, speaking instead of "V-ing" and "anti-V-ing" "values" and "disvalues." He explains what "V-ing" is by giving a list of "V" verbs: bringing about, maintaining, saving from destruction, prizing, protecting, nurturing, and many others. All these verbs connote a positive orientation toward an object in either desire, action, or feeling. Nozick then defends the recursive claims that V-ing values is valuable, V-ing disvalues disvaluable, anti-V-ing values disvalu-

---

37. Ross, *The Right and the Good*, p. 161.

38. Chisholm, "Brentano's Theory of Correct and Incorrect Emotion," "The Defeat of Good and Evil," and *Brentano and Intrinsic Value*, pp. 62–67. See also Zimmerman, "On the Intrinsic Value of States of Pleasure"; Carson, "Happiness, Contentment and the Good Life"; and Lemos, *Intrinsic Value*, pp. 34–37, 73–77.

39. See, e.g., Blum, *Friendship, Altruism, and Morality*; Noddings, *Caring*; Trianosky, "Rightly Ordered Appetites"; Martin, *Virtuous Giving*, p. 31; and Swanton, "Profiles of the Virtues."

40. Nozick, *Philosophical Explanations*, pp. 429–33; see also Nozick, *The Examined Life*, pp. 91–95.

able, and anti-V-ing disvalues valuable, claims that match the clauses I have labelled (LG)–(HE). At the same time, Nozick imposes a very strong condition on these clauses. He says it would be "trivial" and merely "ad hoc" to add them to a list of base-level values, as my formulation of the recursive account does. Instead, the recursion-clauses must be shown to follow from the base-clauses, so that the nature of what is initially valuable and disvaluable entails that certain attitudes to them are also valuable and disvaluable.[41] I will discuss this strong condition of Nozick's in chapter 2. The condition aside, Nozick gives a fully general statement of the same recursive account affirmed with varying degrees of completeness by philosophers from Aristotle through Rashdall and Brentano to the present.

Given this extensive history, one would expect the recursive account to be well known among philosophers. Yet it is still widely assumed that consequentialism cannot treat virtue as more than instrumentally good. In addition, even those philosophers sympathetic to the account have not developed it in much detail. In my view, these are both reasons to explore the account further, as I will do in the remainder of this book.

---

41. Nozick, *Philosophical Explanations,* p. 430.

2

Merits and Implications

That a consequentialist account of the intrinsic values of virtue and vice is possible does not show that it is attractive. In this chapter I will defend this further claim by again considering the account's two components in turn. I will argue that both the recursive characterization of good and evil and the definition of virtue and vice contain attractive general principles, make attractive particular claims, and use the former to explain and illuminate the latter. This done, I will discuss some implications of incorporating the account within a consequentialist framework.

1. *The Recursive Characterization: Merits*

The most important part of the recursive characterization is its recursion-clauses (LG)–(HE), which assign intrinsic values to attitudes to intrinsic goods and evils. These clauses can have attractive implications only if combined with attractive base-clauses, and I hope (BG)'s and (BE)'s claims that pleasure, knowledge, and achievement are good and their contraries evil do strike readers as attractive. As we have seen, however, these particular values are not essential to the recursive view and could be replaced. What is distinctive in this view are its clauses identifying higher-level intrinsic values, and of these, (LG)–(HE) have priority over the instrumental and other relational clauses. Though adopting the former should lead us to adopt the latter, the recursion-clauses come first. If the recursive characterization as a whole is to be attractive, it must primarily be because (LG)–(HE) are attractive.

These clauses are indeed attractive, first, when considered on their own and apart from any further implications. Consider one claim of clause (LG): that it is intrinsically good to desire what is intrinsically good. Surely this claim has positive intuitive appeal. Desire for what is intrinsically good is morally appropriate desire; it is directed where desire should be directed. Is it not fitting that this appropriate desire should also be good and therefore also an object of appropriate desire? The claim's appeal is heightened by its connection to two parallel claims about the goodness of pursuing and taking pleasure in what is good—claims that are likewise attractive on their own—and by the subsumption of all three under a more general claim that explains them: that it is intrinsically good to love, or to be positively oriented toward, whatever is intrinsically good. This more general claim is in turn made more appealing by its subsumption, along with parallel claims about loving evil, hating good, and hating evil, under a yet more general one: that morally appropriate attitudes to goods and evils are intrinsically good and morally inappropriate ones intrinsically evil. This last, most abstract claim is logically contingent. It can be denied without self-contradiction, and many theories of value do deny it. But surely it is intrinsically appealing. If attitudes to objects can be fitting or unfitting, it is attractive to hold that the one orientation makes them intrinsically good and the other intrinsically evil.

The attraction of these clauses depends partly on their recursive form. It would already be plausible to hold, as Aristotle does, that love of a good activity is good, even though the love is not an activity and therefore not itself a potential object of valuable love. But this core idea becomes more appealing when it is formulated recursively, so that good love is also good to love. This formulation makes the core idea more abstract, which in my view makes it a better candidate for a foundational idea about value. It is more likely to be a fundamental truth of ethics that love of any good is good than that love of some restricted type of good is good. The formulation also gives the core idea more unifying power, enabling it to explain the goodness not only of attitudes to base-level goods, but also of an infinite series of nested attitudes to higher-level goods. As recursively formulated, Aristotle's idea is both more attractive in itself, because more widely applicable, and more explanatory of other attractive claims.

The appeal of these clauses contrasts sharply with that of the superficially similar view Sidgwick discusses—that any disposition to act that is instrumentally good is on that basis intrinsically good (see chapter 1, section 1). Like the recursive view, this instrumental view identifies certain higher-level goods by their relation to base-level goods. But the relations the two views focus on are importantly different.

The instrumental relation Sidgwick considers is always to something external to the state that has it—for example, to the pleasures of others that will result from a given person's beneficence. Given the strict view of intrinsic goodness, this makes the instrumental view logically impossible; even given the looser view, it makes that view hard to accept intuitively. It may be that actions that are already good because they are directed at a good object will be better if their object is achieved, as when a person's efforts to preserve Venice succeed. But it is going too far to ground a state's intrinsic goodness entirely on an external relation. Surely that goodness must have some basis in the state's intrinsic properties.

This difficulty does not arise for the recursive characterization, which identifies its higher-level goods by an internal relation. Each of these goods is a desire *for* a lower-level good, a pursuit *of* it, or a pleasure *in* it and cannot be fully described without reference to this internal intentional object. Consider a desire for knowledge. It is not a compound consisting of a desire on the one side, existing independently of any object, and knowledge on the other, with some merely external relation between them. A desire cannot exist apart from any object; one cannot desire without desiring something. And when one does desire, one's object typically does not exist; one desires knowledge because one does not or believes one does not have it. A desire for knowledge is therefore a single state, a desire directed internally at knowledge and made the particular desire it is by that particular object. The same is true of the pursuit of knowledge. Since one cannot pursue without pursuing some thing, this, too, is a single state, and again one whose object usually does not exist. The point even holds for pleasure in knowledge. Though one can feel a simple pleasure such as that of suntanning apart from any object, one cannot do the same for pleasure *in* some thing. And though in this case the object of one's attitude often does exist, it need not, since one can take pleasure in what one falsely believes is knowledge, or in knowledge as a merely intentional object.[1] For all three forms of love, therefore, their directedness to a particular object is not an external but an internal fact about them, one neces-

1. For more on attitudes to objects believed falsely to exist, see chapter 6, section 1.

sary for their being the particular attitudes they are. This point is not always recognized by defenders of the recursive account. Moore, for example, sometimes speaks as if pleasure in a good object is a whole composed of pleasure on one side and the object on the other, with the recursive characterization affirming a value in this whole that is additional to any values in its parts.[2] But this analysis, which is clearly impossible for desire for or pursuit of a good, does not even fit pleasure in a good when the latter's intentionality is properly understood. It is a crucial feature of the recursive characterization that it identifies higher-level values not by an external relation, such as an instrumental one, but by an intentional and therefore internal relation.

For a similar reason, the recursive characterization avoids a difficulty the instrumental view faces about the spread of its higher-level goods. Sidgwick is interested in this view as possibly grounding the claim that virtue is intrinsically good, and he therefore applies it only to human dispositions to act. But if what makes a disposition to act intrinsically good is just its being instrumentally good, one would expect the same intrinsic goodness to be found in other instrumental goods, including non-intentional states such as healthy digestion, sunny weather, and vintage wine. Their causing base-level goods should make them, too, intrinsic goods. If the instrumental view accepted this extension, it would be committed to an implausibly long list of higher-level goods, one containing many items other than virtue. Yet there seems to be no principled way it can avoid the extension. Once again, the recursive characterization does not face this difficulty. Since the relations it values are intentional, its higher-level goods extend only as far as intentionality does. There can be intrinsic values in human desires, actions, and feelings, as well as in similar states of animals, but not in features of human bodies or of the physical world. Rashdall emphasizes this point in his commentary on Sidgwick. What partisans of virtue such as himself value, he says, is "the settled bent of the will towards that which is truly or essentially good, and not a mere capacity or potentiality of pleasure-production such as might be supposed to reside in a bottle of old port."[3] When the ground of higher-level goodness is an intentional relation, that goodness is found only in intentional states.

---

2. Moore, *Principia Ethica*, pp. 190–91, 199, 208, 211–12, 216–22.
3. Rashdall, "Professor Sidgwick's Utilitarianism," p. 224; see also Rashdall, *The Theory of Good and Evil*, vol. 1, p. 65.

Alongside their intrinsic appeal, the recursion-clauses have attractive implications. Combined with the base-clauses (BG) and (BE), they imply that feeling pain at another's pain for itself is intrinsically good, desiring that a person have false beliefs for itself is intrinsically evil, and striving for achievement for itself is intrinsically good. These and a host of other claims that follow from the clauses are intuitively appealing, and it is a great merit of the characterization that it entails them. In fact, at a series of points, the recursive characterization corrects flaws in simpler theories of value containing only base-level goods and evils.

Consider two possible worlds.[4] In the first world, natural conditions are benign and people therefore lead very pleasant lives. But they are all entirely self-concerned: they do not desire or pursue each other's pleasure for itself, and their hearts are cold to any enjoyments not their own. In the second world, resources are less plentiful and there is some disease, but people are benevolent. They try to promote each other's pleasure as an end in itself and are pleased when their fellows experience pleasure. Their benevolence increases their pleasure, but not enough to overcome their natural disadvantages. Despite their mutual concern, people in the second world enjoy slightly less pleasure than those in the first.

A theory affirming only base-level values, and especially hedonism, which holds that only pleasure is good and pain evil, must judge the first of these worlds as better than the second. But surely most of us would reverse this ordering. If we could bring either world into existence, we would prefer the second. Even hedonists should feel pressure in this direction: people in the second world have more of the attitude to others' pleasure that agent-neutral hedonism says is appropriate. Should this fact not be reflected in the value ascribed to the second world? It is reflected by recursion-clause (LG), which says that by their benevolence people in the second world display a greater love of what is good, where the value of this love can outweigh their shortfall in pleasure.

The recursive characterization also corrects another flaw in hedonism. Imagine that a torturer takes sadistic pleasure in the intense pain he causes his victim. Hedonism says that, considered in itself, the torturer's pleasure makes the overall situation better than if he were indifferent to his victim's pain or, worse, pained by it. As an

---

4. Compare Ross, *The Right and the Good*, pp. 134–35.

instance of pleasure, it is only good and in no way evil. Hedonism can say the torturer's pleasure is instrumentally evil if it makes him torture more diligently now or more likely to do so again in the future, but it holds that considered in itself, that pleasure is good. Surely most of us cannot accept this claim. We believe the torturer's pleasure, even apart from its effects, makes the situation worse.[5] Again, the recursive characterization can explain why. In enjoying his victim's pain, the torturer loves for itself something intrinsically evil, which is by clause (LE) intrinsically evil. If he were instead pained by this evil, that would by clause (HE) be intrinsically good. The torturer's pleasure is still good as a pleasure, by base-clause (BG), and it remains to be seen how its positive and negative values weigh against each other. But unlike hedonism, the recursive characterization can hold that sadistic pleasure is in one respect intrinsically evil.

The characterization also corrects theories that make only base-level claims about knowledge. Consider a great intellectual figure who for all his brilliance in research ended up with empirical beliefs that were largely false—for example, Aristotle in his career as a biologist. A theory that values only knowledge must say that in his biological investigations Aristotle achieved little of intrinsic intellectual worth—less, probably, than an undergraduate biology student today. This is an unwelcome implication, and the recursive characterization again avoids it. It says that by actively seeking biological knowledge rather than merely acquiring it from a textbook, Aristotle showed a greater love of knowledge than an undergraduate, and that the value of his love of knowledge may compensate for his false beliefs. More generally, the recursive characterization can explain the widespread view that there is special value in the search for, as opposed to the mere possession of, knowledge. As Ross writes, "While in its own nature knowledge seems to be a better state than inquiry, the moral virtue of desire for knowledge may be more fully present in many an unsuccessful search for difficult knowledge than in the successful attainment of knowledge that is easier to get."[6]

Analogously, the recursive characterization corrects theories making only base-level claims about achievement. According to base-clause (BG), there is special value in achievements that are difficult,

---

5. See, e.g., Broad, *Five Types of Ethical Theory,* pp. 234–35; and Brandt, *Ethical Theory,* pp. 315–18.
6. Ross, *The Right and the Good,* p. 152. A different account of the value of the search for knowledge treats it as an instance of achievement; see my *Perfectionism,* p. 102.

in the sense of complex and intricate. But for people with highly developed skills, a complex activity can be less difficult, in the colloquial sense of requiring less effort and dedication, than a simpler activity is for someone with ordinary or impaired skills. Thus, it can be less difficult for a linguistically gifted person to write creditable poetry than for a handicapped person to read simple prose. Yet many of us think that because of its greater difficulty in the colloquial sense, the handicapped person's achievement is in one respect more valuable. The recursive characterization can again explain why: like the search for difficult knowledge, the pursuit of achievements that are difficult in the colloquial sense involves a greater love of achievement than a less taxing pursuit of achievements that are in themselves more complex.

Nor does the characterization value only research and difficulty as such. Imagine that Aristotle pursued biological knowledge actively but only as a means to intrinsically valueless goals such as money and prestige. Many of us would then think his pursuit intrinsically less good than if he had sought knowledge for its own sake. Again, the recursive characterization endorses this view. It likewise implies that if an athlete pursues a difficult goal, such as leading his team to a championship, only in order to increase his salary, his doing so is less good than if he valued the championship and the skilful play it demands in part for their own sakes.

At the same time as they imply these attractive claims, the recursion-clauses unify and explain them. At first sight, the judgments that compassion for suffering and love of a sport are intrinsically good and pleasure in malice is evil seem unconnected. Given the recursive characterization, however, we can see them all as instantiating a single abstract idea about appropriate and inappropriate attitudes to intrinsic goods and evils. This on the one side increases our confidence in the particular claims: they are more firmly grounded when, no longer just items on a list, they have a unifying rationale. On the other side, its ability to explain the claims counts in favour of the abstract idea: that it can unify appealing judgments increases its own appeal.

To further illustrate this unifying power, consider the value of personal relationships such as friendship and love. Many theories of value include these relationships as a base-level good, and it is certainly plausible that they have intrinsic worth.[7] But it would be more

---

7. See, e.g., Griffin, *Well-Being*, pp. 67–68.

satisfying to derive their worth from that of other goods, so that loving relationships embody not a distinct intrinsic value but more general values to a high degree. A reductive account of this kind is possible to some extent using only the base-level goods in (BG). Intimate relationships involve intense pleasure in the company and doings of a loved one and the most thorough knowledge of another's character we attain. They also involve achievements of just the kind (BG) finds specially valuable. The goals friends or lovers pursue are cooperative, extending beyond their individual selves to include states of each other; they are tailored to each other's needs; and over time they form a hierarchical structure, with more particular goals serving overarching ones that define the relationship.[8]

Suggestive though it is, this reductive account of the value of personal relationships leaves out the crucial element of love or affection. One can take pleasure in another's company only because one finds her amusing or useful, without caring about her for her own sake. One can likewise understand her character without feeling any concern for her and cooperate with her extensively while taking no interest in how she fares in ventures not involving oneself. In these cases, one's relationship, however much it instantiates the base-level values in (BG), surely lacks the full intrinsic value of friendship or love. But this omission is repaired if the reductive account can also appeal to the higher-level goods identified by clauses (LG)–(HE). It can then say that the most valuable relationships involve not just pleasure but pleasure in another's good, that is, pleasure in her pleasure, knowledge, and achievement, as well as in higher-level goods such as her compassion and benevolence. It can also say that the most valuable relationships involve desire for and pursuit of another's good for its own sake. In fact, the reductive account can make these higher-level goods the central goods in love and friendship. Our friends and loved ones, it can say, are above all people whose good we desire, pursue, and take pleasure in for its own sake, and any further goods these relationships involve, such as pleasure and knowledge, are infused and guided by these forms of virtuous love.[9]

I have argued that the recursion-clauses are attractive both in

---

8. For this account, see my *Perfectionism*, pp. 134–36.
9. For a similar account of the value of personal relationships, which likewise appeals to both base-level and higher-level goods, see Ross, *The Right and the Good*, p. 141.

themselves and for their implications. The first of these claims is implicitly rejected by Nozick, who finds it "ad hoc" to merely add recursion-clauses to a list of base-level goods.[10] Instead, he demands that these clauses be shown to follow from the base-clauses, so that the nature of what is initially good entails that loving it is also good, and for the same reason.

This demand is audacious. A theory that satisfied Nozick's condition and derived its recursive from its non-recursive claims would be a philosophical tour de force and a triumph of explanatory integration. In my formulation, the recursive characterization involves an ineliminable dualism between base- and higher-level values. On one side are the initial intrinsic goods of (BG) and evils of (BE); on the other side, irreducibly distinct from them, are the higher-level goods and evils identified by (LG)–(HE). Satisfying Nozick's condition would involve eliminating this dualism, generating an infinite hierarchy of intrinsic goods and evils from a single foundational idea about value.

Nozick thinks his own theory of value satisfies his condition, perhaps uniquely. His candidate for the fundamental intrinsic good is "organic unity," and alongside it his fundamental evil is disunity. There is organic unity in a collection of states when they are both intimately related to each other and diverse. Their unity is a matter of the closeness of their connection to each other; its being organic requires them to be initially independent or distinct. What is valuable, then, is not just unity but unity in diversity, or bringing into an organized structure elements that are strongly individual, so their successful integration is a surprise. Nozick argues that this ideal of unity in diversity successfully unifies base- and higher-level values: "The V-ing [or loving] verbs are verbs of unification; the relationships they specify establish and embody complex unities of the person with (what realizes) the values. The situation when these relationships hold will have some (positive) degree of organic unity, and so be ranked as valuable by the dimension of organic unity as underlying value."[11] If an intrinsic good exists, in other words, an organic unity exists. And if a person loves this good for itself, she unifies herself with it, creating a further or greater organic unity. By the same criterion that makes the initial state intrinsically good, her loving it is also intrinsically good.

10. Nozick, *Philosophical Explanations*, p. 430.
11. Nozick, *Philosophical Explanations*, p. 432.

To assess Nozick's theory, we must first determine whether it yields an acceptable list of base-level values. Here the theory has some notable successes, implying, for example, that knowledge and achievement are intrinsically good. Each of these states involves a relation of correspondence, or what the theory calls unity, between a mind and the world. The theory also makes attractive claims about the degrees of value in these goods. If someone knows a scientific law, for example, and has used it to explain many other truths, there is more unity both between her mind and the world and among her beliefs than if she knew a single isolated fact. The same holds if she has accomplished a complex series of goals. The theory also successfully affirms the intrinsic evils of false belief and failure, which involve not just a lack of unity between a mind and the world—which would give them neutral value—but positive disunity, or the opposite of correspondence, between them.

Nozick's theory has more difficulty, however, with the base-level values of pleasure and pain. If these are sensations distinguished by introspectible qualities of pleasantness and painfulness, how can a theory valuing only organic unity find either good or evil?[12] Denying that pleasure is intrinsically good is not unimaginable, especially if the value of pleasures with good objects is affirmed by (LG). But that pain is intrinsically evil has seemed to many as compelling a claim as any about intrinsic value. If Nozick's theory cannot capture this claim, its base level will strike many as unacceptable.

Aside from this initial difficulty, Nozick's theory does not succeed in deriving higher-level from base-level values, because of an ambiguity in its concept of unity. When Nozick affirms the value of knowledge and achievement, he understands unity as a relation of correspondence, with no requirements about attitude or directedness. The object of a true belief must exist; one can have knowledge only of what is real. But one need neither love nor hate, be pleased

---

12. Nozick acknowledges this difficulty *(Philosophical Explanations*, p. 418), but there is a different view of pleasure and pain on which he could find them good and evil. It identifies pleasures as sensations people desire to experience given just their qualities as sensations, and pains as sensations they desire not to experience. On this view, when a person enjoys pleasure there is unity between his sensations and his desires about them, and when he suffers pain there is disunity. I do not find this view of pleasure and pain as persuasive as one in terms of introspectible qualities. But even if Nozick's theory included it and successfully valued pleasure and pain, it would still face the difficulties I raise later about its derivation of higher-level from base-level claims.

nor displeased, by what one knows. As valued in the recursion-clauses, however, the relation of unity does involve intentional directedness. In clause (LG), for example, it involves love of or a positive orientation toward an object for its own sake. And unlike an object of knowledge, this intentional object need not exist, since one can desire, pursue, and even take pleasure in something that is not real. In the base-clauses of Nozick's theory, "unity" means one thing, correspondence to something real, whereas in the recursion-clauses it means another, a positive orientation toward what need not be real. And Nozick cannot jettison one of these meanings in favour of the other. If he uses only the correspondence relation, his theory cannot value appropriate loves as instances of organic unity and therefore cannot even affirm the recursion-clauses. But if he uses only the directedness relation, his theory does not have a remotely plausible list of base-level goods. It cannot value knowledge and achievement intrinsically, since they involve the wrong kind of unity, but instead must value only directedness as such—for example, valuing only desiring as such, regardless of its object or of whether it is satisfied. But surely the mere existence of a desire, with no further conditions, is not on any credible view intrinsically good. Nor, finally, can Nozick just admit that "unity" has two meanings, for that would mean abandoning his pursuit of explanatory integration. His theory would then by its own lights use one relation in its base-clauses and another in its recursion-clauses, with the phrase "organic unity" only papering over this dualism.

This difficulty about connecting base and higher levels arises especially sharply at a particular point in Nozick's theory. Consider recursion-clause (HE), about the intrinsic goodness of hating what is evil. As Nozick himself notes, hating is a relation of (directed) disunity. So how, on his theory, can it be intrinsically good? He writes, "The disunifying character of the anti-V [or hating] verbs can match the disunity of the disvalues. In taking an anti-V stance towards disvalues, our relationship mirrors its object, and so the total situation has its own degree of unity."[13] Here Nozick claims that a disunifying response to evil involves an element of unity with that evil, through "mirroring." But he does not show that this unity will always outweigh the disunity present in any instance of hating, as it must do if the hating is to be on balance good. Nor would it be sufficient if he

13. Nozick, *Philosophical Explanations,* p. 433.

did show this. Considered as an intentional state, hating evil seems to be purely good, with no admixture of evil. Yet Nozick's theory implies, implausibly, that it is always in one respect evil. And there is still the ambiguity of the term "unity." Imagine that the initial intrinsic evil is *B*'s false belief about his own motives. For a state of *A* to "mirror" this evil, it should involve the same relation to the same or a parallel object, as when *A* has a false belief about *B*'s or, better, his own motives. But in Nozick's theory, the "mirror" is a state that has a different relation (negative directedness rather than non-correspondence) to a different object (*B*'s false belief rather than anyone's motives). How are these fundamental disanalogies consistent with a single meaning of "unity"?

I believe these difficulties warrant our rejecting Nozick's condition and continuing to explore the recursive characterization, even though we cannot derive its higher-level from its base-level claims. Such a derivation would indeed be a tour de force, but for precisely this reason, it cannot reasonably be demanded. Perhaps we can only formulate the recursive characterization dualistically; even so, we can find its distinctive clauses and the particular claims they imply immensely intuitively attractive.

2. The Definition of Virtue and Vice: Merits

The second component of the recursive account is its definition of the virtues and vices as attitudes to goods and evils that are, respectively, intrinsically good and evil. This definition, too, has attractive features, beginning with several general ones.

First, the definition meshes with our everyday understanding of the virtues as somehow desirable states of a person and the vices as somehow undesirable. The definition specifies this understanding in a particular way, making the virtues intrinsically rather than instrumentally or all things considered good, and the vices intrinsically evil. It is therefore not uniquely consistent with that understanding, which can also be specified in different ways. But it does fit it and give it a plausible rationale.

Second, the definition clearly distinguishes the virtues and vices from other desirable and undesirable states. Even if the virtues are intrinsic goods, they seem intuitively to form a distinct category from goods such as pleasure and knowledge, and the vices likewise seem distinct from pain and false belief. The definition sets the virtues apart as higher-level goods, ones that consist in attitudes to other values, and the vices as higher-level evils. Although they are among the intrinsic values, virtue and vice have a distinctive character because of their distinctive place in a hierarchy of values.

Third, the definition captures widely accepted claims about the kinds of state that embody virtue and vice. It is usually held that virtue is centrally manifested in a person's actions, so he can act virtuously, or from virtue. Thus, Aristotle defines virtue as a state "concerned with choice," by which he means primarily the choice of how to act.[14] Our definition endorses this view by holding that one form of virtue is action either in pursuit of a good or to prevent an evil. It gives virtue an active form, involving a person's intentional behaviour. The definition also captures widely accepted claims about what makes actions virtuous. It is usually held that actions are virtuous not because of their physical properties or even their consequences, but because of their connection to inner states such as motives and desires. Thus, Aristotle says that virtuous actions, as against ones merely in accordance with virtue, must be done from a virtuous motive.[15] Our definition agrees, saying that virtuous action must issue from a desire directed positively toward a good or negatively toward an evil. Finally, it is widely held that although virtue has one manifestation in a person's actions, it can also be expressed in purely inner states such as feelings. Thus, Aristotle identifies a virtuous person in part as one who feels pleasures and pains at the right times and toward the right objects.[16] Our definition again agrees, finding virtue in desires that never issue in action, such as wishes and regrets about the past, and in appropriate pleasures and pains. It makes inner states not only the ground of virtue in action but also forms of virtue themselves. Its capturing these various claims distinguishes the recursive definition sharply from Sidgwick's definition of virtue as any disposition to act that is instrumentally good. As we saw, Sidgwick's definition both ignores the many forms of virtue other than virtuous action and counts as virtuous actions that issue from unworthy motives. Our definition avoids both these flaws, affirming virtues of mere desire and feeling while also denying that a storeowner who gives accurate change only from a selfish motive is acting virtuously.

Finally, the definition captures the difficult status of virtue as both

14. Aristotle, *Nicomachean Ethics,* 1106b36.
15. Aristotle, *Nicomachean Ethics,* 1105a33.
16. Aristotle, *Nicomachean Ethics,* 1106b16–23.

a derivative and an independently important moral property. In my view, virtue cannot plausibly be treated as morally primitive: it consists in an appropriate response to other moral considerations and must be analyzed in terms of those considerations. At the same time, virtue has its own intrinsic significance. Its presence contributes to a life's goodness not just as a means, but also in itself. This delicate balance is captured perfectly by the recursive account, according to which virtue is a response to other values but, as that response, is a further value itself.

Despite these merits, the definition may be faulted for ignoring another widely accepted claim about virtue: that it involves stable dispositions. Aristotle says that to count as virtuous, an action not only must be done from a virtuous motive but must "proceed from a firm and unchangeable character."[17] For him, the virtues are not short-term but persisting states, ones realized in long stretches of a person's life. Our definition, by contrast, treats virtue atomistically, finding it in occurrent desires, actions, and feelings regardless of their connection to more permanent traits of character.

The difference between Aristotle's and an atomistic view should not be exaggerated. Though Aristotle defines virtue as a stable disposition, he does not think the existence of this disposition is what is centrally valuable. Since mere virtue can be had by a person "who is asleep or in some other way quite inactive," the chief good must consist in the active exercise of virtue, found precisely in occurrent desires, feelings, and especially actions.[18] But Aristotle does not count an occurrent attitude as virtuous unless it issues from a stable disposition, so the latter is at least a condition for the central good. As formulated to this point, the recursive account imposes no such condition.

The account can easily be amended so that it does value dispositions. Most simply, it can say that alongside the values in occurrent attitudes to goods and evils, there are further intrinsic values in dispositions to have these attitudes. There is some intrinsic goodness and virtue in dispositions to consciously desire, pursue, and take pleasure in the good, and some intrinsic evil in dispositions to love evil. This is the line Ross takes, saying that the state of mind of a habitually unselfish person is intrinsically better than that of a habitually selfish one even when neither is exercising his disposition. What

---

17. Aristotle, *Nicomachean Ethics*, 1105a34–35.
18. Aristotle, *Nicomachean Ethics*, 1009a1–2; see also 1095a32–33.

is morally good, according to Ross, is not just occurrent "acts of will, desire, and emotion," but also "relatively permanent modifications of character even when these are not being exercised."[19] If it adopts this view, the recursive account should agree with Aristotle that there is a separate and greater value in occurrent good attitudes, so the active exercise of a virtuous disposition is considerably better than its mere possession. But it can and in my view should find some value and virtue in appropriate dispositions.

What about Aristotle's stronger claim that virtuous actions and feelings must issue from a stable disposition? To make more than a verbal point about "virtue," this claim must imply one about value. Aristotle must and apparently does believe that actions aimed at what is good are better, or even are good only, when they issue from a stable disposition; if done out of character, they have little if any worth. The recursive account can again in principle be amended to incorporate this claim, but I do not believe it should be.

Imagine that *A* acts kindly from a long-standing disposition to be kind, while *B* does so just once, without this reflecting anything permanent in his character. In comparing the values of these two actions, we must not be distracted by extraneous facts. *A*'s virtuous disposition will lead him to act kindly on many other occasions, making his life as a whole far more virtuous than *B*'s. So on any view *A*'s disposition is at least instrumentally good. And we have just allowed that his disposition may be to a degree intrinsically good, that is, good just as a disposition. But in assessing Aristotle's claim we must abstract from these facts and ask whether, considered just in itself, *A*'s kind action has more value than *B*'s. Apart from the values in any associated actions and in his disposition itself, is *A*'s action morally preferable? I see no reason to believe this and therefore no reason to accept Aristotle's stronger claim. *A*'s kind action may be accompanied by more valuable actions at other times in his life and by a more valuable disposition now, but I do not see that it is any better in itself.[20] So although the recursive account can and should find some value in dispositions considered on their own, it should not make these dispositions a condition for the value of occurrent attitudes. A long tradition beginning with Aristotle centres the

19. Ross, *The Foundations of Ethics*, pp. 291–92.

20. For similar arguments against the centrality of dispositions for virtue, see Blum, *Friendship, Altruism, and Morality*, pp. 112–15; Garcia, "The Primacy of the Virtuous," pp. 82–84; Solomon, "The Virtues of a Passionate Life," pp. 92–95; and Montmarquet, "An Asymmetry Concerning Virtue and Vice," pp. 150–51, 153–54.

analysis of virtue on permanent traits of character, but in my view this tradition is misguided. The concept of virtue is essentially that of a kind of desirable state. If what is most desirable in the relevant area required stable dispositions, it would make sense to define virtue in terms of dispositions. But if this is not so, virtue should mainly be found in occurrent attitudes.[21]

Alongside these general merits, the recursive definition of virtue and vice has attractive implications. It implies that a benevolent desire for another's pleasure and compassion for her pain are virtues and that malice and pleasure in one's malice are vices. Obviously, these are highly intuitive claims. And when the recursive account has been developed more fully, in chapter 3, we will see that it captures an immense variety of commonly recognized virtues and vices. The recursive definition is especially impressive in its ability to accommodate different categories of virtue and vice. For example, it recognizes both self-regarding virtues, such as love of knowledge and the desire to be virtuous, and other-regarding virtues, such as compassion. It also recognizes both virtues whose objects are base-level values, such as pleasure, pain, and knowledge, and higher-level virtues whose objects are themselves forms of virtue and vice. These higher-level virtues include the desire that one's child grow up to be benevolent and shame at one's malice. Cutting across these initial divisions, the definition recognizes three further categories each of virtue and vice. When the recursive account has been elaborated, we will see that it recognizes what I call pure vices, such as malice, sadism, and self-hatred; vices of indifference, such as callousness, sloth, and shamelessness; and vices of disproportion, such as selfishness, cowardice, and pride. It also recognizes what I call simple virtues, such as benevolence, compassion, and shame; virtues of proportion, such as temperance, patience, and modesty; and virtues of self-control, such as courage (in one form) and control of one's anger. Though these different virtues and vices are made such by different aspects of the recursive account, they are all accommodated within it.

At the same time, the recursive definition unifies the virtues and vices. Instead of unordered lists of good traits—benevolence, cour-

---

21. There are also empirical reasons to doubt whether the stable dispositions of character central to the Aristotelian tradition actually exist; see Ross and Nisbett, *The Person and the Situation.* For relevant philosophical discussion, see Harman, "Moral Philosophy Meets Social Psychology"; and Campbell, "Can Philosophical Accounts of Altruism Accommodate Experimental Data on Helping Behaviour?"

age, compassion—and evil ones, it offers a single explanation of why the virtues are virtues and the vices, vices. In all their manifestations in desire, action, and feeling, and in all their categories, the virtues involve appropriate attitudes to intrinsic or other values and the vices inappropriate attitudes. This unification is much to be desired. If we confidently recognize benevolence and other traits as virtues, they must have some common feature that makes them virtues, and one task of an account of virtue is to say what this is. The recursive account fulfills this task, taking the virtues to share one broad orientation to other values and the vices an opposite orientation.

As I emphasized in chapter 1, the recursive account satisfies the defining assumptions of consequentialist theories by characterizing virtue and vice in terms of intrinsic goodness and evil. It also ascribes these consequentialist properties to virtue and vice themselves. It holds that virtue has the same kind of goodness—intrinsic goodness—as pleasure, knowledge, and other consequentialist goods, and vice has the same kind of evil. This has an important implication. Unlike judgments about rightness and wrongness, judgments about intrinsic values make no assumption about voluntariness or choice. It is not a condition of a state's being intrinsically good or evil that it result from a person's choice or be something she could have prevented. Pleasure and knowledge are desirable whether or not they are chosen; pain is no less evil when it afflicts a person against her will. According to the recursive account, the same is true of virtue and vice. Virtue is good and vice evil when they are voluntary, but also when they are an unchosen part of a person's character. John Stuart Mill holds that humans are so constituted that "the idea of the pain of another is naturally painful; the idea of the pleasure of another is naturally pleasurable."[22] If this is true, then on the recursive view, humans are at least in part naturally virtuous and naturally good. Similarly, if a person finds herself feeling, against her will, pleasure in thoughts of brutality and domination, her pleasure is, despite its involuntariness, evil. Because the recursive account values virtue as good rather than right, it has no special interest in one particular question that has concerned philosophers, namely, how far people are responsible for their emotions or attitudes.[23] If emotions could be evaluated only as right and wrong, it would be crucial

22. Mill, "Sedgwick's Discourse," p. 60.
23. This issue is discussed in Sankowski, "Responsibility of Persons for Their Emotions"; Kupperman, *Character*, pp. 54–64; and Oakley, *Morality and the Emotions*, chap. 4.

to know whether people can exercise control over them. If they are valued as good and evil, however, this is not a vital issue.

This is not to say that on the recursive account, control of one's emotions is irrelevant. If some emotions are voluntary, then they or the actions of producing them can be not only good or evil, but also right or wrong, and people who have them can deserve praise or blame for them as they cannot for emotions that are innate to their personalities. Voluntary emotions can also embody greater intrinsic values. If a person chooses to produce a good attitude in herself from a good motive, such as a desire for the attitude for itself, her producing it involves a form of loving the good that is not possible for someone who merely finds the attitude within herself. Though the latter person can be pleased to have the attitude, she cannot actively pursue it, which on some versions of the recursive account is a further intrinsic good (see chapter 4, section 3). But these points concern only refinements of the recursive account and not its core claim, which is that attitudes can be intrinsically good or evil regardless of whether a person controls them.

Against this claim, some contemporary views define virtue and vice as voluntary states, so the virtues not only issue in choices of how to act but must also themselves at least partly result from choice.[24] This demand for a voluntary origin is clearly implausible if the virtues are occurrent attitudes, since no one can produce or eliminate these attitudes in herself from one moment to the next. It therefore usually goes with a view of the virtues as stable dispositions, so that what must in part involve choice is not the current exercise of a good disposition, but its initial formation and development. But even in this form the demand is implausible. If a person is habitually disposed to seek others' pain for itself, do we need to know her disposition's origin to know whether it is malicious and mars her life? If she habitually seeks others' pleasure, does that not by itself make her benevolent? She may not deserve praise or blame for a disposition she did not voluntarily develop, but praiseworthiness and blameworthiness are different properties from virtue and vice or good and evil. It is therefore a merit in the recursive account that its core claim does not require that the virtues and vices be voluntary.[25]

---

24. Zagzebski, *Virtues of the Mind,* pp. 102–6, 116–28; and McKinnon, *Character, Virtue Theories, and the Vices,* pp. 30, 60–62, 73–76.

25. For a similar view about virtue and voluntariness, see Slote, *From Morality to Virtue,* chap. 7.

The account also satisfies consequentialist assumptions by allowing and even encouraging a standard consequentialist characterization of right action in terms of the quantity of good and evil it results in. The account makes its own claims about actions, namely, that those done from virtuous motives are intrinsically good and those done from vicious motives evil. But these claims concern goodness and evil rather than rightness, which can be characterized, as in standard consequentialisms, in terms of an action's outcome. The account does not strictly require this characterization. It is logically possible to combine it with the view that actions are right when they fulfill duties framed independently of goodness and evil, and even with a characterization of rightness in terms of virtue, so right actions are those that either do or might issue from virtuous motives.[26] But the account does not combine well with these views. By making goodness and evil central for the analysis of virtue, it strongly suggests that they are central for morality generally, including the theory of right action. And goodness and evil are most clearly central if rightness is characterized directly in their terms, through the quantities of good and evil actions result in.

If the account is combined with this characterization of rightness, the resulting consequentialism uses the properties of goodness and evil in two independent ways. It uses these properties and the intentional relation of loving or hating to identify the virtues and vices; and it uses these properties and the largely causal relation of resulting in outcomes to identify right and wrong actions. It contains two parallel derivations, of virtue and vice by one relation to its core properties and of rightness and wrongness by a different relation. Because these derivations are independent, the judgments they issue in are also independent. Whether an action is virtuous depends only on the motive from which it is done, regardless of its outcome; whether an action is right depends only on its outcome. It is therefore possible for a virtuous action to be wrong given its consequences, and for a right action to be vicious. This mutual independence of rightness and goodness is a central theme in Ross's *The Right and the Good*: "the doing of a right act may be a morally bad action, and . . . the doing of a wrong act may be a morally good action; for 'right' and 'wrong' refer entirely to the thing done, 'morally good' and 'morally bad' entirely to the motive from which

---

26. The second type of characterization is found in some versions of virtue ethics; see chapter 8, section 1.

it is done."[27] A standard consequentialist theory incorporating the recursive account shares this view. By using distinct derivations to identify virtue and rightness, it allows that what has these properties may also be distinct.

This independence does not mean that virtue is irrelevant to rightness. On the contrary, if what is right is what results in the most good, and virtue is good, then in evaluating actions as right or wrong, we must consider any virtue they will embody or produce. There are two ways in which, within a consequentialist theory, the goodness of virtue can affect judgments about right action.

In an important range of cases, this goodness supplies an additional reason to perform an action that is right but not a reason that can change which action this is. These cases include, most centrally, ones where the relevant virtue will be embodied in the action a person is about to perform. Imagine that of the actions available to a person, one will produce the greatest total of all other intrinsic goods except her own virtue now. Any plausible version of the recursive account will say that the most virtuous action she can perform now is one directed in the appropriate way at these greatest goods. Though there is some virtue in pursuing lesser goods for themselves, there is more virtue in doing the same for greater goods (see chapter 3). But this means that the most virtuous action she can perform now, assuming she has the relevant motives, is one that is already on other grounds right. The value of her virtue gives her an additional reason to perform this action and magnifies the difference between the goodness of its outcome and that of its next-best alternative. But it cannot change which action is right. On the contrary, the very facts that make the action most virtuous also make it, independently, right.

The same is true in some cases where the virtue in question will be embodied in a person's actions at other times or in the actions of other people. But virtue does not always have this limited relevance to rightness; sometimes its goodness can change which action is right. For example, sometimes a person cannot, given her present attitudes, perform the action that will produce the greatest goods other than her own virtue now from a virtuous motive; she does not

---

27. Ross, *The Right and the Good,* p. 7. Ross carries this independence so far as to use "act" to refer only to behaviour viewed independently of its motive and "action" to refer to it only in light of its motive. In this usage, acts can only be right and actions can only be good.

have that motive within her. But she can produce some slightly lesser goods for the goods' own sakes. Here the greater virtue embodied in the second action can make it all things considered right, with the extra value it embodies as virtuous outweighing the lesser value it will produce. This fact may be unable to motivate the person to action. If she could be moved by thoughts of the overall good an action will result in, why could she not perform the first action from a virtuous motive? But it can motivate other people. If they have a choice between making either the first or the second of her actions available, considering the value of her virtue can make them prefer the second. A similar point applies to social institutions. It may be that under one set of institutions, people will produce slightly fewer base-level goods but act from better motives, with the latter fact making those institutions on balance preferable. We will later consider two competing arguments to this effect: that the welfare state and a free market in blood undermine individual charitable action and are therefore undesirable (see chapter 5, section 3). These arguments can allow that the welfare state and the sale of blood are slightly more efficient than the alternatives at producing goods other than virtue while at the same time claiming that their destructive effects on charitable action outweigh their other benefits.

This more substantive relevance of virtue to rightness is even clearer for forms of virtue not involving action, such as virtuous desire and feeling. On the recursive account, it can be right to absent oneself from an otherwise valuable activity to feel regret for a lost good or compassion for another's pain. It can also be right to encourage such feelings in others at the expense of some base-level goods. Perhaps educating a child to desire and feel appropriately requires not allowing it some possible pleasure or knowledge, where the loss of these base-level goods will not be made good through the future effects of her greater virtue. Even so, this moral education can be on balance right, as producing the best life overall for the child.

Certain of the recursive account's claims about the goodness of virtue may be disputed. For example, some may deny that the account succeeds in making virtue intrinsically good. The account makes the value of an attitude depend on that of its object—for example, the goodness of a desire for pleasure on the goodness of the pleasure. How is this consistent with the attitude's being *intrinsically* good?

This objection is clearly unpersuasive given the looser view of intrinsic goodness, which allows such goodness to be affected by a state's relations (see chapter 1, section 1). But it is also not persuasive given the strict view. This latter view does not allow a state's intrinsic goodness to depend on the *existence* of another state; that is why adherents such as Moore test for intrinsic goodness by asking whether a universe containing only a given state and no other is good.[28] But the view does not preclude a state's intrinsic goodness depending on the *goodness* of another state. A desire for pleasure, for example, can exist and be good in a universe where no pleasure exists; it can pass Moore's "isolation" test. Hence Moore himself, despite his strict view, happily makes recursive claims. One could propose an even stricter view of intrinsic goodness, on which such goodness cannot depend even on the goodness of other states. But it is hard to see what purpose this view would serve other than to rule out an otherwise perfectly intelligible account of virtue. On all useful understandings of "intrinsic" goodness, what the recursive account ascribes is just that.

Rather differently, it may be objected that the account ignores an important distinction between moral and non-moral goodness. Pleasure, knowledge, and achievement, it may be said, are non-moral goods, but virtue is, distinctively, a moral good, and vice a moral evil. In treating both base-level and higher-level goods as simply intrinsically good, the account ignores the special moral value of virtuous states of mind.

The recursive account can certainly distinguish verbally between moral and non-moral goodness. Ross says that unlike pleasure and knowledge, virtue is "morally good," where "morally good" means "good either by being a certain sort of character or by being related in one of certain definite ways to a certain sort of character."[29] In his usage, "moral" goodness is distinguished only by the objects that possess it. It is intrinsic goodness—the very same property—when had by traits of character or their expressions. The recursive account can take a similar line. It can say that moral goodness is intrinsic goodness when had by attitudes to other goods and evils; it is higher-level goodness, and moral evil is higher-level evil. This usage is in fact attractive. One merit of the recursive account is to distinguish the virtues and vices clearly from other intrinsic values, a dis-

---

28. Moore, *Principia Ethica*, pp. 91, 93, 95, 187–88; see also Ross, *The Right and the Good*, p. 75.

29. Ross, *The Right and the Good*, p. 155. There is a similar merely verbal definition of "moral" goodness in Frankena, *Ethics*, p. 62.

tinction we can signal by calling higher-level values "moral" and base-level ones "non-moral." I shall do this in what follows, calling virtue alone morally good and vice morally evil. But this will leave untouched the substantive point that on the recursive account, virtue has the same kind of goodness as pleasure and knowledge.

One may reply that a verbal distinction is not enough: moral goodness is not the same property when had by different objects, but a distinct moral property. I see no need to postulate this distinct property. If we can distinguish benevolence, compassion, and other attitudes verbally, why complicate the metaphysics of value? But let us grant for argument's sake that there is a distinct property of moral goodness. The recursive account does not deny that virtue has this property; it does not affirm this, but it does not deny it. It says only that whatever other properties virtue has, it has the same kind of goodness as pleasure and knowledge. And there are powerful reasons to accept this claim. The non-moral goodness of pleasure and knowledge makes it appropriate to love these states and gives agents reason to promote them; surely the same is true of the goodness of virtue. The non-moral goodness of pleasure and knowledge contributes to the overall goodness of states of affairs; surely the goodness of virtue does as well. Recall the two possible worlds discussed above, one with slightly more pleasure and the other with more virtue. If the second world is on balance better, as intuitively it is, the virtue it contains must compensate for its shortfall in pleasure, which requires virtue to contribute the same kind of goodness as pleasure. Though the recursive account does not deny that virtue has a distinct property of moral goodness, it is surely on firm ground in granting virtue ordinary goodness.

The recursive account, then, makes claims about the intrinsic goodness of virtue that are both attractive and consistent with consequentialism. This last fact is important in part because many philosophers still believe consequentialism can only value virtue instrumentally. Their view is false to the history of consequentialism: such notable consequentialists as Brentano, Rashdall, and Moore give virtue a central place in their lists of intrinsic goods. The view is also false in itself, given the clear possibility of a recursive account. But some may question the larger significance of these facts. Though the recursive account may be attractive to philosophers who accept consequentialism, many, probably the majority, do not. These non-consequentialists usually agree that part of morality concerns intrinsically good and evil states of affairs, so there are moral duties to promote the one and prevent the other. But they hold that there are other duties that can conflict with these and sometimes outweigh them, such as duties to tell the truth, keep promises, and so on. Of what interest to them is the recursive account?

Non-consequentialists should not reject the recursive account; instead, they should think about extending it. They should see the account as giving a characterization of virtue appropriate to the part of morality concerned with good and evil states of affairs, but as needing to be supplemented by other accounts appropriate to whatever other parts of morality there are. If there are situations where telling the truth is right even though it does not result in the most good, then desiring, pursuing, and taking pleasure in telling the truth in these situations should be virtuous and good. And there should be other non-consequentialist virtues corresponding to other non-consequentialist grounds of rightness.

This is the approach Ross takes. He is, famously, no consequentialist, affirming several moral duties other than ones to promote good and prevent evil. This is reflected in his account of virtue. He takes virtue to consist partly in action from the desire to produce something good or to produce pleasure for another being—both forms of recursive virtue—but also partly in action from the desire to do one's duty.[30] And given his non-consequentialism, he allows that this third form of virtue can conflict with and outweigh the other two. If a person tells the truth at what he knows is some cost in base-level goods, because he believes that doing so is right, Ross would say his acting from this motive is more virtuous than if he lied from a desire to produce the greatest goods. In fact, Ross's non-consequentialism should lead him to recognize more forms of virtue than he does. If it can be virtuous to desire another's pleasure without thinking pleasure is good, as Ross explicitly allows, it should likewise be virtuous to desire to tell the truth without thinking truth-telling is right. In both cases, a direct impulse to the good or right should have value alongside one based on a moral belief. But then there should be a distinct virtue corresponding to each non-consequentialist duty Ross recognizes—that is, a distinct virtue of loving each of fidelity, reparation, gratitude, and so on.

Non-consequentialists should follow Ross's lead and see the recursive account as giving a picture of virtue appropriate to the part of morality concerned with intrinsic goods and evils. If this part is the whole of morality, as consequentialism maintains, the account gives

---

30. Ross, *The Right and the Good,* pp. 157–60.

a complete picture of virtue and vice. Even if the part is not the whole, the account still gives an important part of the picture and is worth studying both for its own sake and for the light it can shed on other forms of virtue. Though I will return to this last point, about implications for other forms of virtue, in chapter 7, I will for the most part examine virtue in a consequentialist setting. There is much to explore in the details of the recursive account, but first there are some general questions about the effect of including it within a consequentialist framework.

3. *Virtue in Consequentialism*

The recursive account's claims about virtue are perfectionist rather than welfarist. They make virtue good and vice evil regardless of a person's attitudes to them; for example, they make benevolence good regardless of how much a person wants or is pleased by his benevolence. It is true that many forms of virtue involve desire for or pleasure in some good—for example, in another person's pleasure—but it is not a condition of their goodness that anyone desire or take pleasure *in them*. On the recursive account, the virtues consist in certain attitudes but are good apart from any further attitudes to them.

At the same time, the account allows a certain rapprochement between welfarism and perfectionism. Imagine that a pure hedonism is supplemented by the recursion-clauses (LG)–(HE). These clauses add a perfectionist element to what before was a purely welfarist theory of value, but what they add is only minimally perfectionist. The new good they introduce, virtue, is defined entirely by reference to welfarist values; it consists initially in loving pleasure and hating pain. The new evil, vice, is likewise defined by reference to welfare. The resulting mixed theory is in several ways more attractive than pure hedonism. It can agree that of the two worlds described earlier, the one with more virtue and slightly less pleasure is better, and it can also agree that a torturer's pleasure in his victim's pain is in one respect evil. But these advantages are gained by the smallest possible departure from hedonism. The mixed theory still holds that pleasure is the only base-level good and pain the only base-level evil, and its higher-level values are all defined in terms of these forms of welfare.

Similarly, the recursive account moves a purely perfectionist theory some distance toward welfarism. Imagine a perfectionism that values only knowledge and achievement. If supplemented by the recursion-clauses (LG)–(HE), it holds that certain pleasures, pleasures in knowledge and achievement, are intrinsically good. These pleasures are not good just as pleasures; they are good only as pleasures in something good. But if the theory affirms their value, it can say that an ideal life, one containing all the goods, must contain pleasure. This life will initially contain knowledge and achievement, and, as a further good, it will contain virtuous pleasures in them. It will also contain the fulfillment of desires for knowledge and achievement. These higher-level claims do not value forms of welfare as such and are therefore consistent with pure perfectionism. But they allow a perfectionist theory to say of welfare in general what Aristotle says of pleasure: though not the only intrinsic good, nor even as such a good, it is nonetheless an essential element in a fully desirable life.[31]

The recursive account, then, allows a welfarist theory to add a perfectionist element while remaining at its base level resolutely welfarist, and also allows a perfectionist theory to hold that an ideal life will contain forms of welfare. But I believe the account has more far-reaching implications. Accepting it undermines the attractions of either pure theory about base-level values.

If the recursive account cannot satisfy Nozick's demand for explanatory unification, it accepts an ineliminable dualism between base- and higher-level values: its base-level goods are good for one reason, its higher-level goods for another. And accepting this dualism weakens any ground for insisting on monism at the base level. Allowing the one element of pluralism makes it less reasonable to resist and more natural to accept further pluralist claims. If a purely welfarist theory is supplemented by the minimal perfectionism of the recursion-clauses, it has less reason to resist the further perfectionism of base-level goods such as knowledge and achievement. And if a perfectionist theory accepts the duality of base- and higher-level perfections, it has less reason to resist non-perfectionist goods such as pleasure. Partly for this reason, I think the most plausible versions of the recursive account start from base-clauses that mix welfarist and perfectionist values, as base-clauses (BG) and (BE) do. (BG) affirms both the welfarist good of pleasure and the perfectionist goods of knowledge and achievement, and (BE) offers a similar

---

31. Aristotle, *Nicomachean Ethics*, 1173a9–12, 1174b15–1175a2, 1175b24–1176a3.

mix of evils. Though there is no logical inconsistency in combining the recursive structure with base-clauses affirming just one kind of value, accepting the dualism between base and higher levels relaxes the objections to pluralism generally and makes a more thorough-going pluralism plausible.[32]

A second consequence of valuing virtue within consequentialism concerns the relation between acting rightly and achieving one's own good, or between what Thomas Nagel calls the "moral life" and the "good life."[33] In agent-neutral consequentialism, what is right is standardly what results in the greatest total good for all persons. Considering only base-level values, this implies that acting rightly often requires an agent to sacrifice her own good. Imagine that she can produce either 10 units of pleasure for herself or 20 for other people. What is right by agent-neutral standards is for her to produce the 20 for others, thereby sacrificing the 10 for herself.

The relation between right action and one's own good changes, however, if virtue, too, is good. Then in pursuing others' pleasure for itself a person acts virtuously, achieving a further good in her own life. And on all plausible versions of the recursive account, pursuing the greater good of others is more virtuous than pursuing a lesser good of one's own (see chapter 3). Assuming the person has appropriate motives, therefore, her acting rightly maximizes her own virtue now, or maximizes her own achievement of one intrinsic good.

Whether her gain in virtue from acting rightly counterbalances her loss in pleasure depends on how much value virtue has compared to base-level goods (see chapter 5). If virtue has infinite value compared to these goods, a sacrifice of them can always be outweighed by right action, and morality and one's own good can always coincide. If virtue has only finite value, however, acting rightly will sometimes involve self-sacrifice. On this more plausible view, the extra virtue involved in pursuing others' greater pleasure can be outweighed in one's own life by the loss of pleasure for oneself. In some cases, acting rightly can maximize one's good; in other cases, it cannot. Even in the latter cases, however, virtue's having value changes the relation between morality and one's good. Pursuing

---

32. Note the converse: given a highly unified theory of base-level values, one has some reason to resist the recursion-clauses and the pluralism they introduce. The theory of value defended in my *Perfectionism* claims to be unified in this way.

33. Nagel, *The View from Nowhere*, pp. 189–200.

others' greater good no longer involves only sacrifice on one's part, but can mean achieving an additional good oneself.

Even if virtue had infinite value compared to other goods, the recursive account would not derive the moral life from the good life, nor would it try to justify the demands of right action in self-interested terms. This has often been an ambition of philosophers: to show that concern for one's own good, taken as the ultimate starting point of practical thought, requires the conventionally moral treatment of others. Hobbes attempts this argument using a welfarist theory of the good, Plato and Aristotle using perfectionist ones. But the recursive account has no such ambition. It starts from base-clauses that are agent-neutral, saying that from each person's point of view, the pleasure, pain, and knowledge of others are good or evil in the same way as her own. Its claims about right action likewise appeal to agent-neutrality: what is right is what maximizes the good of all. Given the strong view that virtue has infinite comparative value, the account could add that acting rightly can maximize the agent's own good, but this would be a separate and subsidiary claim. The account's reasoning would not be, "Agents ought to maximize their own good, which requires being virtuous, which requires conventionally right action towards others." It would be, "Agents ought to maximize the good of all, which requires conventionally right action, and as a side effect can maximize their good." Morality would not be derived from self-interest; instead, self-interest or one's own good would involve an independently grounded morality as a component. We can imagine a version of the recursive account that starts from agent-relative base-clauses, ones saying that each person should care only about his own pleasure, pain, and knowledge. This account can then give virtue, as it defines virtue, infinite comparative value. But virtue as so understood has no connection to conventionally right action; it consists only in loving one's own lower-level goods. In the most plausible versions of the recursive account, virtue is in large part a response to agent-neutral values, and these values themselves ground claims about the right. Even if these versions held that morality and one's good can coincide—which requires a very strong assumption about virtue's comparative value—they would not reduce the former to the latter. Virtue is part of the agent's good, but only because he already has independent reason to care about the good of others.

A final implication of the recursive account concerns supererogation. Supererogatory actions are ones that go beyond an agent's duty; they are morally worthy actions, but not ones she is required to do or would be wrong to omit. The most familiar, maximizing versions of consequentialism notoriously leave no room for supererogation. If each person's duty is always to produce the most good possible, she can never exceed that duty. Some philosophers, seeing this as a flaw, propose amending consequentialism to allow for supererogation. One possibility is to switch from a maximizing to a satisficing principle of right action, according to which each person's duty is only to produce outcomes that are satisfactory or reasonably good.[34] Another is to give agents moral permission to weigh harms and benefits to themselves more heavily than equal harms and benefits to others, so that when maximizing the good is especially costly to them, they may, though they need not, omit to do so.[35] But though these proposals allow in one sense for supererogation, they do not by themselves capture the idea that supererogatory actions are especially morally worthy. On neither proposal can we say that these actions are more right than their alternatives, since they are not. And though they may produce more good than their alternatives, this is a fact about their consequences rather than about the actions themselves and can be shared by actions that are not supererogatory—for example, actions that accidentally and without the agent's foreknowledge produce great goods. A complete account of supererogation must explain how supererogatory actions are specially admirable in themselves, and here the recursive account can help. Since these actions aim at greater goods than other equally right actions, they manifest greater virtue on the agent's part and are therefore intrinsically better. Their special moral worth is a matter of the special intrinsic value of their motive. Though supererogatory actions are not more right than their alternatives, they are intrinsically better because they are directed at greater intrinsic values.

34. Slote, *Common-Sense Morality and Consequentialism;* chap. 3.
35. Scheffler, *The Rejection of Consequentialism;* and Davis, "Abortion and Self-Defense."

3

Degrees of Virtue and Vice

As formulated to this point, the recursive account says only that certain attitudes are intrinsically good and others evil, but not how good or evil they are. Yet surely some instances of loving good are better or more virtuous than others, and some instances of loving evil are worse. There are *degrees* of virtue and vice, and a complete account must explain how this is so.

At least two factors seem relevant to an attitude's degree of value, of which one is its *intensity*. One can desire a state of affairs more or less fervently,[1] pursue it more or less vigorously, and take more or less pleasure in it, and these differences seem intuitively to affect the attitude's value. In at least many cases, loving a good more intensely seems better than loving it less intensely, and hating it more intensely seems worse; thus, desiring another's pleasure more intensely seems better, as does being more intensely pleased by his pleasure. The second relevant factor is the *value of the attitude's object*. In many cases, loving a greater good with a given intensity seems better than loving a lesser good with the same intensity, and loving a greater evil with a given intensity seems worse; thus, taking pleasure in another's agonizing pain seems worse than taking similar pleasure in his mild pain. A complete recursive account must explain how an attitude's degree of value depends on these two factors, its intensity and the degree of good or evil of its object.

---

1. Intensity of desire can be understood in two ways: as the intensity with which a desire is felt or as its motivational force or likelihood of issuing in action, especially in competition with other desires. If these two forms of intensity always go together, the recursive account can use just one measure of the intensity of desire. If they can diverge, as seems plausible, it needs two. But I will ignore this possibility and speak simply of intensity of desire as a single thing.

At the same time, the account must address a related *problem of division*. None of us can love all good things with infinite intensity. We all have finite capacities for desiring, pursuing, and taking pleasure in what is good, and the question therefore arises of how best to divide our love among good objects. If there are two good states of affairs, one better than the other, what is the best division of love between them? What is the ideal combination of attitudes to the two states? As stated, this problem of division involves a degree of abstraction. It is not as if each person always feels the same total quantity of virtuous love, so all that can change is how that total is parcelled out. On the contrary, she can often feel more or less love, and on many views her feeling more is always, other things equal, intrinsically better. It can even be an effect of a given division to increase her total concern for the goods involved, so that a change in one dimension of her attitudes leads to an improvement in another. But however a combination of attitudes comes about, one factor relevant to its value is how it divides its concern between good objects. We can isolate this factor by taking its total quantity of love as fixed and asking how that quantity is best divided: this is what I call the problem of division.

It may seem that a complete solution to this problem will follow from an account of the degrees of value in individual attitudes. For any combination of attitudes, this account will assign a value to each component attitude, given its intensity and the value of its object. Given the atomistic assumption that the value of a combination of states always equals the sum of its components' values, the best combination of attitudes will always be the one whose constituent attitudes' values sum to the greatest total. I will explore this atomistic approach in the first two sections of this chapter, examining a series of views about the values of individual attitudes with special attention to their implications for the problem of division. It will emerge in the third section, however, that this approach cannot capture all plausible claims about combinations of attitudes and must be supplemented by a further, holistic principle.

Before I begin, a methodological comment is in order. In the discussions to follow I will sometimes speak of "units" of intensity of love and hate and even of "units" of value in virtuous and vicious attitudes. I do not intend this mathematical language to suggest that virtue and vice can be measured with numerical precision or placed on anything like a complete cardinal scale. On the contrary, I believe our judgments about virtue and vice, like our judgments about other goods and evils, can at best be rough and imprecise. We can say that one person is much more virtuous or slightly less vicious than another, but we cannot make more determinate claims than these. My working assumption is only that we can deepen our understanding of these rough judgments by asking, hypothetically, which precise principles for measuring virtue and vice would be most attractive if precise measurement were possible. The principles I will formulate in this chapter are not ones we can apply in practice, but they express especially clearly ideas that can be present in and influence our everyday thinking about degrees of virtue and vice.[2]

1. *Indifference and Proportionality*

Let me start with a minimal claim about the problem of division: given two goods, one greater than the other, it is best to love the greater more intensely than the lesser. If one person is enjoying a very intense pleasure and another only a mild one, it is best to be more pleased by the first person's pleasure than by the second's. This minimal claim is somewhat vague, since it does not specify by how much more one should love a greater good. But partly for this reason, it seems intuitively undeniable. Surely, if what is good is responding appropriately to values, one should respond more intensely to what has greater value.

This minimal claim can be derived from several views about the values in individual attitudes, of which the simplest is a *linear view*. It holds that, other things equal, love of a greater good is always better than love of a lesser good, and hatred of a greater good always worse. It also holds that, other things equal, a more intense love of a

---

2. A fuller defence of this methodology would show how the rough judgments can arise out of precise cardinal ones by the logical device of supervaluations (see my *Perfectionism*, pp. 86–88). For any two people, we can in principle construct cardinal measures of their virtue, in the sense that we can write those measures down. Of the infinitely many possible such measures, however, some are morally unacceptable. If the first person is Gandhi and the second Stalin, any measure that makes Stalin more virtuous than Gandhi is unacceptable, as in any that makes him as much as 90 percent as virtuous. If we eliminate all cardinal measures that are in this way unacceptable, we will have left a set that are not morally unacceptable, and we can then say that those claims about the two people's virtue are true that are true on all the measures in this set. Thus, it can be true that Gandhi was much more virtuous than Stalin even if there is no one correct numerical measure of either's virtue; this will be so if all acceptable measures yield that conclusion. And we can formulate precise principles about virtue, imagining them to apply to all the precise measures in the set and to yield firm conclusions whenever their implications on all those measures are the same.

good is always better and a more intense hatred always worse. More specifically, the view treats both these relationships as constant or linear, so that the value of a fixed increase in either the value of an attitude's object or the attitude's intensity is always the same. In its simplest version, it holds that if state x is twice as good as state y, loving x with a given intensity is always twice as good as loving y with that intensity, and loving either x or y with twice a given intensity is always twice as good. This version of the linear view is represented in figure 3.1. In this graph and the six that follow, the horizontal axis represents the intensity of an attitude, with positive attitudes of loving to the right of the origin and negative ones of hating to the left, while the vertical axis represents value, with good attitudes above the origin and evil ones below. The top right quadrant therefore represents loving attitudes that are good, the top left hating attitudes that are good, and so on. Each line on the graph shows how the value of an attitude is a function of its intensity, given a fixed value for its object. The lines for attitudes to good objects, ones with the values m, $2m$, and so on, therefore run from the top right quadrant to the bottom left, since loving these objects is good and hating them evil, whereas the lines for attitudes to evil objects run from the top left to the bottom right. And the specific properties of these

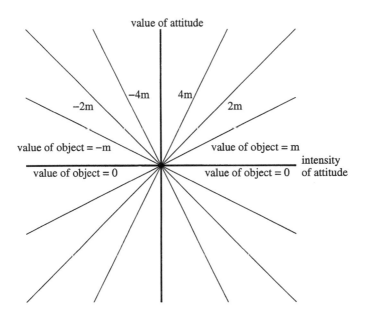

FIGURE 3.1

lines reflect specific features of the linear view. For example, that the lines in the top right quadrant have constant positive slopes shows that more intense loves of goods are always better, and in a linear way; that the lines for greater goods have steeper slopes shows that loves for these goods are, again, always better.

This graph of one version of the linear view brings out especially clearly some unstated implications of the original recursive account. One concerns the value of attitudes to objects that are intrinsically neutral, that is, neither intrinsically good nor evil. The line for attitudes to these objects lies between those for objects of value m and $-m$, that is, along the horizontal axis. Given this line, any attitude to a neutral object for itself, that is, love, hate, or indifference to it, is itself of neutral or zero value. If fame, for example, has no value, then loving and hating fame for itself also have no value. As we will see below, this is not the only possible view of attitudes to the neutral, but it does have intuitive appeal. It seems fitting that the lack of value in a neutral object should be reflected in a similar lack of value in any attitude to it.

This view of attitudes to the neutral does not imply that they are always on balance intrinsically neutral. Consider pleasure in something neutral. Though neutral as an attitude to an object, it has positive value as a pleasure and is therefore on balance good. Similarly, pain at something neutral, though neutral as an attitude, has negative value as a pain and so on balance is evil. Chisholm proposes acknowledging these facts by supplementing the recursive characterization with the clauses "Pleasure in the neutral is intrinsically good" and "Displeasure in the neutral is intrinsically bad,"[3] but these clauses confound two distinct ideas. If the recursion-clauses give the values of attitudes as attitudes to objects, they should treat both pleasure and pain in the neutral as neutral. That these states may also be good or evil as pleasures or pains is a matter not for any recursion-clauses but for the base-clauses (BG) and (BE), which affirm the goodness of all pleasures as pleasures and the evil of all pains as pains.[4]

A second implication concerns the value of indifference for itself to what is intrinsically good or evil. The indifference at issue here is

3. Chisholm, *Brentano and Intrinsic Value*, p. 64. See also Zimmerman, "On the Intrinsic Value of States of Pleasure," p. 35; Carson, "Happiness, Contentment, and the Good Life," p. 387; and Lemos, *Intrinsic Value*, pp. 75–77.

4. Brentano, from whom Chisholm derives the recursive characterization, himself clearly distinguishes between the value of a pleasure or pain as an attitude and as a pleasure or pain; see *The Origin of Our Knowledge of Right and Wrong*, pp. 23 n., 90–91.

not just the negative state of neither loving nor hating an object, as when one is neither pleased nor pained by an object one does not know exists. It is the indifference of neither loving nor hating when one has the cognitive states that make those attitudes possible, such as knowledge that an object exists. A view concerning this kind of indifference is implicit in the original recursion-clauses (LG)–(HE). If clause (LG) makes all instances of loving a good good and clause (HG) makes all instances of hating it evil, it follows that the intermediate state of being indifferent to that good has intermediate or zero value. If clauses (HE) and (LE) make all instances of hating an evil good and of loving it evil, indifference to it likewise has zero value. This view is reflected in the fact that all the lines in figure 3.1 pass through the origin, so attitudes involving neither love nor hate have neither positive nor negative value.

This view about indifference is not completely unacceptable, and the recursive account could perhaps retain it. But I do not find it in the end most plausible. Imagine that B knows A is suffering intense pain but feels no compassion whatsoever for A; though aware of A's pain, he is utterly unmoved by it. His indifference to another's evil seems to involve not just the absence of a good response, but the presence of a bad one; it manifests callousness, which is a vice and therefore evil. Similarly, if B fails to be in any way pleased by a great pleasure of A's, this seems not just not good, but evil. Indifference to intrinsic goods and evils, especially to great goods and evils, seems positively inappropriate and therefore a vice.

If we are to capture these judgments, we must supplement the recursive characterization with the following clauses about *indifference to intrinsic goods and evils for themselves*, (IG) and (IE):

(IG) If x is intrinsically good, being indifferent to x (neither loving nor hating x when, given one's cognitive states, one could do so) for itself is intrinsically evil.

(IE) If x is intrinsically evil, being indifferent to x for itself is intrinsically evil.

These clauses in turn require revisions to the original recursion-clauses (LG) and (HE).[5] Since the scale of intensity in attitudes is

---

5. They also need to be supplemented by instrumental clauses making indifference to instrumental goods and evils as means intrinsically evil, as well as by other relational clauses.

continuous, running from intense through mild hatred and indifference to mild and intense love, the scale of value based on it should likewise be continuous. But then if indifference to a good is evil, the very mildest love of that good must also be, though to a lesser degree, evil. Otherwise there will be a discontinuity in the scale of value, a jump from the evil of indifference to the goodness of the mildest possible love. To avoid this discontinuity we must hold, contrary to the original formulations of (LG) and (HE), that very mild loves of goods and hatreds of evils, even if appropriately oriented, can be intrinsically evil. And this revision does seem plausible. If it is callous and therefore evil to be entirely unmoved by another's pain, it should likewise be evil to feel compassion for his pain to an entirely insufficient degree; this, too, is a form, though a lesser one, of callousness. If it is evil to be entirely unmoved by another's pleasure, it should likewise be evil to be moved by it only minimally. If we accept these claims, we will say that for every good and evil there is a threshold or zero-value intensity such that only love or hatred above this intensity is good. Attitudes below the threshold, though oriented in the right direction, are inappropriately weak and therefore evil. They are not as evil as complete indifference to a good or evil or as attitudes that are wrongly oriented, but they do have some negative value. To reflect this view, the recursion-clauses (LG) and (HE) must be rewritten to value not all instances of loving good and hating evil but only those above a threshold intensity. And (IG) and (IE) must be extended to make intrinsically evil not just strict indifference to goods and evils, but also seriously inadequate loves and hatreds of them. The result is a graph whose lines do not pass through the origin but cut the vertical axis below it, giving zero-intensity attitudes negative value, and cut the horizontal axis to the left and right of the origin, giving zero-value attitudes positive or negative intensities.[6]

There are further claims that an adequate account of indifference should capture. One is that indifference to greater goods and evils is more evil, and in a specifically linear way, so that callousness about a pain that is twice as intense is always twice as evil. A second claim is that the threshold intensities for attitudes to greater goods and evils are higher, so a degree of compassion that is good for a mild pain can

---

6. Zimmerman, Carson, and Lemos all affirm analogues of (IG) and (IE) but retain (LG) and (HE) in their original, unrestricted forms (Zimmerman, "On the Intrinsic Value of States of Pleasure," p. 35; Carson, "Happiness, Contentment, and the Good Life," p. 387; and Lemos, *Intrinsic Value*, p. 37). Their theories therefore all involve unacknowledged discontinuities in the scale of value.

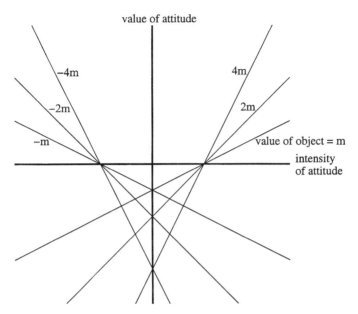

FIGURE 3.2

be insufficient and evil for an intense one. These threshold intensities are also linearly related, so the threshold for compassion for a pain that is twice as great is twice as high. The first of these further claims concerns the spacing of the points where the lines cut the vertical axis, which it says must be linear; the second concerns the spacing of the cuts on the horizontal axis. Unfortunately, the two claims cannot be simultaneously accommodated within a linear view. If this type of view accepts the first claim and makes linear claims about the degrees of evil in indifference, it must hold that the threshold intensities for all goods or evils are the same. A version of the view with these features is represented in figure 3.2. If a linear view makes the threshold intensities for greater values higher, it must hold that indifference to values that are twice as great is more than twice as evil. We will see later whether a different view of individual attitudes can capture both these claims about indifference.[7]

---

7. The versions of the linear view that incorporate (IG) and (IE) no longer claim that loving a good that is twice as great and loving the same good twice as intensely are always twice as good. But they retain the linear claims that an additional unit of love for a good that is twice as great is always twice as good, and that adding two units of love for a given good is always twice as good as adding one.

In addition to this difficulty, the linear view has highly contentious implications about the problem of division. It implies the minimal claim that it is best to love the greater of two goods more, but does so in a very strong form, one saying it is best to devote all one's love to the greater good and none at all to the lesser. This *concentration view* of division says that if neither of two goods exists, one should desire the greater as fervently as possible and the lesser not at all; if both of two evils do exist, one should be as pained as possible by the greater and not at all by the lesser. This concentration view follows from the linear view's claims that at any level of intensity, a unit of love for a greater good is better than a unit for a lesser good, and that for any good, the value of an additional unit of love is always the same. Together these claims imply that a unit of love for a greater good is always better than a unit for a lesser good, which in turn implies the concentration view. Given a fixed quantity of love, it is always best to give as much as possible to the greater of two goods and as little as possible to the lesser.[8]

This concentration view may seem attractive for one form of loving the good: actively pursuing it. Imagine that a person has 10 units of active pursuit available, say, 10 hours of activity. If he devotes all 10 hours to good x, he will produce x, which has 10 units of value. If he devotes all 10 hours to good y, he will likewise produce y, which has 5 units of value. But if he gives any less than all 10 hours to either x or y, he will produce nothing. Surely what is most virtuous for him in this situation is what will also produce the best outcome, namely, directing all his available activity to the greater good x.

But a recursive account should not apply its view about division directly to the active pursuit of goods. Pursuit is a distinct form of love and may have distinct value, so that desiring a good and pursuing it is better than merely desiring it (see chapter 4, section 3). But pursuit is sufficiently derivative from desire that claims about its division should follow from claims about the division of desire, so the best combinations of active pursuit are those that issue from the best combinations of desire. And to yield the right conclusion in the example above, a view about desire needs only the weak claim that the

---

8. Given clause (IG), giving no love at all to a lesser good involves indifference to that good, which is intrinsically evil. But avoiding this evil by giving a unit of love to the lesser good would be less good overall, according to the linear view, than giving the same unit to the greater good. Given linear principles, it can be better to accept the intrinsic evil of indifference if that allows one to produce a sufficiently greater good of virtuous love.

person should desire *x* somewhat more than *y*, not the strong claim that he should desire *x* exclusively. So long as he has even a weak preference for *x*, he will desire the outcome in which *x* exists more than those in which *y* or nothing exists, and to secure that outcome he will direct all his efforts at *x*.

To assess the concentration view, then, we should consider only its claims about the other forms of love: that one should concentrate all one's desire and pleasure on the greatest among a group of goods. These claims do not strike me as utterly unacceptable. They are at least intelligible, in the sense that I can imagine someone's accepting them. Consider, for example, some well-known claims of Aristotle's.

In his discussion of temperance, Aristotle says, strikingly, that when a temperate person forgoes a bodily pleasure such as that of an extra dessert, she feels no regret about missing this pleasure and would not enjoy it were she somehow to experience it.[9] Some commentators take this claim to rest on the idea that the forgone pleasure would not be a good in the temperate person's life,[10] but this idea is hard to defend. Often what makes it intemperate to choose a bodily pleasure is only that it conflicts with a greater good, such as health. And how can the mere presence of a competing good make a pleasure not only not the greatest good on offer but not a good at all? Aristotle can avoid this dubious idea by applying the concentration view to attitudes to bodily goods. He can then say that when one chooses a greater over a lesser bodily good, as the temperate person does, it is best and most virtuous to direct all one's concern to the greater good. Since one's attitude to this good should be only positive, this leaves no room for any regret.

The concentration view can also explain some claims of Aristotle's about attitudes to existing goods. He holds that the best possible activity is the admiring contemplation of the best objects in the universe.[11] Since these objects are the gods, this implies, on one well-known interpretation, that an ideal human life will be devoted entirely to contemplating the gods. Similarly, the best of the gods,

---

9. Aristotle, *Nicomachean Ethics*, 1118b34–35, 1119a12–16. Aristotle extends this claim to some other virtues but not to courage, which he says involves pain and therefore regret at the thought of one's death (1117a33–b16). Whereas Aristotle's account of temperance fits the concentration view, his remarks about courage come closer to what I later call the proportionality view.

10. See McDowell, "The Role of *Eudaimonia* in Aristotle's Ethics," pp. 369–71.

11. Aristotle, *Nicomachean Ethics*, 1141a18, 1177a21–22.

the prime mover, manifests his perfection by having as his sole activity the admiring contemplation of himself, with no attention to other objects.[12] Aristotle does not deny that other beings are good and can be the objects of virtuous contemplation. It is just that when there is a better object, which in the prime mover's case is himself, it is best to devote as much love as possible to it.

Since these claims of Aristotle's are intelligible, the concentration view that fits them is also intelligible. But I do not find this view nearly as attractive as a rival *proportionality view*. It holds that the best division of love between two goods is proportioned to their degrees of goodness, with as much more for the greater good as its value exceeds that of the lesser. This view agrees with the concentration view that one should love the greater of two goods more but holds that one should also love the lesser to some degree, one that reflects its comparative degree of goodness. If x is twice as good as y and neither exists, one should desire x twice as fervently but also y one-half as fervently; if x and y do exist, one should take twice as much pleasure in x but half as much pleasure in y. The best response to a world of existing goods is not, as Aristotle holds, to take all one's available pleasure in the best among them, but to take graduated pleasures in them all.

This proportionality view does not claim that combinations of attitudes that are less than perfectly proportioned are evil. Though not as good as they could be, these combinations can still be significantly good. Compare a person who feels intense compassion for another's pain but not quite as much compassion as he could. Though not the best possible, his compassion can still be notable for its goodness. Similarly, attitudes that do not exhibit ideal proportionality can, by coming close to proportionality, be notably good. Nor does the view claim to yield complete evaluations of attitudes. If A and B both divide their loves proportionally but B's loves are more intense, B's loves can be on balance better. They can even be on balance better if they are slightly out of proportion, so long as their greater intensity makes up for their slight departure from ideal divi-

---

12. This interpretation, whose claims about the prime mover are based on *Metaphysics*, 1072b18–22 and 1074b15–34, is given in Ross, *Aristotle*, pp. 182–83. The interpretation is rejected by many current commentators, but for our purposes it matters less whether it is exegetically correct than whether the view it ascribes to Aristotle is intelligible. Surely it is intelligible to hold that if the world contains different good objects, it is best to direct all one's love and admiration to the very best among them.

sion. Finally, the proportionality view does not presuppose more precise measurement than is realistically possible. If we cannot assign precise numbers to two goods, as we often cannot, we cannot precisely specify an ideal division of love between them. But we can often still make rough judgments about proportionality, as when one good is only slightly better than another but a person loves it far more intensely.

The proportionality view of division is highly appealing when considered in itself. If what is good is responding appropriately to values, surely the best combinations of attitudes must be attuned to their objects' degrees of value.[13] The view also has attractive implications. For example, it captures a plausible claim about regret defended by Bernard Williams, Ronald de Sousa, Michael Stocker, and others. These philosophers claim that when one had a choice between two goods and chose the greater good over the lesser, one should still feel some regret for the forgone lesser good.[14] For example, if one chose some more valuable pleasure over some less valuable knowledge, one should feel some regret for the forgone knowledge. They do not deny that one should feel pleasure in the greater good one chose, and even more pleasure than regret. Nor do they claim only that one should regret having had to choose between the two goods rather than being able to produce both. Though this latter regret, about one's situation, is certainly appropriate, they claim that one should also feel some regret that in one's situation one did not produce the lesser good. This claim, in its most plausible form, follows directly from the proportionality view.

After a choice between goods, the ontological status of these goods is different: one exists while the other does not. This means the forms of love possible for the goods are also different: pleasure that it exists for the one, regret or a wish that it existed for the other. But proportional division between the two is still possible. Just as one could desire the greater good more intensely before one chose, so one can afterwards feel more pleasure in it than regret for the lesser good. Since this is just what the proportionality view recommends, the view derives an attractive claim about regret from a more abstract view about division. The desired claim does not follow from the rival concentration view. Since that view makes it best to

13. The proportionality view is also defended in Nozick, *The Examined Life*, pp. 118–19, 258–66.
14. Williams, "Ethical Consistency," pp. 172–75; de Sousa, "The Good and the True"; and Stocker, *Plural and Conflicting Values*, chap. 8.

concentrate one's love, it says one should feel only pleasure in the greater good one chose and no regret at all. The two views also differ over the case in which one somehow chose the lesser of two goods. Here, the concentration view says one should feel only regret for the forgone greater good and no pleasure at all in the chosen lesser good. The proportionality view says, again more plausibly, that one should feel more regret for the forgone good but still some pleasure in the lesser good one did produce.

Some of the philosophers mentioned above argue that regret is appropriate only after a choice between different kinds of goods— for example, a choice of more valuable pleasure over less valuable knowledge, but not of a greater over a lesser pleasure. In the latter case, everything present in the lesser good is also present in the greater, so there is no ground for any regret.[15] But this restriction of the scope of the proportionality view is not persuasive. If one has chosen a greater pleasure for one person over a lesser pleasure for another, it is surely appropriate to regret the forgone pleasure for the second person. One can likewise feel appropriate regret after choosing a greater pleasure at one time over a lesser pleasure at another, or a greater pleasure with one set of accompanying introspectible qualities over a lesser pleasure with another set—say, a greater pleasure of suntanning over a lesser one of eating ice cream. So long as two goods are distinguishable in some way, even if not in their good-making properties, it is possible and appropriate to divide love between them proportionally.[16]

Despite these claims, the proportionality view does not imply that our lives should be consumed by regret for forgone goods. On the contrary, a recursive account incorporating this view can explain why there are limits on the regret one should feel. First, one should never feel more regret for a forgone lesser good than pleasure in a chosen greater good; that would precisely not be proportional. Second, even when regret is proportional and therefore intrinsically best, it can be instrumentally and even on balance evil. If intense regret for a forgone good will prevent one from vigorously pursuing

15. De Sousa, "The Good and the True," pp. 536, 548; and Stocker, *Plural and Conflicting Values*, chap. 8. See also Wiggins, "Weakness of Will, Commensurability, and the Objects of Deliberation and Desire," pp. 254–61; Nussbaum, *The Fragility of Goodness*, pp. 106–17; Dancy, *Moral Reasons*, pp. 120–23; Kekes, *The Morality of Pluralism*, pp. 57–58; and Landman, *Regret*, p. 9.

16. For a fuller version of this argument, see my "Monism, Pluralism, and Rational Regret."

some greater good in the present or future, it can be all things considered best to forgo the regret and pursue the greater good. Third, regret that takes the form of pain at the absence of a good is, though good as an attitude, evil as a pain, with the second property sometimes outweighing the first and making the feeling on balance evil. A further limit on desirable regret, especially for goods in the distant past, follows from a modal condition to be discussed in chapter 4. It is true that regret for a forgone good can also be instrumentally good, for example by strengthening one's commitment to goods it will be important to choose in the future, and that its instrumental goodness can outweigh the various limits on its desirability.[17] But the main point is that the desirability on balance of regret for a good depends on all the reasons for and against such regret, of which its satisfying proportionality is only one.

The proportionality view, then, is attractive both in itself and for its implications. But to include it in the recursive account, we must replace the linear view about the values of individual attitudes with either of two alternative views, which I call the *asymptotic* and *optimality views*.

2. *The Asymptotic and Optimality Views*

Both the asymptotic and optimality views agree with the linear view that, other things equal, love of a greater good is always better than love of a lesser good. The first of them, the asymptotic view, also agrees that a more intense love of a good is always better than a less intense love, but it denies that this relationship is linear.[18] Instead, it holds that the value of a fixed increase in the intensity of love for a good gets smaller as that love's intensity increases, so the more one cares about a good, the less value an extra unit of love for it has. More specifically, the asymptotic view holds that the value of a fixed increase in the intensity of love for a good diminishes asymptotically toward zero, so there is an upper bound on the value love of that good can have. A version of this view is represented in figure 3.3. For simplicity's sake, this graph and the three that follow ignore the

17. For a survey of arguments for and against regret, most instrumental but some intrinsic, see Landman, *Regret*, chap. 1.

18. Its most plausible versions also deny that the first relationship is linear, that is, they deny that loving a good that is twice as great with a given intensity is always twice as good.

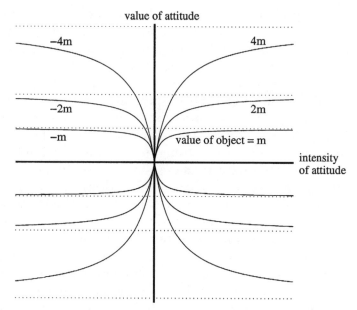

FIGURE 3.3

revisions required to accommodate the clauses about indifference, so their curves again pass through the origin. (The issues involved in accommodating these clauses will be taken up later.) The curves for attitudes to good objects therefore again run from the top right quadrant to the bottom left, whereas those for evil objects run from the top left to bottom right. But this time the curves' properties reflect features of the asymptotic view. That the curves in the top right always have positive slopes shows that more intense loves of goods are always better, but since the curves flatten toward a slope of zero, the value of increments of love diminishes. And there is a similar flattening in the other quadrants. An asymptotic view need not imply the proportionality view about division, but the version in this graph does because its curves satisfy what I will call the *proportionality constraint* on slopes. This constraint says that whenever state x is n times as good as y, and for any intensity i, the slope at point ni on the curve for love of x must be the same as the slope at point i on the curve for love of y. For example, if x is twice as good as y, the slope at $2i$ on the curve for love of x must always equal the slope at i on the curve for love of y; that way, combinations giving x twice as much love can be optimal. Since the curves in the top right of figure 3.3 do satisfy this constraint, the asymptotic view in this graph implies that the best divisions of love are proportioned to their objects' degrees of goodness. And since analogues of the constraint are satisfied in the other three quadrants, this view also implies that the best divisions of hatreds of evil—for example, of pains at others' pains—are likewise proportioned to their objects' degrees of evil, and that what we can call contraproportional divisions, such as loving an evil or hating a good that is twice as great twice as intensely, are worst. Just as proportional divisions maximize goodness in a combination of virtuous attitudes, by maximizing their total movement up the vertical axis, so contraproportional divisions maximize evil in a combination of vicious ones, by maximizing their total movement down.[19]

The version of the asymptotic view in figure 3.3 retains the linear view's treatment of attitudes to the neutral, holding that all such attitudes are themselves neutral. (The line for these attitudes still lies along the horizontal axis.) This version of the view also makes linear claims about the upper bounds on the values of attitudes: the asymptote for the curve representing love of an object that is twice as good is always twice as far above the horizontal axis. Finally, this version of the asymptotic view is like the linear view in treating virtuous and vicious attitudes symmetrically. It places upper bounds not only on the goodness of virtuous attitudes, but also on the evil of vicious ones; there are asymptotes below the horizontal axis as well as above it. It also relates these bounds symmetrically: the asymptote for a vicious attitude to a given object is always the same distance below the horizontal axis as the asymptote for a virtuous one is above it. And this version of the view makes the evil of a vicious attitude of a given intensity to an object always the same as the goodness of a virtuous attitude of that intensity to the object. In the asymptotic view represented in figure 3.3, virtue and vice are exact mirrors of each other.

The second of the views that can satisfy proportionality, the optimality view, departs further from the linear view by denying that a

---

19. Many formulas will generate a family of asymptotic curves satisfying the proportionality constraint; assuming V is the value of an attitude, i its intensity, and m the value of its object, a simple such formula is

$$V = \frac{im}{|i| + |m|}.$$

The implications of these formulas vary given different scales of measurement for i and m, but for any pair of scales and any judgments satisfying proportionality, there is some formula that yields those judgments.

more intense love of a good is always better than a less intense one. It holds that the value of a fixed increase in the intensity of love of a good not only diminishes but eventually becomes negative, so an attitude can lose value by gaining in intensity. For any good object, there is an optimal intensity of love, and just as love can be less than the best because it is not strong enough, so it can be less than the best because it is too strong. Nozick defends this view, saying that a "disproportionately intense response to a small value itself is of lesser value than a more proportionate response would be," and, likewise, a disproportionately intense hatred of a small evil is of lesser value.[20] One version of the optimality view is partially represented in figure 3.4, where the curves not only flatten as they rise from the origin but slope downward from a peak or optimal point. This version again implies the proportionality view about division, since its curves satisfy the proportionality constraint on slopes, and its doing so leads to two further claims. First, the optimal love of a good that is twice as great is always twice as intense, so the peak for love of this good is twice as far to the right of the origin. This is an obvious requirement of proportionality, but the view also makes optimal love of a good that is twice as great itself always twice as good, so the peak for this love is also twice as high. This, too, is a requirement of proportionality and is intuitively plausible. Imagine that one person feels optimal compassion for others' intense pains but none for their mild pains, while another feels optimal compassion for mild pains and none for intense pains. Surely the first person's attitudes are better overall. If so, ideal responses to greater values must be better than ideal responses to lesser ones, as figure 3.4 implies.

Though both imply the proportionality view, the asymptotic and optimality views are clearly different, and the recursive account must choose between them. This choice is somewhat complex.

Though the asymptotic view denies that more intense appropriate attitudes can be intrinsically less good, it agrees that they can be instrumentally and even on balance less good. If a person with a limited capacity for virtue loves a trivial good very intensely, she prevents herself from directing the bulk of that love to greater goods, which the asymptotic view says would be intrinsically better. So this view agrees with the optimality view that appropriately oriented attitudes can be in some way excessive. It allows them to be only instru-

20. Nozick, *Philosophical Explanations,* pp. 431–32; see also Nozick, *The Examined Life,* pp. 89, 124.

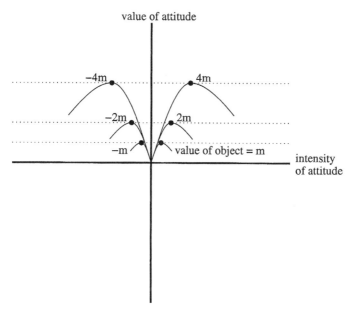

FIGURE 3.4

mentally rather than intrinsically excessive, but it shares the general idea that they can be too intense for ideal virtue. To discriminate between the views on this point, we need a sharply focused example.

Imagine that *A* and *B* have the same total capacity for virtuous pleasure, but whereas *A* lives in a very good world with many very good objects, *B* lives in a much less good world with only slightly good objects. The asymptotic view says it is best for both *A* and *B* to divide all their available pleasure among their worlds' good objects. If these objects' goodness is proportioned in the same way, *B* should love the best object in his world as intensely as *A* loves the (much better) best object in his, and likewise for all other objects. But the optimality view can say it is best for *B* not to feel some possible pleasure in goods. If his capacity for virtuous pleasure is sufficiently great, his using all of it could mean his loving only slightly good objects more intensely than is optimal, which would be less good than loving them less.[21] This claim—that it can be best to hold back some

---

21. It may be objected that the views' disagreement about this case disappears if we consider not just one form of virtuous love—pleasure in existing goods—but all three forms together. Then the optimality view can say that although *B* should not take as much pleasure in existing goods as *A,* he should compensate by having more intense desires for nonexistent goods and in particular should desire the

possible love—is what most centrally distinguishes the optimality from the asymptotic view, but it is hard to assess intuitively. I suspect some readers will find it attractive and on that basis prefer the optimality to the asymptotic view, whereas others will hold that it is always best to take the greatest possible pleasure in existing goods, however modest. My own intuitions run slightly in the second direction and therefore slightly in favour of the asymptotic view. This is also the position of one classical defender of the recursive account, Brentano. "It can never be reprehensible," he writes, "to feel the greatest joy possible in what is good, to enjoy it, as we say, with all one's heart. Descartes observed that the act of love when it is directed upon what is really good can never be too intense. And he was obviously right."[22]

In my judgment, the optimality view's appeal is further limited by the fact that its plausible versions must relativize their claims about optimal intensities to beings' differing capacities for love. Consider the biblical claim that God feels intense concern for every sparrow that falls (though he feels even more concern for humans).[23] If the optimality view assigned the same ideal intensities to all beings, and if these intensities were low enough that humans can sometimes exceed them, it would have to say that God's love for the sparrow is excessive and suboptimal; it would be better if the deity cared less about birds. Since this claim is not plausible, the view has to assign different optimal intensities to beings with different capacities, so God's ideal love of a sparrow is more intense than a human's. This relativization does not eliminate what is distinctive in the optimality view, which can still say there are cases like that of B above where a human should not use all his capacity for virtuous love. But it does make the view less simple than if its optima were fixed just by the

---

goods in A's world as intensely as A takes pleasure in them. But, first, there is no guarantee that B can transfer his love from the form of pleasure to that of desire; if he cannot, there is still some capacity for love the optimality view says he should not use. Second, even if B can transfer his love, a modal condition to be discussed in chapter 4 can tell him not to use all his capacity for desire either. Given this modal condition, the optimality view can tell B to hold back not only some of his capacity for pleasure, but also some of his total capacity for virtuous love.

22. Brentano, *The Origin of Our Knowledge of Right and Wrong*, p. 25; see also pp. 16–17 n. The Descartes reference is to *The Passions of the Soul*, part 2, article 139: "when the things which [our knowledge] constrains us to love are truly good, and those which it constrains us to hate are truly evil, love is incomparably better than hatred; it can never be too great, and it never fails to produce joy."

23. Matt. 10:29.

value of their objects, and this, in my judgment, makes it less plausible as a general view about value. It also raises the question whether any attraction we feel for the view may not reflect a more familiar concern, captured equally by the asymptotic view, about the best uses of finite capacities for love.

More serious difficulties emerge if we try to complete the representation of the optimality view in figure 3.4 by extending its curves further beyond their peaks in the top right and top left quadrants. There seem to be three main possibilities here. The curves can flatten out above the horizontal axis, so excessive appropriate attitudes such as excessive benevolence, though not ideally good, are still always positively good; they can flatten out below the horizontal axis, so these attitudes can become evil but only to a limited degree; or, rather than flattening, they can continue down to negative infinity, so excessive appropriate attitudes can become evil without limit. I find the first of these possibilities more attractive than the second, which is more attractive than the third. It is more plausible that intense pleasure in another's pleasure is always good than that it can become evil, and more plausible that its evil is limited than that that evil has no bound.[24] But these possibilities are not all available if the optimality view has to imply the proportionality view in its most plausible, which is an unrestricted, form.

It is in principle possible to restrict the proportionality view so it applies only to attitudes at or below their optimal intensities, and not to ones beyond them. But this restriction is implausibly ad hoc; surely, if proportionality matters up to a set of optimal points, it should matter beyond them as well. And a proportionality view that applies also to excessive attitudes has very strong implications. It does not allow the optimality curves to flatten anywhere past their

---

24. Nozick proposes a mixed selection from these possibilities, saying that even the most intense love of a good is always good, but intense hatred of evil can be evil (*Philosophical Explanations*, pp. 431–32). This yields a graph with curves that flatten out above the horizontal axis in the right half but drop below it in the left. Nozick gives no justification for this mixed view, and his endorsement of it may be influenced by the fact that some forms of love and hate—intentional pleasure and pain—have value not only as attitudes but also as pleasures and pains. It may be that both excessive pleasures in goods and excessive pains at evils are always good as attitudes, but the latter's evil as pains can make them on balance evil. Or perhaps both types of excessive attitudes can be evil as attitudes, but the former's goodness as pleasures makes them always on balance good. On either supposition, the pleasure and pain have the same values as attitudes and differ on balance only because of their additional values as hedonic states.

peaks, since that would violate the relevant constraint on slopes. Instead, it requires the curves to run down to negative infinity, so excessive appropriate attitudes can become evil without limit. If these attitudes can increase indefinitely in intensity, they can increase indefinitely in viciousness. And this initial requirement brings others in its wake. Consider the curves on the opposite sides of their peaks, where they run down to the origin. When they are extended below the origin, these curves represent the intrinsically vicious attitudes of hating good and loving evil, and although, consistently with proportionality, they could flatten out below the horizontal axis, this would not be intuitively plausible. It would not be plausible to place limits on the evils of hating good and loving evil but none on those of excessively loving good and hating evil, that is, limits on the forms of malice but none on those of excessive benevolence and compassion; the former are the intuitively worse attitudes. So a plausible optimality view must have curves that run down to negative infinity on both sides of their peaks, as in figure 3.5. The view must also change its treatment of attitudes to the neutral. It would be implausible to hold that intense loves of goods can become evil but intense loves of neutral objects remain neutral; the former are the intuitively better attitudes. And the completed optimality view cannot

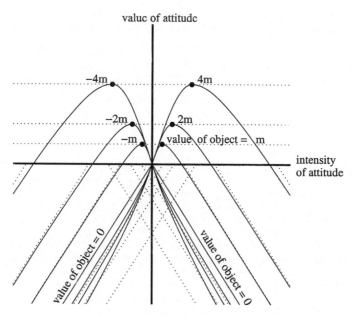

FIGURE 3.5

retain this treatment of attitudes to the neutral if it is to make the value of an attitude a continuous function of its object's value. Its curve for these attitudes can no longer lie along the horizontal axis but must be an inverted V with its apex at the origin, as in figure 3.5. Given this curve, there is an optimal attitude to neutral objects—namely, strict indifference—and while this attitude has zero value, all other attitudes to the neutral are evil. Though different from the asymptotic view's treatment, this one again has some intuitive appeal. If there is an appropriate attitude to the neutral, it is presumably indifference, and the completed optimality view makes this attitude intrinsically best. In addition, this view gives a simple account of the moral vice of fetishism. Fetishism consists precisely in loving for itself what is not intrinsically but at best instrumentally good, and the optimality treatment makes doing so intrinsically evil.

This completed proportional optimality view is a coherent and integrated alternative to the asymptotic view of individual attitudes, but it has several problematic features. First, it implies that intense appropriate attitudes such as pleasure in another's pleasure can become not just evil, but evil without limit. As I have said, I find this very hard to accept. How could attitudes as good as benevolence and compassion become that bad? Second, the view entirely abandons the asymptotic view's symmetrical treatment of virtue and vice—most importantly by denying that there is an upper bound on the evil of vicious attitudes as there is on the goodness of virtuous ones. (There are limits on how high the optimality curves go in figure 3.5 but none on how low they go.) As we will see in chapter 5, this rules out an attractive view about how the evil of vice compares to other values. Finally, the view's treatment of attitudes to the neutral seems unduly harsh. Imagine that someone has a mild desire for a neutral object such as the Montreal Canadiens' winning the Stanley Cup. Though his desire is not intrinsically good, it seems puritanical to call it evil. The optimality view could avoid this implication by moving its curve for attitudes to the neutral up the graph, so the curve's apex is above the origin.[25] But this would imply, counterintuitively, that mild loves and hatreds of the neutral are good. Worse, it would imply that contrary attitudes to a neutral object, mild love and hatred of it, can both be good. Nor, finally, is the opti-

---

25. This revision, which requires moving the other curves up as well, is not consistent with proportionality if the curves have to pass through the origin, but it is if the optimality view is revised to make indifference to goods and evils evil.

mality view's treatment of attitudes to the neutral needed to explain the vice of fetishism. This vice consists, we can say, in disproportionate love of the neutral, and its evil can be explained by principles specifically about disproportion (see section 3, below, and chapter 4, section 1).[26]

These various difficulties are not decisive objections to the optimality view, which does have some intuitive appeal. But I think that, on balance, an asymptotic structure is more plausible for judgments about virtue and vice, and I will assume that structure in what follows, with only brief references to the optimality view when it would make a difference.[27] It remains to be seen how the asymptotic view can be modified to accommodate clauses (IG) and (IE) about indifference to goods and evils. There are two ways in which, consistently with proportionality, this modification can be done.

If indifference to goods and evils is to be evil, the asymptotic curves must cut the vertical axis below the origin. The first modification achieves this by retaining the curves' original shapes but moving them all down the graph; this also requires moving their asymptotes down. In its most attractive version, it moves the curves down in proportion to their objects' values, so the curve for an object that

26. These problems may suggest reconsideration of an optimality view that implies only the restricted proportionality view, and whose curves can therefore flatten past their peaks. But this view faces numerous other difficulties. If its curves have determinate shapes past their peaks, it not only fails to mandate proportional division beyond the optimal intensities; it says that some other division of excessive love is best. This division may give more love to the greater of two goods but cannot do so proportionally. And how can any other division be better than a proportional one? In addition, specific versions of the view face more specific difficulties. If an optimality view makes all its curves flatten out above the horizontal axis, it has to make the drop-off from the peak to the flattening point smaller for attitudes to smaller goods and evils. (For a very trivial good, the peak is so close to the horizontal axis that there is no room for more than a tiny drop-off.) But then the view implies that it is best to give the bulk of any great excess of love to the lesser of two goods, since then the loss compared to optimality will be less. But surely it is unacceptable to say that one should love the lesser of two goods more! An optimality view could avoid this difficulty by having constant drop-offs for attitudes to all goods and evils, or a constant distance from the peak to the flattening point for all curves. This has the perhaps attractive implication that excessive loves of small goods can become evil while those of great goods remain always good, but the resulting view cannot give a treatment of attitudes to the neutral that avoids discontinuities. It may be that every version of the optimality view with flattening faces some such additional specific difficulty, alongside the general one of implying that some division of excessive love other than a proportional one is best.

27. By contrast, an optimality structure is clearly preferable for judgments about desert; see Kagan, "Equality and Desert."

is twice as good is moved down twice as far. This results in cuts on the vertical axis that are linearly spaced, so indifference to a good or evil that is twice as great is always twice as evil. If the curves satisfy proportionality, it also results in cuts on the horizontal axis that are linearly spaced, so the threshold or zero-value intensities for values that are twice as great are always twice as high (see fig. 3.6). The resulting asymptotic view therefore captures both of the plausible claims about indifference that could not be simultaneously accommodated in the linear view; in fact, if it captures one, it must capture the other. The second modification of the asymptotic view retains the original placement of the asymptotes but changes the shapes of the curves so that, staying within those asymptotes, they cut the vertical axis below the origin (fig. 3.7). If the resulting curves satisfy proportionality, as in figure 3.7, the cuts on both axes must be linearly spaced, so the two plausible claims are again, and this time both unavoidably, captured.

Both these modifications abandon the symmetrical treatment of virtue and vice found in the original asymptotic view. They do not do so as radically as the optimality view, however, since they still place upper bounds on the values of both virtue and vice. The first modification denies that these bounds are symmetrical; in figure

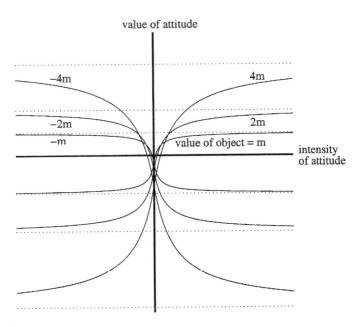

FIGURE 3.6

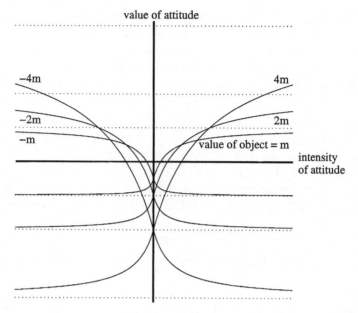

FIGURE 3.7

3.6, the asymptote for a vicious attitude to an object is always further below the horizontal axis than that for a virtuous attitude to the object is above it, so for any object there are vicious attitudes to it that are more evil than any virtuous attitude to it can be good. The second modification departs less from symmetry, retaining equal upper bounds for virtuous and vicious attitudes. But it holds, as does the first modification, that a vicious attitude of a given intensity to an object is always more evil than a virtuous attitude of the same intensity to it is good. And at least this weaker asymmetry is required by the combination of proportionality and the idea that indifference to goods and evils is evil. Any view combining these features must hold that in at least this minimal sense, vice is a greater intrinsic evil than virtue is a good.

This asymmetry between virtue and vice is not intuitively implausible, just as it is not implausible to hold that pain is a greater evil than pleasure is a good.[28] The recursive account can adopt either of the modified asymptotic views that implies this asymmetry, and it

28. Moore, *Principia Ethica*, pp. 212–12, 222–23; and Mayerfeld, "The Moral Asymmetry of Happiness and Suffering."

does not matter greatly which. But I will assume the second modification, the one in figure 3.7, which retains asymptotic symmetry. The resulting asymptotic view departs less from a symmetrical treatment of virtue and vice and, as we will see in chapter 5, allows a simpler formulation of an attractive view about how they compare to other goods and evils.

With this version of the asymptotic view, the recursive account makes attractive claims about the values of individual attitudes and also implies the proportionality view about the best divisions of virtuous love. But there are other claims about division that the account in its present form does not imply. Capturing these claims requires a different kind of principle.

3. *The Proportionality Principle*

Imagine that a person is extremely selfish, caring much more about lesser goods of his own than about greater goods of other people—for example, more about his own mild pleasure than about others' intense pleasure. His extreme selfishness and the disproportion it involves make his combination of attitudes less good than if he divided the same concern proportionally. His selfishness therefore involves at least a loss of goodness in his attitudes, or what I will call a *shortfall in his virtue.* Does it also involve, more strongly, a vice?

The concept of a shortfall in virtue is an important one for the theory of virtue. Often people's attitudes, though intrinsically good, are less good than they could be, and we need a term for the features that make them so. For example, a person may feel just mild compassion when he can and should feel intense compassion. If his compassion is above the threshold intensity, his failure to feel more compassion does not make his attitudes evil and is not a vice, but it does involve a shortfall in virtue. The same is true of some cases of disproportionate division. If a person is just mildly selfish, caring a little more about his own goods than about equal goods of other people, it seems right to say that despite their disproportion, his attitudes are on balance good. But the concept of a shortfall in virtue does not fit more serious disproportions such as extreme selfishness, which seems intuitively to be evil and a vice. The recursive account makes a very mild desire for another's minor pain evil, as well as indifference to his minor pain. If these petty forms of malice and callousness are vices, surely so is extreme selfishness. Can the recursive account capture this claim?

In its present form, the account takes the value in a combination of attitudes to equal the sum of its components' values as calculated by the asymptotic view. So let us apply this view to the two components of extreme selfishness, beginning with a person's intense love of his own good. Since this love is directed at a good object, the asymptotic view says it is intrinsically good, and in fact better than any less intense love of the same good. The view also says mild love of others' good is good if it is above the threshold intensity, as it surely can be. So on the asymptotic view, even extreme selfishness involves two components each of which is good, making it at most a shortfall in virtue and not a vice. On the rival optimality view, such selfishness could sometimes be a vice: if a person's love of his own good was so excessive as to be evil, it could makes his attitudes on balance vicious. But even apart from its other difficulties, the optimality view does not yield this conclusion in all cases. It allows that a selfish person's concern for his own good can be excessive but still good, or even below the optimal intensity but still much more intense than his concern for others' good. In both these cases his extreme selfishness still seems intuitively a vice, yet the optimality view finds it only a shortfall in virtue.

To make extreme selfishness always a vice, the recursive account must supplement its atomistic account of the values in individual attitudes with a holistic principle evaluating combinations of attitudes as combinations, or in light of the relations between their components.[29] More specifically, it must adopt a version of the following *proportionality principle*, (PP), which says that any disproportion in one's division of love between goods is, as that disproportion, intrinsically evil. The individual attitudes in a disproportionate combination retain their original values, which must be included in an overall evaluation of it. But the new (PP) holds that any mismatch between the ratio of one's intensities of love for two goods and the ratio of those goods' values is a separate intrinsic evil.

> (PP) If x is n times as intrinsically good as y, loving x for itself any more or less than n times as intensely as y is intrinsically evil as a combination.

This principle says that if x and y are exactly equal in value, loving either more intensely than the other is intrinsically evil; if x is one-half

---

29. The importance of evaluating combinations of attitudes as combinations is also stressed in Smith, "Varieties of Moral Worth and Moral Credit," p. 280.

as good as y, loving it anything other than half as intensely is evil. Whatever values one's attitudes to x and y have on their own, there can be a further evil in their combination if their intensities are out of proportion.

The proportionality principle reinforces the asymptotic view's claims about the best divisions of love but makes stronger claims about other divisions. If a combination of attitudes is perfectly proportioned, (PP) finds no intrinsic evil in it, and the value of the combination equals, as before, the sum of its components' values. Once there is a disproportion, however, (PP) finds this a separate holistic evil, and we should understand this evil to be greater when the disproportion is greater. If x is exactly as good as y, loving x much more intensely than y is worse than loving x a little more intensely, and in general, greater departures from proportionality make for greater intrinsic evils. Given this last claim, mild selfishness, or loving one's own good a little more than other people's, involves just a small holistic evil, whereas extreme selfishness involves a great evil. This means the former combination of attitudes can be on balance good while the latter is on balance evil. If a person is only mildly selfish, the evil (PP) finds in his loves is small and may be outweighed by the goodness they have on their own. As his selfishness becomes more extreme, the holistic evil increases until eventually his combination of attitudes is on balance evil. Whereas mild selfishness involves on balance just a shortfall in virtue, extreme selfishness is, as it intuitively should be, a vice.

A similar analysis is possible for vices such as cowardice. A coward cares about his comfort or safety, which is good in itself or as a means, but he cares more about his comfort or safety than about some greater good he could achieve by risking them. There is therefore a disproportion in his attitudes that makes for only a loss of goodness given the asymptotic view but involves an additional evil given the proportionality principle. If the good the coward forgoes is only a little greater than his comfort or safety, his cowardice may even, given (PP), be on balance only a shortfall in virtue. But if this good is much greater, as when it involves saving several people's lives at the cost of mild discomfort for himself, the disproportion between his concerns outweighs any good they contain individually, and his cowardice is, again intuitively, a vice.

The proportionality principle, then, allows the recursive account to find extremely disproportionate combinations not just less than ideally good but evil. And there is a related point where (PP) improves on the original account. Imagine that having started out extremely selfish, a person changes his attitudes so that he is no longer so. If he makes this change only by increasing his concern for other people's good, the asymptotic and optimality views will say his attitudes have improved or become more virtuous. But what if he reduces his selfishness only by decreasing his concern for his own good, leaving his concern for that of others unchanged? The asymptotic view then says his attitudes have only become worse. He has replaced a more intense love of his good with a milder one, which is less good, and has made no compensating change in his love of others' good. The optimality view agrees with this conclusion so long as his initial love of his good was below the optimal intensity, as it easily may have been.[30] Given this last assumption, his abandonment of extreme selfishness has on both views involved only a reduction in his virtue. But this claim is counterintuitive, and (PP) again lets us avoid it. With this principle we can say there is something good even in the person's second way of reducing his selfishness. Though his resulting individual attitudes are less good, their combination is less evil as a combination because it is less disproportionate. It remains an open question whether the second change results in attitudes that are on balance better; that depends on how the values identified by (PP) compare with those of individual attitudes. But given the proportionality principle, there is at least some extra good, or some less evil, in any move away from disproportionate division.[31]

As these various claims illustrate, the proportionality principle introduces a holistic element into a previously atomistic account of virtue and vice. The resulting account still characterizes a person's virtue at a particular time in terms just of his attitudes at that time, without tying them to longer-lasting dispositions. But with (PP), it denies that his virtue at a time depends just on the values of his individual attitudes at that time; it also depends on the relations between those attitudes. With (PP), the recursive account embraces Moore's "principle of organic unities," according to which "the value of a whole must not be assumed to be the same as the sum of the values of its parts."[32] Its claims can therefore be clarified by Moore's distinction between a combination's intrinsic value "as a whole" and its intrinsic value "on the

30. In this argument, his initial selfishness need not have been so extreme as to be on balance vicious; it can have been just a shortfall in virtue.

31. This argument is modelled on one of Kagan's about desert; see "Equality and Desert," p. 302.

32. Moore, *Principia Ethica,* p. 28; see also pp. 27–36, 92–96, 183–225.

whole."[33] A combination's intrinsic value *as a whole* is its intrinsic value just as a whole or as a combination, independently of any values in its parts. Its intrinsic value *on the whole* is its intrinsic value on balance or all things considered, that is, the value that results from adding its intrinsic value as a whole to any intrinsic values in its parts. In this terminology, (PP) gives the value as a whole of a combination of attitudes such as mild selfishness; it says this value is slightly negative. The value on the whole of mild selfishness is then arrived at by adding this slight negative value to the positive values in the combination's component attitudes, and this value on the whole is positive. Mild selfishness, though it is as a whole of negative value and therefore a vice, involves on the whole only a shortfall in virtue. (Having introduced the concept of a shortfall by reference to on-balance judgments of value, I will continue to describe mild selfishness and similar traits as only shortfalls in virtue, without explicitly noting that as wholes they are minor vices.) Extreme selfishness, by contrast, is vicious not only as a whole but also on the whole, or considering all factors relevant to its value.

My initial statement of the proportionality principle has been only partial, concerning only loves of good objects. The principle needs to be extended to other attitudes and must also be able to measure departures from proportional division. To see how all this can be done, consider a graph whose horizontal axis measures the intensity of love or hate for one object, while its vertical axis does the same for another (fig. 3.8). Whatever these objects' values, there will be a ray starting from the origin that represents proportional divisions of love and hate between them; I will call this the proportionality ray. In figure 3.8, the two objects are both goods, with the first twice as good as the second. The proportionality ray therefore lies in the top right quadrant, with a slope of $+\frac{1}{2}$. If the objects were both evils, this ray would lie in the bottom left quadrant; if one was good and the other evil, it would lie in the top left or bottom right. But wherever the proportionality ray is located, (PP) gives all the points on it zero value as combinations. Now consider the contrary ray, the one running in the opposite direction from the origin. It represents contraproportional divisions, such as hating twice as intensely a good that is twice as great. These are the worst divisions, and (PP) gives them some fixed negative value, say, -10. The values of other divisions are then determined by their angular distances from these two

33. Moore, *Principia Ethica*, p. 214f.

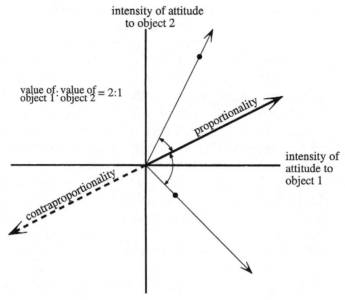

FIGURE 3.8

rays. For any division that is not proportional or contraproportional, (PP) draws the ray from the origin on which the point representing it is located, measures how far that ray is rotated around
from proportionality to contraproportionality, and uses that angular
distance to give the division a value between 0 and –10. The closer
the ray in question is to proportionality, the closer the division's
value is to 0; the closer to contraproportionality, the closer to -10. In
figure 3.8, this procedure is represented for two points, one in the
top right, representing excessive love of the lesser good, and one in
the bottom right, representing love of the greater good but hatred
of the lesser. Since in this case the point in the bottom right is rotated further around—the arc from its ray to the proportionality ray
is longer—its evil as a combination is greater.

As so extended, the proportionality principle makes judgments
about many more combinations of attitudes than just loves of goods.
It says it is disproportionate and therefore evil to hate a lesser evil
more than a greater one—for example, to care more about one's
own mild pain than about another's intense pain. This, too, is a
form of selfishness, though about evils rather than goods. It is likewise evil to love an evil more than a good. Here one's love of the evil
object is already evil by recursion-clause (LE), but there is a further

evil in the mismatch between one's division of concerns and the values of their objects. Finally, (PP) says it is evil to love a neutral object more than one loves a good. Imagine that a person cares more about fame, which is intrinsically neutral, than about knowledge. Given the asymptotic view, her desire for fame is in itself neutral, but its being more intense than her desire for knowledge makes for evil in her attitudes as a combination. This is how the recursive account can explain the vice of fetishism without adopting an optimality treatment of attitudes to the neutral: though not in themselves evil, these attitudes always make combinations containing them evil.

More complex formulations of the proportionality principle are possible. For example, it can be revised to make the evil in a disproportionate combination depend not only on its ratio of intensities, but also on their absolute levels. Imagine that A and B are both selfish in the same ratio or to the same degree—for example, both caring twice as much about their own goods as about equal goods of other people. But B cares more intensely about all goods than A, so whereas A has 10 units of love for his own good and 5 for other people's, B has 20 units for his own and 10 for other people's. (Call A's a more anemic and B's a more passionate selfishness.) Given (PP) as formulated above, B's combination of attitudes is on balance considerably better than A's. It involves the same evil of disproportion but better, because twice as intense, loves of the good. (Given the asymptotic view, B's loves cannot be twice as good as A's, but they can still be considerably better.) Some may question this implication, arguing that B's selfishness should be equal or closer to equal in evil to A's. I do not find the stronger of these claims, that B's selfishness should be equal in evil to A's, persuasive. If A and B both divided their loves in perfect proportion but B's were more intense, B's attitudes would be on balance better. (Compare a human's ideally proportioned loves with God's.) And some version of the parallel claim about A's and B's forms of selfishness is likewise attractive. That B loves his own and especially others' good more intensely makes his more passionate selfishness less of a vice. But our current version of (PP) may exaggerate this difference, making A's more anemic selfishness too much worse. We can reduce the difference by making the evil of a disproportionate combination greater when the total intensity it involves is greater. Then the evil of a point on the graph will depend not only on the angular position of its ray, but also on its distance along that ray from the origin; for example, its evil can be an asymptotic function of the total intensity it represents. And this revision can reverse (PP)'s judgment about the two points in figure 3.8, so the greater distance from the origin of the point in the top right makes that point worse than the one in the bottom right, despite the latter's greater disproportion. The revision also has the attractive feature of eliminating discontinuities through the origin. Instead of a jump from, say, +5 to −5 when the proportionality and contraproportionality rays meet, there can be a gradual decline from 5 to zero and a gradual ascent from zero to −5.

The principle can also be revised to give points on the proportionality ray not a value of zero but some positive value, say, +2. In that case, perfectly proportioned combinations of attitudes are positively good as combinations, as to a lesser degree are mildly disproportionate ones, and only significantly disproportionate ones are evil. What have zero value are moderate disproportions, ones moderately close to the proportionality ray. The resulting (PP) makes perfect divisions of concern on balance intrinsically better, since they involve not only the goods in their component attitudes but also the holistic good of proportional division. It also raises the level of disproportion at which traits such as selfishness and cowardice pass over from shortfalls in virtue to vices, making a degree of selfishness that would be on balance evil given the original (PP) now on balance good. The revised principle therefore allows a more optimistic view of people's characters, holding that there is more virtue and less vice in the world than if perfect proportionality had zero value; moving the zero-value point in (PP) makes certain vices less prevalent. Finally, the revised (PP) makes more moderate claims about fetishism. It was an objectionable feature of the optimality view that it treated even a mild desire for a neutral object, such as a team's winning a championship, as evil. But the original (PP) does something similar, holding that any such desire makes for evil in a person's attitudes as a whole. The revised principle is more moderate, holding that mild loves of the neutral make, even at the holistic level, only for shortfalls in virtue.[34]

It may seem that a principle revised in this second way allows the recursive account to dispense with any view about the values in individual attitudes. If the principle's zero point is set in the right place, it will count precisely those combinations of attitudes as evil that

---

34. The revised principle also no longer holds that zero/zero divisions, where one is indifferent to both of two goods, are ideal as combinations. These divisions are not evil as combinations and are most naturally given a holistic value of zero. Given the initial (PP) they are therefore optimal as combinations, but given the revised (PP) they are not.

seem intuitively on balance to be so and leave all others as good. But just as the asymptotic view needs to be supplemented by the holistic (PP) to make seriously disproportionate combinations evil and reductions in disproportion good, so (PP) needs to be supplemented by something like the asymptotic view to make more intense combinations of attitudes better or worse. If *A* and *B* divide their loves proportionally but *B*'s loves are more intense, *B*'s loves are better in a way that no claims about proportionality can explain. The atomistic asymptotic view and the holistic (PP) coincide at two points: their claims about the best and worst divisions of fixed quantities of love. But beyond that, they make contrasting and complementary contributions to an overall recursive account.

As elaborated so far, the recursive account contains three elements: the original recursion-clauses (LG)–(HE), supplemented by the clauses about indifference (IG) and (IE) and revised as those clauses require; the asymptotic view about the degrees of value in individual attitudes; and the proportionality principle (PP). Together these elements make a series of attractive claims about the values both of individual attitudes and of combinations of attitudes. Given clauses (LG)–(IE), certain attitudes, such as loving goods and hating evils, are intrinsically good and others intrinsically evil. Given the asymptotic view, an intrinsically good attitude can be instrumentally evil if, by being disproportionately intense, it prevents a person from having another, better attitude, such as a more intense concern for a greater good or evil. Finally, given (PP), an intrinsically good but disproportionate attitude can be instrumentally evil in the stronger sense of making for intrinsic evil in a person's combination of attitudes as a combination and even, if the disproportion is sufficiently great, on balance. These various claims, attractive in their own right, also allow illuminating analyses of the individual virtues and vices. They yield something close to our everyday list of virtues and vices and explain why the list has that particular content. This topic is one of considerable importance in itself. Having elaborated the recursive account in an abstract way, I will next explore its implications for particular virtues and vices.

4

Varieties of Virtue and Vice

Our everyday moral thinking focuses less on the general nature of virtue and vice than on particular traits such as benevolence, courage, and malice. An acceptable account of virtue must cohere with this thinking, capturing at least many commonsense virtues and vices and explaining both what they have in common that makes them virtues and vices and what distinguishes them from each other. In this chapter I will show that the recursive account meets this condition, by applying it to a series of particular traits of character. I begin with the vices, which divide into categories more fundamentally than do the virtues.

1. *Categories of Vice*

The recursive account identifies the vices as those attitudes to goods and evils that are themselves intrinsically evil. Given the account as developed up to now, this means there are three categories of vices, which I call pure vices, vices of indifference, and vices of disproportion. All involve attitudes that are intrinsically evil, but in each the attitudes are made evil by a different element of the recursive account.

The *pure vices* involve attitudes that are inappropriately oriented to their objects, either love of an evil or hatred of a good. These vices are therefore made evil by the recursion-clauses (LE) and (HG) or their relational counterparts. Malice is a pure vice in this sense, in fact the central other-regarding one. A malicious person desires, pursues, or takes pleasure in another's evil, for example, her pain or failure, for its own sake, or desires for its own sake to destroy another's good. His attitude has the contrary orientation to one that is virtuous and is therefore simply and purely vicious. A malicious person need not desire another's pain *as* something evil; it may be impossible to desire an object as evil. But he can desire her pain *as* pain, wanting as an end in itself that she suffer, or he can take pleasure in her pain *as* pain. Then he loves something evil for the very property that makes it evil, which makes his love vicious by clause (LE). There are more specific other-regarding pure vices. One is anger, at least when it involves, as intense anger can, a desire to strike out at another or in some way cause her pain. Such anger is a specific form of malice, distinguished both by its cause—a belief that the other has mistreated one—and by its high intensity and short duration. Related forms of malice include *Schadenfreude*, or pleasure at the misfortunes of others, and sadism, where one enjoys both another's pain and the process of inflicting it. There are also self-regarding pure vices, such as self-hatred and masochism. Given agent-neutral base-clauses such as (BG) and (BE), desiring one's own pain and hating one's own pleasure and achievement are evil in the same way as are the comparable attitudes to other people's pleasure and achievement; in both cases, one is wrongly oriented to a base-level value. So self-hatred, too, is a pure vice. Of course, self-hatred and masochism are often instrumentally evil because they cause their subjects pain, but they are also disfiguring in themselves. Someone who injures himself out of self-hatred is in a worse state overall than if the same injury had befallen him accidentally.

These initial pure vices are directed at base-level values such as pleasure, pain, and failure, but there are also higher-level pure vices. A person who acts maliciously can also love his own malice, desiring and taking pleasure in the fact that he seeks others' pain for itself and wants to destroy their pleasure. This higher-level pure vice—let me call it "moral depravity"—is an essential part of complete viciousness. Stock fictional villains such as the Joker in the movie *Batman* combine malice toward others with delight in their own malice; they cackle as they perform their nasty deeds. They also delight in the malice of others, such as their corrupt underlings, and hate the compassion, benevolence, and other virtues of the heroes they battle. In the most total moral depravity, represented by Satan, a villain not only loves his own vice but wants to propagate it, by corrupting other people's characters. This total depravity combines an initial pure vice of malice with higher-level pure vices that extend up the hierarchy of attitudes and encompass all people, for a maximum of purely vicious love and hate.

A more subtle pure vice is cynicism. A cynic believes the world and people's lives are less good than they are commonly taken to be and, let us assume, actually are. His cynicism can concern base-level goods such as pleasure and knowledge, which he claims are only rarely found. But its more common subject is virtue, so he claims that people are less virtuous and more prone to vice than in fact they are. This undervaluing of existing goods is not itself a vice, though it involves the non-moral evil of false belief. But in cynicism it has a vicious origin. The cynic wants people not to be good—he in that sense hates good—and persuades himself, by wishful thinking or self-deception, that they are evil. For example, he wants people not to be benevolent and concludes against any evidence that they are ultimately selfish. His cynical belief issues from a purely vicious attitude and therefore itself reflects pure vice.[1] This analysis fits the *Oxford English Dictionary* definition of a cynic as "one who doubts or despises human sincerity or merit," though it adds that the doubting follows from the despising. The analysis can be confirmed by contrasting cynicism with pessimism. A pessimist, too, believes the world is less good than in fact it is, but pessimism is not cynicism and we react to the two very differently. This is because pessimism does not issue from a vicious attitude. Though the pessimist believes the world is evil, he wishes it were good and feels gloom because it is not. Hence our sympathy for him as against our resentment of the cynic, whose belief is not accompanied by love of the good but expresses hatred of it.

As a category, or holding the values of their objects fixed, the pure vices are the worst among the vices. In both their self-regarding and other-regarding forms and with base- or higher-level objects, they are most simply and thoroughly evil. The second category, the *vices of indifference*, are as a class less evil. They involve not a positively inappropriate orientation to a good or evil, but the absence, at least to a minimum threshold intensity, of an appropriate one. They are therefore made evil by the clauses about indifference, (IG) and (IE). Callousness, or caring not at all or insufficiently about another's pain, is an other-regarding vice of indifference, in this case of indifference to evil. So too, though it lacks a special name, is indifference to another's false beliefs or to her failing in important life projects. Remaining unmoved by these harms is vicious in the

---

1. The cynic also often takes pleasure in seeing through illusions that others do not and so being cleverer than they. His cynicism therefore involves a coordinate vice of pride and may in part be motivated by it.

same way as indifference to another's pain. There are also vices of indifference to good, including apathy and sloth. Though these two vices are closely connected, they can perhaps be distinguished as follows: an apathetic person is moved not at all by the thought of goods attainable by action, while a slothful person is moved a little, but not enough for his concern to reach the threshold intensity for virtuous love, and certainly not enough to move him to action. In the one case there is total indifference to goods, in the other seriously inadequate concern for them.

The vices of indifference also have higher-level forms, such as shamelessness. A person who has acted from an evil or insufficiently good motive should feel pain and especially shame about this fact. If he does not but is instead shameless about what he has done, he exhibits a higher-level vice, involving indifference to a higher-level evil. He is likewise shameless if he is in no way pained by an evil desire or feeling. Shamelessness is not as great a vice as the delight in moral evil that I have called moral depravity. In fact, shamelessness stands to depravity as callousness stands to malice: it involves the absence of hatred for an evil rather than, what is more vicious, positive love of it. But shamelessness is still a higher-level vice, though in the lesser category of vices of indifference.

Callousness, apathy, and shamelessness involve indifference to a good or evil one is aware of, but other vices of indifference involve not bothering to be aware. Thoughtlessness is one such vice. A thoughtless person does things that harm others because he does not take time to consider his actions' consequences in advance. His attitude is not as evil as that of someone who knows his action will harm others and callously performs it anyway. But if he cared seriously about avoiding harming others he would scrutinize his actions more carefully, and his failure to do so is a vice. As cynicism is a cognitive expression of malice, so thoughtlessness is a cognitive expression of indifference. A higher-level form of thoughtlessness is smugness or moral self-satisfaction. A smug person is satisfied that his moral character is good because he has not seriously considered the possibility that it is not. Because his favourable self-assessment reflects a lack of genuine concern for the goods of character, it too is a vice of indifference.

Some vices straddle the division between pure vices and vices of indifference. Consider cruelty, defined by the *Oxford English Dictionary* as a disposition to inflict suffering with either "delight in or indifference to another's pain." If cruelty involves delight in pain, it is a pure vice; if it involves only callous indifference, it is a vice of indifference. A similar analysis applies to hypocrisy. In one form of this vice, a person knows his moral character is not as he publicly presents it to be. If he takes pleasure in either his own vice or others' false beliefs about it, or both, his hypocrisy, is a pure vice; if he is merely unconcerned about them, it is a vice of indifference. In another, perhaps more common form of hypocrisy, a person has deceived himself into believing his character is indeed good; here again he is indifferent to his own vice and, in this case, to his own false belief.[2]

The third category of vices, the *vices of disproportion*, involve two or more attitudes both of which are appropriately oriented and above the threshold intensity, so that on their own they are good. But the intensities of these attitudes are so out of proportion to their objects' values that their combination is evil not just as a combination, as in some shortfalls in virtue, but on balance. These vices are therefore made evil by the proportionality principle, (PP), or by (PP) as weighed against the goodness found by (LG) and (HE).

In chapter 3 I argued that selfishness and cowardice, at least in their extreme forms, are vices of disproportion. An extremely selfish person cares much more about his own lesser goods than about greater goods of other people; a coward cares much more about his safety or comfort than about some greater good he could achieve by risking them. These initial vices of disproportion are accompanied by two contrary vices of self-abnegation and foolhardiness. Given agent-neutral base-clauses, it is just as evil to care too little about one's own good as it is to care too much. A person who discounts his good to an extreme, or is extremely self-abnegating, has a combination of attitudes that is on balance evil. Such a person need not be self-hating or even indifferent to his own good; he need have no self-regarding attitude that on its own is evil. But he does lack a kind of self-respect, respect for his own good as equal in importance to other people's, and this lack of self-respect is a vice of disproportion. A similar point applies to foolhardiness. Just as it can be on balance evil to care too much about one's safety, so it can be evil to care too little about it or to risk it in foolhardy actions aimed at trivial goods. Quite apart from its effects, such foolhardiness involves an intrinsically vicious preference for lesser over greater values.

---

2. A recursive account whose base-clauses are supplemented by claims about desert (see chapter 7, section 1) can say there is a further evil in the combination of vice and an undeserved reputation for virtue. Hypocrisy can then also involve love of or indifference to this further evil.

There are many other vices of disproportion, including intemperance (with the more specific forms of gluttony, drunkenness, and lust), pedantry, and nepotism. A person with one of these vices loves an object that he should love to some degree much more intensely than its value relative to other goods makes appropriate. He cares disproportionately about the pleasures of eating, drink, or sex, about small points of detail, or about the welfare of his own children, and there are again contrary vices of caring too little about these objects. Yet another vice of disproportion is laziness, if that is distinguished in a certain way from sloth. A slothful person does not care more than minimally about goods achievable by action; a lazy person may care more than minimally, but his caring is outweighed by his stronger love of the pleasures of idleness. It is not a lack of interest in goods that prevents him from acting, but excessive fondness of inaction. Fetishism, too, is best understood as a vice of disproportion. Loving for itself what is neutral in value is not itself evil, given the asymptotic view, but loving something neutral more than one loves a good is evil, by the proportionality principle. Thus, loving fame more than one loves knowledge is evil because it fails to recognize the greater value of the knowledge. It is not that any love of a neutral object is on balance vicious. If one's love of the object is mild it is only a shortfall in virtue, making one's overall combination of attitudes only slightly less good. But loving a neutral object much more than some good is on balance evil, and the same evil is present in more specific vices such as miserliness and avarice. An avaricious person cares more about his own money and therefore his own instrumental good than about other people's. His avarice is in that respect a form of selfishness, but he may also care about his money for its own sake, as the miser does, and do so with sufficient intensity that his combination of attitudes just to his own states is on balance evil. In overvaluing wealth as against genuine goods such as pleasure and knowledge, he manifests a self-regarding vice of disproportion.

Given its basis in the holistic principle (PP), the disproportion in these vices always involves two or more attitudes. A different view holds that vices such as intemperance and its opposite involve an attitude that is disproportionate to its object considered on its own, so that, for example, a person cares too much or too little about pleasure given just the value of pleasure. The recursive account as I have developed it captures the part of this view about deficiency: if a person cares too little about a good such as pleasure, his attitude on its own involves a vice of indifference. The account could also capture the other part, about excess, given an optimality view that makes excessive appropriate attitudes evil. But I rejected that type of view in favour of the asymptotic view; in my account, vices of disproportion involving excessive love arise only in combinations of attitudes.

A different vice of disproportion is pride, which involves excessive pleasure in certain aspects of one's own good. At the lowest level, one can take pleasure in one's knowledge or achievement; this becomes pride in the sense connoting vice when one is much more pleased by one's own knowledge or achievement than by similar or greater achievements of others. At a higher level, one can be pleased by one's virtue—by one's love of good and hatred of evil—and more so than by the similar virtue of others. This is specifically moral pride, or excessive love of one's own moral qualities, and is likewise a vice. Pride normally involves a specific kind of love, based on a belief that a state of oneself is admirable or good. (In chapter 6 I will call this "intellectualized" as against "simple emotional" love.) Some philosophers equate pride with this belief, so excessive pride just is the belief that one is superior to others when one is not. But this belief on its own is neither necessary nor sufficient for the vice of pride. Imagine that someone knows his achievements are no greater than other people's but dwells on them constantly, taking intense pleasure in them and expressing that pleasure in boasting. He is objectionably proud despite not having the relevant belief. Conversely, someone who does have the belief is not objectionably proud if he does not dwell on his achievements or take much pleasure in them. If he does not have a proud attitude, his belief does not make for moral vice.[3] This is not to deny that an exaggerated belief about one's merits is a common element in pride. But when this belief contributes to a vice of pride, it is because, like the cognitive states in cynicism and thoughtlessness, it originates in a vicious attitude. In the relevant cases, a proud person wants to be better than other people, or else wants to be good himself more than he wants others to be good, and by wishful thinking or self-deception persuades himself that what he wants is indeed so.[4] At the root of his vicious

---

3. See Stocker, *Valuing Emotions*, p. 250.

4. In a different kind of case, the proud person's false belief originates in thoughtlessness. He believes he is better than others because, while attending closely to his own achievements, he pays little or no attention to theirs. But this thoughtlessness, which involves more concern for his own than for others' good, is likewise a vice of disproportion and perhaps also of indifference.

pride is an excessive concern for his own as opposed to others' good.

Among more specific forms of pride, arrogance involves a standing or unquestioned assumption of one's own superiority. It is expressed less in specific episodes of proud feeling than in a continuous sense of satisfaction with oneself and often involves a smug indifference to one's real level of achievement. Conceit, by contrast, does involve specific episodes of proud feeling, as well as a constant effort to substantiate one's superiority through comparisons with other people. This last aspect of conceit suggests an origin in a desire to be better than others coupled with a perhaps subconscious recognition that one is not. A similar combination of attitude and belief lies behind vanity, where the specific evidence of superiority one seeks is the admiration and approval of others.[5] We can also distinguish between local and global pride. Local pride is pride in a particular feat or in one's achievement in a particular domain such as music; global pride is pride in one's self or life as a whole. Though either form of pride can be excessive, a common vice of global pride involves a false generalization from local pride. A person has excelled in a specific domain such as music and takes, let us assume, appropriate local pride in having done so. But, eager to be globally excellent, he exaggerates the importance of musical achievement in his life as a whole, or as weighed against other traits, and so takes excessive pride in his life on balance; though properly pleased by his music, he is excessively pleased with himself because of his music. A similar false generalization can occur in the opposite vice of excessive shame. A person has failed in some domain and feels shame at having done so. But then, from self-hatred or a similar emotion, she exaggerates the significance of this failing and concludes that her whole life and person are worthless, moving from a proportionate local shame to an excessive and disfiguring global one.[6]

Other vices, such as envy, straddle the division between pure vices and vices of disproportion. An envious person lacks some good that another person has and is troubled by this fact. In addition to his interest in the good considered on its own, he resents the disparity between his state and the other person's and wants that disparity removed. In one form of envy, called emulative envy, he seeks to remove the disparity by acquiring the same good for himself, desiring it more intensely and pursuing it more vigorously than if he were

5. I borrow these distinctions from G. Taylor, *Pride, Shame, and Guilt*, pp. 48–49.
6. Stocker, *Valuing Emotions*, pp. 221–30.

not spurred by the other's possession of it. This emulative envy is at worst a vice of disproportion; the envious person desires a good, but more intensely than its intrinsic merits make appropriate. A more vicious form, malicious envy, seeks to remove the disparity in the other way, by destroying the other person's good; it can also take the form of pleasure when that good is destroyed by other forces. Malicious envy is a pure vice, involving hatred of another's good, and in its worst form, which we can call spite, involves a double pure vice. A spiteful person prefers a situation where neither he nor another has a given good to one where he has it to a lesser degree and the other to a greater. Here his desire to avoid a disparity in standing makes him hate not only the other's but also his own good, or to take a purely vicious attitude to two people's goods.[7]

A similar analysis applies to a related vice sometimes called jealousy and sometimes begrudgingness. The jealous person, as I will call her, is likewise concerned with a disparity in goods but starts from the superior position of having a good that another lacks. In a less vicious form of jealousy, she loves her own good more because the other lacks it, taking a greater pleasure in it or wanting more intensely to retain it than if she cared only about its intrinsic qualities. This form of jealousy is a vice of disproportion, involving excessive love of something good. The more vicious form of jealousy involves desiring that the other not acquire the good one has, so that one's possession of it will remain exclusive, or taking pleasure in her not having it. Like malicious envy, this second form of jealousy is a pure vice, involving hatred of another's good.[8]

To summarize: the recursive account recognizes pure vices, made evil by the recursion-clauses (LE) and (HG); vices of indifference, made evil by the clauses about indifference, (IG) and (IE); and vices

---

7. It is probably most accurate to define envy and related vices as Nozick does, in terms of attitudes to conjunctions of goods and evils (*Anarchy, State, and Utopia*, pp. 239–40n). Then the emulatively envious person prefers a situation where both he and another have a good to one where he does not have it and the other does, but prefers the first situation by more than the difference in value between it and the second—which is just the difference between his having and not having the good— makes appropriate. The maliciously envious person prefers a situation where neither he nor the other has the good to one where he does not have it and the other does, thereby preferring a worse conjunctive situation to a better, or hating the better.

8. On envy and jealousy, see G. Taylor, "Envy and Jealousy." Taylor is mainly interested in how these vices are instrumentally evil, destroying other goods in an envious or jealous person's life. I am exploring the different view that they are intrinsically evil.

of disproportion, made evil by the proportionality principle, (PP). As a category, or abstracting from the values of their objects, the pure vices are worse than the vices of indifference, which are worse than the vices of disproportion. It is more evil to love an evil or hate a good than to be indifferent to it, and, holding one's other attitudes fixed, it is more evil to be indifferent to a good or evil than to love or hate it with disproportionate intensity.[9] This ranking of the vices, and especially the primacy of pure vices, has been affirmed by several philosophers. Schopenhauer says of *Schadenfreude* that "to feel envy is human, but to indulge in such malicious joy is fiendish and diabolical. There is no more infallible sign of a thoroughly bad heart and profound moral worthlessness than an inclination to a sheer and undisguised malignant joy of this kind."[10] More recently, Judith N. Shklar writes that "liberal and humane people, of whom there are many among us, would, if they were asked to rank the vices, put cruelty first" and proposes that treating cruelty as the *summum malum* is what distinguishes liberalism as a position in political theory.[11] But the ranking of vices I have suggested should not be treated as more significant than it is. It concerns the categories of vice only as categories and does not imply that every instance of a worse kind of vice is more evil than any instance of a lesser kind. Maliciously desiring a small evil for another person, such as a small pain, can be less vicious than being indifferent to his great pain. Hannah Arendt's concept of the "banality of evil," applied initially to Adolf Eichmann, is precisely that of moral evil that involves not sadism or malice but mere callous indifference. But callousness about an evil as immense as the Holocaust is still an immense evil, and far worse than petty malice.[12] Similarly, indifference to a minor good or evil can be less vicious than a huge disproportion among virtuous attitudes. It can be less evil to be unmoved by another's minor pain than to be moved above the threshold by his greater

9. Remember that the disproportion in a vice of disproportion is exceeded by an even greater disproportion in a vice of either of the other two kinds. Someone who is indifferent to a good or, worse, hates it and loves an evil has a massive disproportion in his attitudes as a combination.

10. Schopenhauer, *On the Basis of Morality*, p. 135.

11. Shklar, *Ordinary Vices*, p. 44, and "The Liberalism of Fear," p. 20. See also Rorty, *Contingency, Irony, and Solidarity*, pp. 146, 176; and Baier, "Moralism and Cruelty," pp. 437, 451.

12. Arendt, *Eichmann in Jerusalem*. Eichmann was also banal because he cared more about minor goods in his own life, such as promotions in the SS, than about the suffering of millions of Jews. This was a mere vice of disproportion but again, given its object, an immense one.

pain but much less than by one's own minor pain. However the categories of vice compare as categories, the values of their specific instances depend on facts about their specific intentional objects. Nor does the ranking I have suggested apply to the vices' degrees of evil on balance, or counting both their intrinsic and instrumental qualities. The latter is surely what matters most for the political issues addressed by liberalism, since the state's concern must be all goods and evils rather than just higher-level or moral ones. But which trait of character is worst on balance, or including its effects, varies from situation to situation. In some circumstances it may be a pure vice such as cruelty, but in others it may be selfishness, laziness, or even misguided benevolence. To the question "Which vice is all things considered worst?" there is, *pace* Shklar, no single answer.[13]

By recognizing these three categories of vice, the recursive account captures a wide range of evil states of character; but it also suggests a certain pessimism about people's characters. If there are many kinds of vice, there are many ways in which human attitudes can be and presumably are morally evil. The account can be contrasted on this score with two others that are more optimistic, implying in different ways that vice is less commonly found.

The first such account recognizes only the pure vices as vices. It rejects the indifference principles (IG) and (IE), holding that indifference to a good or evil is itself neither good nor evil and that all love of good and hatred of evil, even the least intense, is positively good. It also rejects the proportionality principle, holding that what I call vices of disproportion involve only shortfalls in virtue, or make an on-balance good combination of attitudes only somewhat less good. This rival account treats callousness, extreme selfishness, and cowardice, which I have said are intrinsically evil, as either positively (though not ideally) good or as at worst neutral. Only a few attitudes, such as malice, sadism, and moral depravity, constitute vice, which is therefore far less widespread.

The second more optimistic account recognizes only vices of indifference and of disproportion. It cannot hold that the pure vices exist but are not evil; that would not be credible. Instead, it denies that such vices exist. This denial is implicit in Aristotle's theory of vice, as stated in his doctrine of the mean. This doctrine holds that every virtue is intermediate between two vices, one of excess and one of deficiency. It is virtuous to have a certain feeling or to love a

---

13. See Kekes, "Cruelty and Liberalism."

certain object to the right degree and on the right occasions, and vicious to love it either too much or too little. The doctrine of the mean assumes that no human feelings are inappropriate or evil whatever their intensity. Since every feeling relevant to moral evaluation is intrinsically good if present to the right degree, vice consists only in exceeding or falling short of this degree. Given Aristotle's acceptance of this doctrine, it is no surprise that the vices he analyzes, such as cowardice, intemperance, and meanness, are all either vices of disproportion or, at worst (like shamelessness), of indifference, and that he never mentions pure vices such as malice and depravity, intuitively the worst among the vices. Aristotle's is a sunny picture of human vice, on which it consists always in aiming in a good direction but missing one's mark rather than in having an evil aim from the start. Aristotle may seem to allow for the pure vices when he says that "not every action nor every passion admits of a mean; for some have names that already imply badness, e.g., spite, shamelessness, envy, and in the case of actions adultery, theft, murder."[14] But examined in context, this remark implies no true departure from the doctrine of the mean and no expansion of the categories of vice. As Aristotle goes on to explain, we can apply a special name to the excess or deficiency of some feeling—for example, "cowardice" to the excess of fear or "gluttony" to the excess of appetite—and there will be no mean associated with this name because there is in general no "mean of excess and deficiency."[15] This is exactly how Aristotle understands his trio of "spite, shamelessness, [and] envy." Shamelessness is only a vice of indifference, involving a lack of regret for but no positive delight in one's evil action.[16] And spite and envy he characterizes as the excess and deficiency of a feeling whose intermediate form is righteous indignation, that is, as themselves involving disproportion.[17] The doctrine of the mean may be under strain at this point—how do indignation, envy, and spite all involve the same feeling?—but Aristotle still employs it. Even when discussing what seem to be purely vicious attitudes, he takes vice to involve too much or too little of a feeling that in an intermediate form is good—that is, he continues to deny the existence of pure vice.[18]

14. Aristotle, *Nicomachean Ethics*, 1107a9–13.
15. Aristotle, *Nicomachean Ethics*, 1107a25.
16. Aristotle, *Nicomachean Ethics*, 1128b33–34.
17. Aristotle, *Nicomachean Ethics*, 1108a35–b6.
18. It may be objected that Aristotle leaves room for the pure vices under the heading of "brutishness," a state he considers worse than vice. But Aristotle's exam-

What is true of Aristotle's doctrine of the mean is true of other classical theories of vice. Consider Plato's view in the *Republic* that vice consists in conflict or disharmony among elements in the soul;[19] it, too, implies that vice consists always in having too much or too little of a desire that in a different, harmonizing form would be consistent with virtue, so it, too, denies the existence of pure vice. Surprisingly, the Christian list of the seven deadly sins does not include malice or, with the possible exception of envy, any other pure vice;[20] this probably reflects the influence on Christian thinkers of Greek ideas that make the same omission. Or consider the view that vice or moral evil is nothing positive but only the privation of moral good.[21] The more general view that all evil is privation is objectionable because it leaves out the intrinsic evil of pain or false belief. Pain is not just the absence of pleasure, but a sensation with its own introspectible quality; false belief involves more than just failing to know. There are similar objections to the more restricted privative view about moral evil. It may apply successfully to vices of indifference, but not without arbitrariness to those of disproportion. If a person loves good x much more than equal good y, we can, holding his intensity of love for x constant, say his failing is not to love y more. But we can equally well hold his love for y constant and say his failing is to love x too much. And the privative view does not apply at all to the pure vices. Malice is not just the absence of benevolence, but a positive contrary attitude; the same holds for sadism and depravity. For all their influence, classical theories like Aristotle's and Plato's express a naive optimism about the possibilities for human evil, one ignoring the pure vices that are, intuitively, the worst vices of all. By contrast, the recursive account makes the pure vices cen-

---

ples of brutishness make no mention of malice or similar traits. Some, such as eating human flesh, result from "injuries to the system"; others involve plucking out one's hair or chewing one's nails *(Nicomachean Ethics,* 1148b15–31). More important, it would be an error to explain the moral evil of malice by saying it reduces us to the level of animals, as the term "brutishness" implies. Malice is a psychologically sophisticated attitude, requiring a capacity to love evils or hate goods for themselves that is beyond non-human animals.

19. Plato, *Republic,* Book 4.

20. Shklar notes the absence of cruelty from the seven deadly sins as well as from Aristotle's theory of vice *(Ordinary Vices,* pp. 7–8). About the former, she suggests that theological assumptions about the supreme goodness of God naturally make pride, or placing oneself above God, the primary vice. These assumptions do make some vices of proportion worse than they would otherwise be, but the worst vice should still be a pure one, namely hating God and his goodness for themselves.

21. For a recent defence of this view, see Midgley, *Wickedness.*

tral, identifying them as vices by the recursion-clauses that are its starting point and always remain its core.

2. *Categories of Virtue*

The virtues cannot be divided into categories as fundamentally as the vices, since they are all made good by the same basic elements of the recursive account. They all involve attitudes that are appropriate to their objects and above a threshold intensity, so they derive their goodness from the same recursion-clauses (LG) and (HE). Whereas there are several ways of being vicious, there is just one basic way of being virtuous.[22] Nonetheless, there are differences in the specific ways virtues satisfy (LG) or (HE), or in the kinds of fact highlighted by their everyday names. On this less fundamental basis, we can distinguish between what I call simple virtues, virtues of proportion, and virtues of self-control.

The *simple virtues* involve a single attitude that is appropriately oriented to its object and above the threshold intensity, so it satisfies (LG) or (HE) independently of its relation to a person's other attitudes. Benevolence is in this sense a simple virtue. A benevolent person desires, pursues, and takes pleasure in other people's good—for example, in their pleasure, knowledge, and achievement—and his doing so is virtuous regardless of its role in combinations of attitudes. Because benevolence is less common than it should be, someone who is more than usually benevolent tends to have combinations of attitudes that are more than usually well proportioned, but the virtue in his benevolence does not depend on this fact. It is a property of his other-concern considered by itself. For the same reason, benevolence and all the simple virtues can be had not only insufficiently but also to excess. If a person cares too much about other people's good, as when he is extremely self-abnegating, his benevolence can make for a combination of attitudes that is less than ideally good and even on balance evil. Even so, his benevolence, considered by itself, remains a virtue, though one he possesses to a fault. On its own it is good, and it is on their own that simple virtues are understood.

---

22. This is not strictly true if the proportionality principle is revised to give proportional combinations positive rather than zero value, since then some virtuous combinations of attitudes derive some goodness from (PP). But I will ignore this possibility in what follows.

More specific forms of benevolence include generosity and kindness. A generous person tries to benefit others by giving them something that would benefit himself, usually something with a market value such as money. His generosity therefore involves a sacrifice, though a willing one, of his own instrumental good. The slightly different virtue of kindness is not similarly tied to the sacrifice of instrumental goods but can be expressed in actions that cost the agent nothing. Thus, helping a stranger across the street is an act of kindness, though not normally of generosity. It is therefore possible for a person to be kind but not generous, as when a childhood of poverty has made it hard for him to part with money but not to act benevolently in other ways. At the same time, kindness often involves, as generosity need not, sensitivity to the details of others' situation and needs. A generous person can be undiscriminating in his attempts to help, but a kind person usually is carefully attentive.

Benevolence is, more specifically, a simple virtue of loving good, as are perseverance, love of knowledge, and dedication to achievement. The central simple virtue of hating evil is compassion, or being pained by and desiring to end another's evil and, especially, pain. Compassion and its more specific forms, such as pity,[23] often make a person's combination of attitudes better proportioned, but their being virtues depends only on their intrinsic character, so again it is possible to have them to excess. A further simple virtue of hating evil is truthfulness, which involves a desire that others not believe or come to believe what is false. This virtue involves hatred of false belief; the stronger virtue of candour or openness adds a positive desire that others come to know relevant truths. As with the pure vices, there are higher-level simple virtues, such as desiring, pursuing, and taking pleasure in one's own or others' virtue and having the opposite attitudes to vice. A special form of hating vice is shame, at least when it involves pain at having acted from an evil motive or having had an evil desire or feeling. Shame of this kind differs from guilt in having an object that is intrinsically evil rather than wrong and that is an attitude rather than an action considered apart from its motive. Whereas one can feel guilt only about actions, one can feel shame at a desire one could not avoid having and that never influenced one's behaviour. Some philosophers claim that

---

23. Blum suggests that pity differs from compassion in involving condescension, a view of the other as, because of his suffering, different from oneself ("Compassion," pp. 177–78). This is a useful way of distinguishing pity, but I will continue to use "compassion" to refer generically to all hatred of another's pain.

shame necessarily involves the thought of an audience, either real or imagined, that views one in a way one does not want.[24] But if shame is a moral virtue, its object cannot be just the reaction of an audience, which may be perfectly justified. It must be their reaction as pointing to something evil in oneself, so that evil is the shame's real object and the audience incidental. As so directed at one's own moral evil, shame is a higher-level simple virtue.

The simple virtues also include prudence, understood as the ability to select effective means to good ends. Prudence in this sense involves the non-moral good of knowledge and contributes to that of achievement, but it can reflect a virtuous attitude if a person's knowing the means to a good end results from his intense desire for that end. Because he wants very much to achieve the end, he carefully seeks out the best means to it. Just as thoughtlessness can be a cognitive expression of indifference to a good, so prudence can be a cognitive expression of intense love for it. The same holds for sensitivity, or knowing subtle facts about another's feelings and what affects them. Such sensitivity again involves the non-moral good of knowledge but can also express the simple virtue of benevolence. It is because one cares deeply about another that one notices just what she is feeling and has learned what specific actions will make her feel better.[25]

Two related virtues are "blind charity"[26] and trust. Blind charity consists in believing that people are morally better than they are and is typified by Jane Bennett in Jane Austen's *Pride and Prejudice*, of whom her sister Elizabeth says, "Oh! you are a great deal too apt, you know, to like people in general. You never see a fault in anybody. All the world are good and agreeable in your eyes."[27] This excessively charitable interpretation of others involves a false belief, which is non-morally evil. But if this belief results from a strong desire that others be virtuous, which is a form of love of their good, it is a cognitive expression of simple virtue.[28] The same holds for the

---

24. G. Taylor, *Pride, Shame, and Guilt,* pp. 57–68; and Williams, *Shame and Necessity,* p. 78. For critical discussion see Stocker, *Valuing Emotions,* pp. 217–19.

25. Compare Blum, *Friendship, Altruism, and Morality,* pp. 129–35.

26. Driver, "The Virtues of Ignorance," pp. 381–82, where Jane Bennett is used as an example. See also Wallace's discussion of "generous-mindedness" in *Virtues and Vices,* pp. 136–39.

27. Austen, *Pride and Prejudice,* p. 14.

28. Blind charity also involves indifference to false belief, which is a moral evil. If we think the blind charity of someone like Jane Bennett is on balance a virtue, it must be because we think this evil is outweighed by the goodness in her motivating desire. Note that the contrary vice of cynicism also involves indifference to false belief and is therefore doubly vicious.

more restricted virtue of trust, which involves believing beyond one's evidence in the virtues of particular people, such as one's friends and family.

Other traits would be simple virtues given the right claims about base-level values. Consider what David Hume disparagingly calls the "monkish virtues" of "celibacy, fasting, penance, [and] mortification," all of which involve denying oneself pleasure and even causing oneself pain.[29] These would be not virtues but vices if pleasure and pain were the only base-level values. But if there are further intrinsic goods of knowledge of or union with God, and bodily pleasure hinders these spiritual goods, then hating that pleasure as an obstacle to these goods is a simple virtue. A similar conclusion follows if, more strongly, pleasure's association with the body makes it intrinsically evil. Then hating pleasure for itself is a simple virtue. What the recursive account recognizes as simple virtues depends on its list of base-level goods and evils, and disagreements about the latter can lead to disagreements about what is and is not a virtue. The same feature of the account can explain historical changes in beliefs about virtue, as traits once regarded as virtuous lose that status after shifts in other beliefs about value.

The second category of virtues, the *virtues of proportion*, involve not just one appropriate attitude but a combination of such attitudes. Though the goodness of these attitudes again derives from (LG) and (HE), it is a condition of their combination's being on balance virtuous that their goodness not be outweighed by a greater evil of disproportion, and the virtues' names often point to this fact. They connote a rough proportionality among attitudes rather than any properties they have on their own. This proportionality need not itself be intrinsically good—given the original proportionality principle, it has at most zero value—but it is often what makes a combination of attitudes on balance good. Because of this, the virtues of proportion, unlike the simple virtues, cannot be had to excess. One can be too benevolent, for example, by being excessively self-abnegating, but can never have attitudes that are too well proportioned.

Since the virtues of proportion contrast with vices of disproportion, one such virtue involves that balance between concern for one's own and others' good that avoids both extreme selfishness

---

29. Hume, *An Enquiry Concerning the Principles of Morals*, p. 270. As an instrumentalist with respect to virtue, Hume condemns the monkish virtues because of their effects rather than, as the recursive account does, intrinsically.

and extreme self-abnegation. Surprisingly, this virtue seems to have no everyday English name, but it can be included as one instance of a more general virtue that I call proportional justice. (A different virtue of holistic justice is discussed in chapter 7.) This kind of justice involves caring proportionally about the goods of all people, one's own not much more nor less than others', and one's friends' and intimates' not much more nor less than strangers'. To be proportionally just is to have appropriate attitudes to many people's goods and, in addition, to divide those attitudes impartially. Proportional justice is a form of distributive justice, concerned with dividing one's concern between people. And it has as one aspect balancing one's own and others' good so as to give each its appropriate weight, avoiding both selfishness and self-abnegation. This aspect is not the whole of proportional justice, but it is one part and therefore one virtue of proportion.

Another such virtue is what I will call proportional courage. Whereas a coward cares much more about his safety or comfort than about some greater good he could achieve by risking them, a person of proportional courage desires the greater good sufficiently that his attitudes are on balance virtuous, with the result that he pursues that good without hesitation. Though he feels some fear, it is not intense enough to prevent or even hinder his acting as is best. Not just any proportioned response to danger counts as courageous in this sense, but only a response to significant danger. We do not call someone courageous who without hesitation accepts the small risk involved in driving a car.[30] Nor are only perfectly proportioned responses courageous. Imagine that the greater good at issue is 100 times as good as a person's safety, but that he cares about it only 80 times as much. His combination of attitudes involves some disproportion and therefore some evil by the proportionality principle, but it is on balance courageous. Nor, finally, is any preference at all for the greater good courageous. Imagine that in the above example the person cares only twice as much about the hundredfold greater good. His division of concern is sufficient to make him pursue the greater good without hesitation, but not sufficient for courage. Though he acts as a courageous person does, he does so with cowardly attitudes.

A central self-regarding virtue of proportion is temperance. A temperate person cares proportionally about the bodily pleasures of

30. Wallace, *Virtues and Vices*, pp. 78–79.

food, drink, and sex, desiring and pursuing them neither more nor less than their value compared to other goods makes appropriate. He therefore avoids both the vices of intemperance, such as gluttony, drunkenness, and lust, and the "monkish" vices of caring too little about bodily pleasures. As in the vices of disproportion, the proportionality that defines this virtue arises between different attitudes. It is not that the temperate person's concern for pleasure is proportioned to the value of pleasure on its own, though given the optimality view, this could be so. His concern is proportioned to his other attitudes, given their intensities and the values of their objects.

Yet another virtue of proportion is patience. In one sense, patience involves the ability to wait. A patient person does not immediately leap for a smaller present good but can hold off for greater ones coming later; he does not overvalue present as against future benefits. (This temporally impartial division of concern is sometimes referred to as "prudence.") In another sense, associated with Job, patience involves the calm endurance of hardship or suffering. Here a patient person does not excessively lament minor evils or feel overly troubled by them. Though great evils should indeed be greatly resented, and failing to do so is a vice, patience avoids excessive concern for what from a larger point of view are not enormous burdens.

Another virtue of proportion is modesty or humility, which involves not taking much more pleasure in one's own achievements and virtues than in the similar merits of others. If modesty is a virtue rather than just the absence of vicious pride, a modest person cannot lack self-respect or take much less pleasure in her own achievements than in others'. (Otherwise, modesty would be something she could have to excess.) Instead, her responses to her own and others' merits must be roughly proportioned to their magnitude. Like pride, modesty is often associated with a cognitive state—either a belief that one's merits are less than they are or the absence of a belief that they are greater.[31] But this cognitive state is, again, not sufficient for the virtue of modesty. A person who seriously underestimates her own merits but takes intense pleasure in and boasts of them is not modest.[32] And when a cognitive state does contribute to

---

31. Driver, "The Virtues of Ignorance"; Richards, "Is Humility a Virtue?"; and Flanagan, "Virtue and Ignorance."
32. Schueler, "Why Modesty Is a Virtue," p. 470.

modesty, it is because, like the false belief in blind charity, it originates in a virtuous attitude. This attitude can be one of several. A
person can be so dedicated to improving herself that she notices
only her failings and ignores her successes; she can be blindly charitable and, while accurately estimating her own achievements, systematically overrate those of others; she can believe that excessive
pride is a temptation and to avoid it can intentionally direct her attention away from herself; or she can dislike inequalities in achievement and the distress they cause the less accomplished, and from
that dislike again avoid noticing her merits. With any of these origins, her modest belief can reflect a virtue, though usually a simple
virtue rather than one of proportion.

The virtues of proportion correspond to those recognized by Aristotle's doctrine of the mean, though with an important difference.
Aristotle's claim that one should have desires and feelings neither
too much nor too little verges on tautology if it does not specify, as
Aristotle never clearly does, how the relevant mean is determined.
The doctrine of the mean is not completely empty, since it implies
that there are no desires that are in all forms evil, that is, no pure
vices. But it says very little substantive about what virtue positively is.
The recursive account remedies this lack, fixing the mean intensities for virtuous desires and feelings by the values of their objects, especially as compared to those of other objects.

The final category, the *virtues of self-control*, likewise involve a combination of attitudes, though in this case the attitudes are not both
good. Instead, one is evil and the other is a higher-level attitude directed at reducing the first's intensity and preventing it from issuing
in action. If this second attitude is strong enough to achieve its aim,
it can be more good than the first is evil, making their combination
on balance virtuous.[33]

The virtues of self-control are typified by control of one's anger. If
an angry person wants to strike out at another, his anger involves a
desire that will be instrumentally evil if it issues in action and is also
intrinsically evil, since it is directed at an evil object. This means that
a higher-level desire to control his anger by reducing its intensity

---

33. On these virtues see Roberts, "Will Power and the Virtues." Since my interest
is in *virtues* of self-control, I consider only cases where the attitude being controlled
is an evil one. There can also be self-control where a vicious person resists a virtuous impulse, but this self-control is not virtuous. There is a similar restriction in my
later discussion of weakness of will, which considers only cases where the desire suc-
cumbed to is evil.

can in either of two ways be intrinsically good. First, the person can want to control his anger in order to avoid hurting the other; here he hates his intense anger as a means, which is good by one of the instrumental clauses. Alternatively or in addition, he can hate his anger for itself or as malicious; this is good by recursion-clause (HE). Either way, his higher-level desire responds appropriately to an evil in the self and is therefore good, and with sufficient strength it can make his combination of attitudes good. It can leave him with a weakened angry desire, which is less evil, and a strong controlling desire whose goodness outweighs that evil. Controlling one's anger usually does not mean eliminating it entirely. If a person hates his anger only as a means, he cares only that it be reduced to the point where it does not issue in action; this is consistent with still feeling some malicious anger. If he hates his anger for itself, he may want to eliminate it entirely, but often he cannot. Often what he can make effective is only a desire to reduce his anger's intensity somewhat, perhaps past the point where it does not issue in action but still not all the way; this too leaves him with some malicious anger. And even if he did eliminate his anger, he would still have a disposition to anger, which is to some degree vicious (see chapter 2, section 2). Even in its best form, then, control of one's anger usually involves some element of moral evil. But this evil has been reduced to the point where it is outweighed by the goodness in a higher-level desire, making for an overall virtue of self-control.

A similar analysis applies to what I will call self-controlling courage, as against the proportional courage discussed earlier. A proportionally courageous person does not care much more than proportionally about his own safety or comfort and therefore risks them without hesitation for a greater good. With self-controlling courage a person does care, at least initially, much more than proportionally about his safety. He is excessively fearful, and to a degree that if unchecked will prevent him from pursuing the greater good. But he also has a higher-level desire to reduce his fear, and this desire can again be in two ways intrinsically good. He can desire to reduce his fear in order to achieve the greater good or because in itself it makes his attitudes disproportionate. Either way, his higher-level desire is good, and with sufficient strength to achieve its aim, it can make his attitudes on balance good. His attitudes may still contain some evil, since he may still feel some disproportionate fear. But his fear has been reduced to the point where it not only does not determine his action but is outweighed by moral good.

Given the difference between its proportional and self-controlling forms, courage straddles the division between virtues of proportion and virtues of self-control. In the one form it involves a roughly proportionate response to danger, in the other an initially disproportionate response that is partly subdued by strength of will. How common these two forms of courage are is an interesting empirical question. An optimistic view says that many people can be proportionally courageous even in the face of great danger, facing it willingly and without inner struggle; a perhaps more realistic view says most of us cannot avoid feeling excessive fear and can at best try to control it.[34]

There are many other virtues of self-control—in fact, one for every pure vice and vice of disproportion. One can control one's sadistic or cynical impulses, or one's gluttonous, impatient, or prideful ones. One can even control a tendency to slacken in one's other efforts at self-control. But in all virtues of this kind, the typical mechanism of self-control is indirect. We usually cannot control a vicious desire just by wanting to, but must instead use indirect tactics such as redirecting our attention.[35] To control intense anger, for example, we direct our attention away from its cause, such as the wrong done us, and concentrate on the harmful consequences of expressing our anger or just on nothing, as when we "count to ten." To control excessive fear, we stop thinking about the danger we face and attend just to the task ahead of us and the routine it involves. The success of these diversionary measures depends on the strength of our higher-level desire as against our anger or fear. If that desire is sufficiently strong, it can keep our attention where we want it; if weak, it cannot. But when we do control an evil desire, it is usually by some such indirect means.

By recognizing simple virtues, virtues of proportion, and virtues of self-control, the recursive account both captures a wide variety of virtues and unifies them more thoroughly than it does the vices. In all three categories, the virtues involve attitudes that are appropriately oriented and in some way of appropriate intensity, so they are all made good by the same clauses (LG) and (HE). Despite this, the account does not endorse the classical thesis of the "unity

---

34. Sometimes the intense fear in self-controlling courage can be instrumentally good, giving a person energy through an adrenalin rush and heightened sensitivity to important information. Here one can speak, as some athletes do, of "channelling" fear, or using it to act more effectively.

35. Milo, *Immorality*, pp. 134–37; and Roberts, "Will Power and the Virtues," pp. 242–46.

of the virtues" discussed by Plato and Aristotle.[36] This thesis holds that the virtues are one not only in what makes them virtues, but also in the sense of always going together, so that a person who has one virtue must needs have them all. Our account joins common sense in rejecting this thesis, holding that a person can be courageous but not kind, or just but not patient. In fact, its categorization of virtues shows how strained the classical argument for the unity thesis is.

This argument equates virtue with knowledge of the good, which, though distinct from love of the good, likewise involves a relation to other goods or evils. It then claims that to have the virtue associated with a particular good, a person must know not only that it is good, but also how its goodness compares with that of all other goods, which requires the same knowledge of those other goods. To stand in the relevant relation to one good, he must stand in it to all goods and so have every virtue.[37] But the premises of this classical argument are highly artificial. The requirement that virtue involve knowledge of comparative goodness in effect stipulates that there are no simple virtues, or virtues relating to a single object; there are only virtues of proportion. But surely we recognize benevolence and compassion as virtues just by their relation to their own objects, independently of issues about proportionality. And the requirement that the knowledge concern all goods stipulates that there are no virtues of proportion between just two or a few goods rather than between them all. This is again strained: we normally call a person proportionally just if he is impartial between himself and others even if he overrates pleasure in all people's good, and temperate even if he is somewhat selfish. In each case, proportionality in one domain suffices for some virtue. It is of course possible to define virtue as the unity thesis does, so that a person has no virtue unless his attitudes are perfectly proportioned to all goods and evils. But this is not our everyday understanding of virtue, and it obliterates important distinctions between the kinds of virtue there are.

Can we rank the categories of virtue as categories, as we did the vices? There seems to be no point in comparing simple virtues and virtues of proportion, since they often overlap. A person can be simultaneously benevolent and proportionally just, with his benevo-

---

36. Plato, *Protagoras*, 329b–334c, 349b–351b, 361a–d; and Aristotle, *Nicomachean Ethics*, 1144b17–1145a2.

37. For recent presentations of this argument, see McDowell, "Virtue and Reason," pp. 143–44; and Annas, *The Morality of Happiness*, pp. 73–76.

lence constituting part of his justice. But there is an important question about the comparative values of self-control and the other categories of virtue, or of self-control and that unadulterated virtue where a person has only good attitudes and no evil ones needing control.

Aristotle ranks self-control below unadulterated virtue, calling the former "a mixed sort of state" that is better than weakness of will and unadulterated vice but less good than what he calls virtue proper.[38] The recursive account certainly endorses the first part of this view, its preference for self-control over weakness of will. Weakness of will is like self-control in combining an evil desire and a higher-level desire to control it, but here the higher-level desire is too weak to achieve its aim, and the person acts on the evil desire. Weakness therefore involves a stronger evil desire and a weaker good desire than does self-control, with the former's evil outweighing the latter's goodness.[39] It is not that weakness of will is in no respect good. Even an ineffective hatred of an evil desire has some value, making weakness better than that unadulterated vice where a person has an evil desire and either no higher-level attitude to it or the positive attitude that makes for moral depravity. But the components of weakness of will are not related in the way that can make self-control on balance a virtue.

The account's attitude to the second part of Aristotle's view, his preference for unadulterated virtue, is less clear. Even after a self-controlled person has subdued his anger or fear, he usually has some evil desire, and he certainly has a disposition to such a desire. So there is an element of moral evil in his attitudes that is not present in unadulterated virtue. But there may also be moral goods in his attitudes that are not present in unadulterated virtue. A self-controlled person hates an evil desire that often was actual in him a short time ago and is still a close possibility, since he would have it now were he not working to control it. A purely virtuous person can also hate a vicious desire, by being glad not to have it and hoping never to acquire it. But if his character is firmly settled, the desire he hates may never have been actual in him and is now only a remote possibility. In addition, the self-controlled person's hatred of an evil desire can take the active form of striving to reduce it, whereas the

---

38. Aristotle, *Nicomachean Ethics*, 1128b34–45; see also 1151b34–1152a6.
39. This claim about outweighing relies on the comparative principle (CP) defended in chapter 5.

virtuous person's hatred involves more passive feelings. Does either of these facts—that the self-controlled person hates an evil that is a closer possibility and that his hatred is more active—mean there is a respect in which his attitudes are better than unadulterated virtue? If so, is the extra value sufficient to make his attitudes on balance better? If the recursive account answers no to both questions, it shares Aristotle's view that self-control is less good than unadulterated virtue. But if it answers either question yes, it can endorse the contrary view that hard-won self-control, where one has struggled against and mastered a strong evil impulse, is better than that easier form of virtue that involves no inner struggle. This latter "battle citation" view of moral goodness holds that although self-control involves an evil not found in unadulterated virtue, it also involves, more significantly, a greater moral good.[40] Though the evil tends to make self-control worse, the higher-level response to that evil does more to make it better.

The recursive account's ranking of categories of virtues depends, then, on two issues we have not yet discussed: the modal status of objects and the different forms of love. We must address these to complete our elaboration of the account; as we will see, they also bear on its most general understanding of what virtue is.

3. *Internalism versus Externalism*

As developed to this point, the recursive account makes the value of an attitude depend on two factors: its intensity and the value of its object. Both the asymptotic view and the holistic proportionality principle consider only these aspects of an attitude and no others. If two objects have the same value, then whatever their modal status and whatever form these attitudes take, loving them with the same intensity has the same intrinsic value.

To see what this implies, let us return to the example from chapter 3 where A and B have the same capacity for virtuous love, but A lives in a world with much better objects. The account as formulated so far, which I will call the simple account, says A's best pleasures in his world's objects are better than B's, because they are directed at

---

40. The term "battle citation" comes from Smith, "Varieties of Moral Worth and Moral Credit," pp. 281–82. For related discussions, see Beardsley, "Moral Worth and Moral Credit"; Henson, "What Kant Might Have Said"; and Roberts, "Will Power and the Virtues."

greater goods. But it does not say *A*'s best attitudes as a whole must be better. If *B* can transfer his love between the forms of desire, pursuit, and pleasure, he can compensate for his less valuable pleasures in existing goods by having more valuable desires for nonexistent ones. More specifically, he can desire the goods in *A*'s better world as intensely as *A* takes pleasure in them and be just as virtuous in doing so. If all the account considers is the value of an object and the intensity of an attitude to it, each of *A* and *B* should desire the goods in the other's world exactly as intensely as the other takes pleasure in them, and if he does, his desire has exactly the same value as the other's pleasure. On the simple account, there is an array of goods in different possible worlds, and all people should divide their love between them in the same way. Facts about their circumstances may affect the form their loves take; thus, *A* can take pleasure in goods *B* can only desire, and vice versa. But if people can transfer their loves between forms, facts about someone's circumstances cannot affect the total value of his virtuous loves taken together.

Given these claims, the simple account expresses what I will call an *internalist* view of virtue. It holds that the value of a person's attitudes depends only on their appropriateness to his circumstances and not at all on what those circumstances are. Though one person can in many ways be more virtuous than another, he cannot be so just because his environment gives him better opportunities for virtue.[41] This internalist view need not hold that a person's virtue must be entirely under his control; it can allow that one person is more virtuous just because he was born with a greater capacity for virtue. (Again, compare God's best use of his capacity for virtue with a human's.) Nor need it deny that a person's virtue can be affected by his past circumstances; one person can be more virtuous because, though born with the same capacity, he had a better moral upbringing. But internalism insists that what determines his virtue now is only the appropriateness of his attitudes to his current environment and not at all what that environment is.

Though this internalist view may be attractive, the simple recur-

---

41. If in the example used earlier *B* cannot fully transfer his love from pleasure to desire, then the best attitudes he is capable of are less good than *A*'s best attitudes. The cause of this shortfall in *B*'s virtue is a fact about the relation between his capacities, or the forms of love they allow, and his world. (If he had more capacity for desire and less for pleasure, his virtue could equal *A*'s.) If this is not a purely internal fact about *B*'s attitudes, then even the simple account is not purely internalist.

sive account that implies it is not. Most important, by considering only the value of an attitude's object, it implies, implausibly, that we should have intense attitudes to what are only very remote possibilities. Imagine that someone has just returned from a tropical holiday marred by unseasonably bad weather. It is certainly reasonable for her to regret the loss of the extra pleasure she would have experienced given normal weather. But the simple account says she should regret even more the greater pleasure she would have enjoyed had a stranger given her a million dollars on the beach, or had aliens abducted her and taken her to an intergalactic pleasure palace. Or consider a similar example involving evils. If her child has just missed being struck by a car, she should feel relief that her child did not suffer the pain of a serious accident. On the simple account, she should feel even greater relief that her child was not abducted by aliens and taken to an intergalactic torture chamber.

Because these claims are implausible, the recursive account must be amended to make the value of an attitude depend in part on its object's relation to actuality. A *first modal condition* concerns attitudes to goods and evils that do not exist. It says that concern for one of these objects has less value when the object's existing is a more remote possibility, or would require greater changes in the world.[42] If a possible good or evil could be actual without much else being different, caring about it has the same value as if the object were actual; for purposes of virtue, close possibilities are equivalent to actualities. As the possibility of an object's existing becomes more remote, however, the value of love for it diminishes. More unlikely possibilities merit less concern and past a threshold of remoteness merit no concern at all. The technical effect of this condition is to depress the curves representing the asymptotic view, so that the curve for a remoter possibility comes lower on the graph than that for a closer possibility of equal value, and the curve for an utterly remote one disappears. (The condition likewise adjusts (PP)'s ideal of proportional division.) This depression of the curves implies that a person with a finite stock of virtuous love should direct less of it at unlikely goods, even those of considerable value. In the examples above, she should regret at most minimally a possibility as remote as getting a million dollars and not at all one as fanciful as intergalactic abduction.

This first modal condition narrows the scope of the recursive account's claims. Instead of requiring attitudes to all possible goods and evils, it now requires them only to a subset of objects, those rea-

42. On closeness of possibility, see Lewis, *Counterfactuals*.

sonably close to reality. This narrowing is attractive, as are the condition's implications for more specific topics, such as regret.

Many discussions of regret focus on the specific context following a choice between goods. The modal condition can explain why: immediately after a choice, the good that one had to forgo is still a very close possibility, since it would exist now had one chosen differently a moment ago. This forgone good therefore satisfies the modal condition to a high degree and is a prime object for attitudes such as regret. The condition also fits some empirical findings about regret. Psychologists report that people feel more intense regret after missing a plane by five minutes than after missing it by thirty minutes, or when their lottery ticket was one rather than many numbers off winning.[43] These attitudes make sense if people feel regret in accordance with the modal condition, caring more about what they believe are closer possibilities. The condition also helps explain the difference between what Janet Landman calls the "romantic" and "ironic" modes of regret. Romantic regret involves a belief that a lost good can still be recovered given sufficient effort; people who feel it devote intense energy to this effort, either actively or in fantasy. Ironic regret, by contrast, views loss as inevitable and irreversible and responds with rueful resignation.[44] Underlying the differing intensities of these two modes of regret are differing beliefs about a lost good's closeness to actuality, both at the time of loss and now. Finally, the modal condition further limits the regret one should feel after a choice. Even appropriate regret can be instrumentally evil if it prevents one from achieving greater goods, and when it involves pain, it is in that respect intrinsically evil (see chapter 3, section 2). We can now add that as time passes after a choice, the intensity of regret appropriate to the forgone good diminishes. What was closely possible immediately after the choice becomes progressively less so later, as the effects of the choice multiply. If a person has just chosen one holiday over another, she may appropriately feel as much regret about the trip she will not take as anticipation for the one that lies ahead. But as she arrives at her destination and accumulates experiences there, the possibility of her being somewhere else becomes one that would take greater changes in

---

43. Kahneman and Tversky, "The Psychology of Preferences," pp. 170–73; and Kahneman and Miller, "Norm Theory," pp. 145–46.

44. Landman, *Regret*, pp. 57–91. She takes romantic and ironic regret to be represented by, respectively, the characters Maggie and Ira Moran in Anne Tyler's novel *Breathing Lessons*.

the world to make actual and is therefore less an object of appropriate concern. It is not that she should care less about a past good because it is past; what she should regret less is in part that she is not on a different holiday now. But she should regret it less because it now has less of a modal property that is necessary for objects at any time to merit serious concern.[45]

This first modal condition can be supplemented by a parallel condition about goods and evils that do exist, one giving concern for these objects more value when their *not* existing is a closer possibility. According to this *second modal condition*, one should feel more pleased by the coming into existence of a good if this was more unexpected or surprising, and by its preservation when this was more seriously under threat. One should likewise feel more pain at a less expected evil. Whereas the first modal condition makes possible objects merit less concern as their existing approaches impossibility, the second does the same for actual objects as their existing approaches necessity.

This second condition has several attractive implications. Combined with the first, it gives an even better explanation of why so many discussions of regret focus on the context following a choice. Now both goods in question satisfy a modal condition to a high degree: one does not exist but would had one chosen differently, the other does exist but would not had one chosen differently. The condition also fits empirical findings about regret, for example, that people feel more upset after having a car accident while driving home by an unusual route than after a similar accident on their normal route.[46] Finally, the condition bears on issues about self-esteem. In a well-known discussion, Nozick argues that self-esteem is necessarily based on comparisons with other people: we do not derive our self-worth from knowing we "have an opposable thumb and can speak some language," but only from ways in which we are superior to others.[47] Nozick's view implies, pessimistically, that self-esteem is

45. That intensity of regret should diminish with time after a choice is also noted by Lemos, *Intrinsic Value*, pp. 17–18. In deriving this claim from the modal condition, I assume the condition is time-relative, so the degree of love appropriate to a good x at time t depends on the degree to which x is a close possibility *at time t*. A different condition says that intense love is appropriate for x at t if x was *at some time* a close possibility; this time-neutral condition does not imply that regret should diminish after a choice. I find the time-relative condition preferable partly because it implies that regret should diminish over time.

46. Kahneman and Miller, "Norm Theory," p. 145.

47. Nozick, *Anarchy, State, and Utopia*, p. 243.

necessarily bound up with jealousy and envy, with wanting to be better or at least not worse than other people. It also implies that unless the members of a community use different standards of merit or are self-deceiving, they cannot all enjoy high self-esteem; some must acknowledge their inferiority. With the second modal condition, we can avoid these implications: the reason we do not find self-worth in our opposable thumb or mastery of language is that these traits are not sufficiently contingent. It is not a need to compare ourselves with others that prevents them from grounding our self-esteem, but the fact that we can hardly imagine ourselves without them. This use of the modal condition separates self-esteem from vices such as jealousy and allows all members of a group to have self-esteem. If they have all achieved a good that was unlikely for them, they can all take pleasure in having done so even if this does not distinguish them from their fellows. Of course, knowing that others have achieved a good may affect one's estimate of how difficult it was for oneself, but this knowledge need not be decisive. One can believe one achieved something unlikely even though others did as well, and can esteem oneself for having done so.

At the same time, the second modal condition has more questionable implications. It implies that a person should take less pleasure in the good aspects of a holiday as time passes after she chose it, since they are becoming less contingent. This is a much less compelling claim than that she should feel less regret about a holiday she did not choose as time passes. The condition also implies that one should feel less compassion for another's pain if it resulted from a genetic and therefore unavoidable disease. This seems implausible; surely one's degree of compassion should depend just on the intensity of the pain. Finally, the condition rules out a view defended by many classical philosophers. Aristotle, Aquinas, and others hold that we should take intense pleasure in metaphysically necessary states such as the law-governed order of the universe and the existence and goodness of God. On a strong version of their view, a good's existing necessarily is an additional reason to love it; on a weaker version, it is just no bar to loving it. But the second condition implies, dubiously, that metaphysical necessities should never be objects of intense appreciation.[48]

48. We could try to avoid this last difficulty by reformulting the second condition to apply only to actual but contingent, i.e., non-necessary, goods and evils. But this reformulation would look ad hoc and in any case would leave the questionable implications about pleasures after a choice and genetic diseases.

These may not be insuperable difficulties for the second condition, but they do suggest that it lacks the unqualified appeal of the first. I will therefore amend the recursive account to include only the first condition, about merely possible goods and evils. Even this one condition, if not accompanied by further amendments, changes fundamentally the account's understanding of what virtue is.

Return to the example of A and B in their different worlds, and add that B has only slightly good objects, not only in his actual, but in all close possible worlds. B's best pleasures still have just limited value, given their objects' limited value, as do his best active pursuits. Without any modal condition B could compensate by having more valuable desires, but with the first modal condition he cannot. Any significant good he desires will now be a remote possibility, which means his desire for it will also have limited value. With the modal condition and no further amendments, B's inferior circumstances make not just one form of his loving goods less good than A's, but all three together. In its amended form, therefore, the recursive account expresses a *partly externalist* view of virtue, on which a person's virtue can be affected by his current circumstances. Just because his environment is less favourable, B's virtue is less. Strictly speaking, it is not B's circumstances as such that limit his virtue, but his beliefs about those circumstances. If he could believe falsely that his actual and close possible worlds contain goods as great as A's, he could have desires, pursuits, and pleasures as valuable as A's. (On attitudes involving on false beliefs, see chapter 6, section 1.) But if he is like most of us, his picture of his environment is largely determined by that environment as it actually is. This means his circumstances, though not the proximate cause of his lesser virtue, are the ultimate cause, and their being any kind of cause requires an externalist view.

Similarly externalist implications follow if the recursive account distinguishes between the values of different forms of love and hate. The simple account holds that given the same intensity, desire for, pursuit of, and pleasure in the same object always have the same value.[49] But the account can be amended to prefer some forms of love, as such, over others.

---

49. How can the intensities of these different attitudes be compared? I take the intensity of a pursuit to equal that of the desire that motivates it. This leaves the comparison between desires and pleasures, which, though it cannot be made precisely, can surely be made to some degree. Surely we can say that a person's mild pleasure in one good is less intense than his fervent desire for another.

The most plausible such amendment makes a mere desire for a good that never issues in action less good than either active pursuit of or pleasure in it. Merely wishing for a good that will never exist is less good than striving to make it exist or being pleased when it does. The implications of this amendment overlap with those of the first modal condition, since the objects of mere wishes are often more remote possibilities than those of actions or pleasures. But the overlap is not complete. On the one side, the amendment does not distinguish between mere desires for close and for remote possibilities. Since this is a crucial distinction, the amendment can at best supplement but not replace the modal condition. On the other side, imagine that a given good is an equally close possibility for *A* and *B*, but that whereas *A* actively pursues it, *B* merely desires it. With only the modal condition, we cannot distinguish between these attitudes, but if we prefer pursuit to desire we can. It may be said that if *B* does not pursue the good, his desire for it must be less intense and therefore already less good. But *B* may have another, greater good closely possible and choose to pursue it instead. Then his desire for the first good can be just as intense as *A*'s, which means that it can be less good than *A*'s pursuit only if mere desire is in general a lesser form of virtue.

The account can also distinguish between the values of active pursuit and pleasure, though here either of two views seems possible. One holds that pleasure in existing goods is the highest virtue and action to create goods merely secondary; the other reverses this ordering. The first equates the ideal moral attitude with the admiring contemplation of securely existing values; the second finds this ideal too passive and prefers an active striving for values. The account can also distinguish within forms of virtue. In chapter 1, I discussed the view that pursuit of a good goal is intrinsically better when the goal is achieved, so if a person's efforts to preserve Venice succeed, his activities are better than if they failed. If it adopts this view, the account can make successful virtuous action intrinsically preferable to otherwise identical action that ends in failure. Both this view and the one preferring pursuit to pleasure must be stated carefully if they are to concern virtue as such. Similar implications, including a preference for striving over contemplation, can be derived from a non-moral valuing of achievement or the attempt at achievement as a base-level good. To distinguish themselves from this valuing, the views we are now considering must make claims about the pursuit and achievement only of good goals. Whatever the value of seeking or achieving neutral or evil goals, they must say, there is a distinctive moral value in achieving good ones.

Any of these preferences among forms of love introduces a further element of externalism into the account. If a person's circumstances offer him greater goods as potential objects of the preferred forms of love, they allow him more virtuous attitudes. In the example above, if *A*'s world lets him pursue and take pleasure in great goods that *B* can only desire, then, modal considerations aside, *A*'s world allows him greater virtue. The same holds if a person's circumstances give him better objects for whichever is preferred among pursuit and pleasure, or if they make his pursuits of goods succeed rather than fail.

This externalist view figures in many theories of virtue. Aristotle, for example, holds that pleasure in a good activity is good and pleasure in a better activity better.[50] This implies that if factors external to a person's attitudes allow her to engage in better activities, they also allow her to have better pleasures. If she has a greater innate capacity for contemplation or lives in circumstances more favourable to contemplation, she can not only engage in better contemplation, but also take better pleasures in contemplation. Aristotle also thinks the central expression of virtue is action from a virtuous motive and, largely for this reason, holds that no one can achieve the complete good related to virtue while stretched on a rack.[51] Someone on a rack can have virtuous desires, for example, to be released from the rack, and can feel virtuous pains, but Aristotle does not think these forms of virtue can compensate for her inability to act from virtue. He also thinks external factors can affect the value of the virtuous actions a person does perform. This is why he thinks the highest virtue requires external goods such as wealth, friends, and political power; these allow a person to actively pursue greater goods, for example, greater benefits to others through her generous actions.[52] Finally, Aristotle holds that action in pursuit of a good goal has its greatest value only when that goal is achieved. His well-known claim that a person's good can be affected by events after her death is consistent with his general view that the good involves activity only if it holds that a person's pursuit of a posthumous goal can have less value if, even through no fault of hers, it ends in

50. Aristotle, *Nicomachean Ethics*, 1175b36–1176a3.
51. Aristotle, *Nicomachean Ethics*, 1153b17–20.
52. Aristotle, *Nicomachean Ethics*, 1099a31–b2.

failure.[53] In all these ways, Aristotle, though insisting that a person's virtue depends crucially on her internal states, allows that it can also be affected by her external environment.

Externalism is likewise endorsed by Moore. His version of the recursive account emphasizes the third form of virtue, pleasure and pain at existing goods and evils. It therefore implies that if a person's circumstances give her only lesser goods to appreciate—less beautiful objects and less virtuous friends—it allows her less valuable attitudes. Moore's most explicitly externalist claim concerns compassion. He holds, plausibly, that compassion for real pain is intrinsically better than compassion for the merely imagined pain of a fictional character, such as King Lear. It follows, he concludes, that a world without real pain could not contain the best form of compassion and would in that respect be less good. A world without pain would not be all things considered less good; it would be all things considered better. But attitudes in that world would be in one respect inferior, because its inhabitants would not have real pain to feel compassion for.[54]

Despite these historical antecedents, externalism may strike some as counterintuitive. Whatever is true of non-moral goods, they may say, a person's virtue can depend only on the appropriateness of her attitudes to her circumstances. Perhaps her justified beliefs have the value of knowledge only if the world is in fact as they picture it to be, but her virtue cannot similarly be affected by her current environment. This internalist view, too, appears in classical theories of virtue. Kant says of a morally good will that even if it "should be wholly lacking in power to achieve its purpose, . . . it would sparkle like a jewel in its own right, as something that had its full worth in itself."[55] Or consider the biblical story of the widow and her two mites.[56] Because she is poor, the widow cannot aim at or achieve as great a good through her contribution to the temple as a wealthy person can. But if her contribution is as great in proportion to her means, her action is every bit as virtuous.

---

53. Aristotle, *Nicomachean Ethics*, 1100a19–31, 1101a21–b9. See also Aristotle's remark that prudence *(phronesis)*, which is also required for fully virtuous action, involves taking means that not only "tend towards" the mark one has set but "hit" it (1144a26; cf. 1142b16–35), and his analogy between virtuous action and winning at, not just competing in, the Olympic Games (1099a3–5).

54. Moore, *Principia Ethica*, pp. 219–21; see also pp. 194–98.

55. Kant, *Foundations of the Metaphysics of Morals*, p. 5.

56. Mark 12:42.

If those who favour this view do not want to revert to the simple account, they can introduce compensating amendments to restore an internalist view of virtue. The result is a three-stage process for evaluating attitudes to values.

The first stage is the existing externalist evaluation, incorporating the first modal condition and perhaps some preferences among forms of love. It assigns different values to equally ideal uses of the same capacity in different circumstances, so A's best attitudes in his good world have, say, a total of 100 units of value, whereas B's best attitudes in his world have 60. The second stage then stipulates that equally ideal uses of the same capacity have the same value. Fixing this value involves some arbitrariness, but let us assume that A's and B's best attitudes now both have a total of 80 units of value. The final stage makes all remaining evaluations by multiplying values from the second stage by fractions derived from the first. Imagine that neither A nor B makes ideal use of his capacity; A's attitudes have only 50 of his possible 100 units on the externalist calculation, whereas B's have 45 of his possible 60. Then A's attitudes have $(50/100) \times 80 = 40$ units of value and B's have $(45/60) \times 80 = 60$ units. Or imagine that a particular attitude of A's has 5 units out of his total of 50 on the externalist calculation. Then this attitude has $(5/50) \times 40 = 4$ units of value on the internalist calculation. This three-stage process yields all the evaluations the recursive account needs while reconciling the modal and other conditions with an internalist view of virtue.

The resulting account is more complex than the one-stage externalist one. In addition, it entirely abandons the atomism of both that and the simple recursive account. Even with the modal and other amendments, the externalist account can always assign a value to an individual attitude given just facts about it (now its intensity and form) and its object (now the object's value and modal status) without considering its relation to other attitudes. Though supplemented by the holism of (PP), this initial atomism remains at the account's core. But the three-stage account cannot evaluate an individual attitude without knowing about a person's overall circumstances, the overall value of his response to them, and the importance of the attitude within that response. The account is entirely non-atomistic and can therefore assign different values to attitudes that are intrinsically identical. Imagine that A and B in their different worlds take equally intense pleasures in two existing goods of equal value. B's pleasure can nonetheless be better than A's because it is a more important part of an equally good response to a less good environment.

That it entirely abandons atomism in this way is not a decisive objection to the three-stage internalist account. If internalism is correct and the simple account with no modal condition is unacceptable, then atomism must be abandoned. But the internalist revisions do make the recursive account much harder to apply, requiring knowledge of a person's total set of attitudes before any one can be evaluated. They also seem in tension with the intuitive foundation of the recursive account, which is the idea that certain attitudes considered on their own are intrinsically good and others evil. If we are attracted by recursion-clauses (LG) and (LE), it is because we think loving goods considered on its own is good and loving evils is evil. But if the general intrinsic value of an attitude can be determined on its own, should its degree of value not likewise be determinable on its own?

As I have said, these are not decisive objections to the three-stage account if internalism is correct, but I do not see that it is. Internalism about virtue may have some initial intuitive appeal, and it certainly distinguishes the moral goods and evils in a striking way. But a partly externalist view also has appeal, as I take Aristotle's and Moore's presentations of it to show. Nor can I see any decisive philosophical argument against externalism. The recursive account already allows a person's virtue to be affected by factors outside his control, such as his innate capacities and past environment. If these factors can affect his virtue, why not also his present environment? The distinction between the voluntary and non-voluntary has seemed vitally important to many moral philosophers, but the distinction between what is now internal to a person and what is not is surely less so. Though the recursive approach requires that the value of a person's attitudes depend in large part on their appropriateness to his circumstances, it can in my view allow that value to be affected by what those circumstances are.

For these reasons, I will reject the three-stage account and assume the partly externalist view that results when the modal condition and preferences among forms of love are not supplemented by compensating amendments. This will simplify the discussion of our next major topic: how the value of virtue compares to that of base-level states such as pleasure and pain. But first we should apply the results of this section to the issue that initiated it: how the value of self-control compares to that of unadulterated virtue.

Though both a self-controlled and a purely virtuous person can hate an intense evil desire, the former hates a closer possibility and does so in the active form of struggling against it rather than by mere gladness at its absence. Does either of these differences make the self-controlled person's attitudes in one respect better? Given the simple recursive account, the answer is no, and Aristotle's view that self-control is inferior to unadulterated virtue is vindicated in a straightforward way. But given either or both the modal condition and preferences among forms, and regardless of further internalist amendments, the answer is yes. Hating a closer evil is better, as is hating it more actively, which means that self-control is in at least one respect superior to unadulterated virtue. Whether self-control is all things considered superior depends on exactly how the modal condition and preference for action are formulated. If the values of attitudes to remoter possibilities diminish only slowly, the extra goodness self-control derives from the modal condition will not be enough to outweigh the evil due to its involving an evil disposition and a weakened but usually still present evil desire; the same is true if active hatred is only slightly better than passive gladness. Then Aristotle's preference for unadulterated virtue will again be vindicated, though in a less straightforward way. But if the modal discount rate is steep or the preference for action very strong, the amended account can endorse the battle-citation view that hard-won self-control is better than the easier virtue not involving inner struggle. This is a welcome result. Both Aristotle's and the battle-citation view of moral goodness have some intuitive appeal and have been endorsed by some philosophers. It is therefore an attractive feature of the amended recursive account that it can explain the difference between them as resting on weaker and stronger specifications of two plausible conditions about the modal status of objects and differing forms of love and hate. Whichever view we prefer, however, we should remember that it concerns only the categories of virtue as categories and not their specific instances. Even if we accept Aristotle's preference for unadulterated virtue, we must allow that some instances of self-control are better than some of pure virtue—for example, self-controlling courage in the face of massive danger is better than very mild benevolence. And even if we accept the battle-citation view, we must allow that intense benevolence is better than successful control of mild fear. As always, any comparison between two specific instances of virtue must consider not only the general categories they fall under, but also specific facts about their intensities, objects, and other properties.

5

How Great a Good Is Virtue?

To say that virtue is intrinsically good is not yet to say how good it is, especially in comparison with base-level values such as pleasure, pain, and knowledge. Is virtue the greatest good, even infinitely more valuable than pleasure or knowledge? Is vice in a similar way the greatest evil? Or are virtue and vice each just one value among others, sometimes outweighing base-level values and sometimes outweighed? In this chapter I will argue that, far from being the greatest good, virtue is in the following sense a lesser good: the value of a virtuous attitude to a good or evil object is always less than the value, either positive or negative, of that object. In a parallel way, vice is a lesser evil. It is not that every instance of virtue or vice has less value than any base-level good or evil; it can outweigh many such goods and evils. But it always has less value than the specific good or evil that is its intentional object. Though important additions to the list of intrinsic values, virtue and vice have in this sense a subordinate status.

1. *Virtue as a Lesser Good*

Some philosophers hold, high-mindedly, that virtue is the greatest intrinsic good. The strongest such view claims that virtue is infinitely superior to other goods, or has lexical priority over them. Ross expresses this view when he writes that "*no* amount of pleasure is equal to any amount of virtue . . . ; in other words, . . . while pleasure is comparable in value with virtue (i.e. can be said to be less valuable than virtue) it is not commensurable with it, as a finite duration is not commensurable with infinite duration."[1] Cardinal Newman makes a similar claim about vice, saying it would be less evil for all humankind to die "in extremest agony" than that "one soul . . . should commit one venial sin."[2] According to this *lexical view*, even the most trivial instance of virtue or vice outweighs the greatest imaginable quantity of any non-moral value such as pleasure, pain, or knowledge.

This view has extremely implausible implications. Consider the two worlds discussed in chapter 2, one with more pleasure and the other with more virtue. The lexical view implies that the second world is better even if it contains vastly less pleasure (its inhabitants suffer agony while those in the first world are blissful) and only slightly more virtue (one inhabitant feels a little more compassion at one moment). Ross and Newman are committed to accepting this implication, but I do not see how they can. Surely an evaluation of the two worlds, while considering their virtue, must give their non-moral features serious weight. Or consider a single life, that of a virtuous person who suffers unremitting and agonizing pain. The lexical view implies that this life is overwhelmingly good, with just an insignificant element of evil. But surely this life is on balance undesirable, one it would be better not to live.

The lexical view has equally implausible implications for cases involving action. As Rashdall asks in a telling critique, must we always prefer directing our charitable contributions to people's moral improvement rather than to their education or material comfort? If the only way to save twenty innocent people from intensely painful torture is by bribing a venal official and further corrupting his character, is bribing the official wrong? Or consider a case involving just the agent's virtue. Someone contemplating a career such as nursing or surgery may know that in it she will do much to relieve others' pain. But she may also rightly fear that the constant exposure to pain will harden her character, changing her from someone who feels deeply for others' suffering to one who handles it efficiently but without accompanying emotion. If virtue had infinite comparative value, it would be wrong for this person to take up nursing or surgery whatever the benefits to other people. But surely that is ab-

---

1. Ross, *The Right and the Good*, p. 150; see also Ross, *The Foundations of Ethics*, p. 275. Ross makes virtue lexically superior to knowledge, his other non-moral good, in *The Right and the Good*, p. 152.

2. Newman, *Certain Difficulties Felt by Anglicans in Catholic Teaching*, vol. 1, p. 240; quoted in Parfit, *Reasons and Persons*, p. 49.

surd.[3] It may be said that an unemotional nurse can still act virtuously in her career, since she can still choose her work for the good it does others. But if compassionate feeling is an additional form of virtue, and if its loss would make her life on balance less virtuous, the lexical view still says her becoming a nurse would be wrong. And we can imagine a more radical example, where the exposure to suffering hardens her character more fully, so that she no longer chooses her work from a virtuous motive but does it only as a job or for money. (Those familiar with careers such as nursing and surgery will know this example is anything but unrealistic.) In this case, and even if there is only the slightest probability of this outcome, the lexical view says she should not take up nursing whatever the benefits to others.[4] The lexical view may seem to derive appeal from cases where it cannot be right to sacrifice virtue for the sake of other goods. These are cases where the only relevant virtue will be that expressed in the agent's action now. As we saw in chapter 2, the action that will produce the most non-moral good in these cases is always also, assuming the requisite motives, the most virtuous action she can perform. So in these cases, the lexical view makes the right claims about action. As Rashdall's examples show, however, the same is not true for cases involving either other people's virtue or the agent's virtue at other times. In these cases, the view's implications are unacceptable.

Despite rejecting the lexical view, Rashdall still holds that virtue is the greatest good: "It seems to me perfectly clear that the moral consciousness does pronounce some goods to be higher, or intrinsically better than others; and that at the head of these goods comes virtue."[5] It is not clear, however, that a non-lexical view of this kind is possible. Consider two non-moral goods, such as pleasure and knowledge. If neither is lexically prior to the other, some very intense pleasures outweigh some trivial items of knowledge, and some very valuable knowledge outweighs some minor pleasures. But if some instances of each good outweigh some of the other, how can

---

3. Rashdall, *The Theory of Good and Evil*, vol. 2, pp. 41–47; for a related discussion, see Maclagan, "How Important Is Moral Goodness?"

4. Alternatively, it may be objected that if the nurse's hardened character results from an initial virtuous choice of career, her actions from that character should still count as virtuous. But again, if compassionate feeling and motivation remain additional forms of virtue, so that choosing the career and remaining compassionate is better than choosing it and becoming hardened, the lexical view can still forbid the career whatever its effects on others.

5. Rashdall, *The Theory of Good and Evil*, vol. 2, p. 37.

we say that either is *in general* greater? If we have measured both goods on cardinal scales, we may have a formula for converting between these scales, and this formula may make, say, 2 units of pleasure equal to 1 of knowledge. But the resulting 2:1 ratio depends on our choice of units on the two scales, which is arbitrary; given different units, there could be a 2:1 ratio in the opposite direction. So if neither of two goods is lexically prior to the other, how can we make any general comparison between them?[6]

This difficulty is not decisive for the specific good of virtue, since every one of its instances is specially connected to another good or evil that is its intentional object. Every lowest-level virtue, to start, has as its object an instance of a base-level value such as pleasure, pain, or knowledge. It is a desire for a pleasure, a pain at a pain, or something similar. We can therefore ask how the value of the virtue compares to that of its specific base-level object. If the virtue's value is always greater, there is a restricted but clear sense in which this form of virtue is a greater good than pleasure or knowledge; if its value is smaller, there is a clear sense in which the virtue is a lesser good. The same approach can be extended to higher-level virtues. Every such virtue is likewise connected to a specific base-level value, through the lower-level attitude that is its object. We can therefore assess the value of virtue as a whole by asking how in general the value of a virtuous attitude compares to that of its object. If the attitude's value is always finitely greater, there is a restricted but clear sense in which virtue is a finitely greater good. It may be that for every instance of virtue there are some instances of pleasure and knowledge that are better and some that are less good. But if there is a constant relationship between the value of the virtue and that of the specific base-level value to which it is intentionally connected, this relationship can underwrite a general claim about the comparative value of virtue. A similar relationship can underwrite claims about the comparative evil of, initially, pure vices and vices of indifference. If the evil of a vicious attitude is always greater than the good or evil of its object, these vices are greater evils in the same sense that virtue can be a greater good. And this claim can be ex-

---

6. We can make informal general comparisons on practical grounds. If a formula for weighing pleasure and knowledge implies that most people should spend more time pursuing pleasure than knowledge, we can say that for these people pleasure is in practice the greater good (see my *Perfectionism*, pp. 85, 90). But I do not think this informal judgment is all Rashdall intends when he says that virtue is the greatest good, nor all that is interesting in that claim.

tended to the vices of disproportion if we can compare the evil in a disproportionate combination of attitudes with the intrinsic values in its components, as we must be able to if we can determine which such combinations are on balance evil. I think a charitable reading of Rashdall's non-lexical view takes it to rest on this kind of restricted comparison. He thinks virtue is a greater good and vice a greater evil because he thinks any virtuous or vicious attitude, though outweighed by some base-level values, has more positive or negative value than the specific base-level state that is its direct or indirect object.

That virtue is a greater good is sometimes argued on the ground that virtue alone is morally good, whereas pleasure, knowledge, and the like are not.[7] (This is also sometimes given as a ground for the lexical view.) But if this argument treats moral goodness as a distinct property from intrinsic goodness, it cannot hold that virtue has only that property and no other. If we can compare the values of the two worlds discussed above, the pleasure and virtue they contain must have the same kind of goodness, namely, intrinsic goodness. And why should the virtue's having a distinct property of moral goodness give it more intrinsic goodness? In any case, there is no reason to treat moral goodness as a distinct property. The more plausible view is that moral goodness is just intrinsic goodness—they are the same property—when had by certain objects, namely, attitudes evaluated in relation to their objects (see chapter 2, section 2). And on this view, the claim that virtue alone is morally good supports no substantive view about virtue's comparative worth. To determine that worth, we must compare virtue directly with other values such as pleasure, pain, and knowledge.

In my view, this comparison supports not Rashdall's view that virtue is a greater good, but the contrary view that virtue and vice are lesser values. This view is expressed in the following *comparative principle*, (CP), about attitudes and their objects:

(CP) The degree of intrinsic goodness or evil of an attitude to x is always less than the degree of goodness or evil of x.

According to this comparative principle, the intrinsic goodness of loving a good is always less than that of the good, as is the intrinsic evil of hating it. Thus, desiring a pleasure is always less good than

---

7. See, e.g., Garcia, "The Primacy of the Virtuous," pp. 78–79, and "Goods and Evils," pp. 407–9.

the pleasure is good, and being pained by the pleasure is less evil. Similarly, the evil of loving an evil is always less than that of the evil, as is the goodness of hating the evil. It is not that every virtuous or vicious attitude has less value than any pleasure or pain. A desire for the immense pleasure of others, though less good than that pleasure, can be better than a mild pleasure of one's own. But every attitude has less value than its object, and virtue and vice are in that sense lesser values.

In making these claims, (CP) assumes there is an upper bound on the value of any attitude to an object, whatever its intensity. (If there were not, a sufficiently intense attitude could be more good or evil than its object.) The principle is therefore inconsistent with the linear view of individual attitudes, which places no bounds on the values of any attitudes, and also with the completed optimality view, which limits the goodness of virtuous attitudes but not the evil of vicious ones (see chapter 3, sections 1 and 2). As it happens, we rejected both these views, and the arguments for (CP) provide a further reason for doing so. But the principle fits perfectly with the asymptotic view, which places bounds on the values of both virtue and vice and which we have already preferred on other grounds. In fact, (CP) helps specify this view by determining where the asymptote for a given attitude must be located: at a point representing a value smaller than that of its object. But exactly how the principle and view combine depends on how the two are formulated.

The simplest formulation of (CP) makes the upper bound on the value of an attitude a constant fraction of its object's value, say, one-half. Whether a good is great or small, the positive value of loving it cannot exceed one-half its value, nor can the negative value of hating it. This simple (CP) could not be adopted if the asymptotic view accommodated clauses (IG) and (IE) about indifference by moving its curves and asymptotes down the graph, as in figure 3.6. Since the resulting version of the view makes the bounds on the values of vicious attitudes higher than those for virtuous ones, it implies that vicious attitudes can have a larger fraction of their objects' values, say, three-fourths as against one-fourth. But the simple (CP) is compatible with the version of the asymptotic view that accommodates (IG) and (IE) by retaining the symmetrical placement of asymptotes and changing the curves' shapes, as in figure 3.7. If we adopt this version of the view, as I proposed doing in chapter 3, we can take (CP) to imply that the value of an attitude can never exceed a constant fraction of its object's value, such as one-half. We need not commit ourselves to any such mathematically precise formulation to assess

(CP), but it will help us understand the principle if we take it to limit the values of attitudes in some such constant way.[8]

The first argument for (CP), which derives from Moore, concerns the combination of an evil and a virtuous response to it, for example, one person's pain and another's compassion for that pain. Moore writes: "There seems no reason to think that where the object [of an attitude] is a thing evil in itself, *which actually exists,* the total state of things is ever positively *good on the whole.* The appropriate attitude towards a really existing evil . . . may be a great positive good on the whole. But there seems no reason to doubt that, where the evil is *real,* the amount of this real evil is always sufficient to reduce the total sum of value to a negative quantity."[9] If the value of a virtuous attitude were greater than that of its object, as Rashdall claims, the combination of pain and compassion for it would be on balance good. But this is intuitively unacceptable. The compassion is indeed good, and makes the situation better than if there were only pain and no compassion, but it cannot outweigh or justify the pain. If so—if a combination of pain and compassion for it is always on balance evil—the goodness of virtuously hating an evil must be less than the evil of its object.

This argument does not claim only that a situation with pain and compassion for it is worse than if there were no pain. A situation with no pain can still contain hatred of pain; someone can be glad that pain does not exist and hope that it does not exist in future. On an internalist view of virtue, these latter attitudes can be just as good as hatred of real pain, and even on a partly externalist view they have significant value. So a situation with pain and compassion can be worse than one without pain, even though in the first the compassion is better than the pain is evil. Moore's argument therefore requires the stronger claim that the combination of pain and compassion for it is on balance evil, or worse than if there were neither

8. In itself, the simple version of (CP) is compatible with either an internalist or an externalist view of virtue, but given the first modal condition, it requires a partly externalist view. To see this, return to the case where *A* lives in a world with many very good objects and *B* in one with only slightly good objects, and add that neither *A* nor *B* has any good objects in close possible worlds. On an internalist view, *B*'s optimal pleasure in his world's good objects is as good as *A*'s optimal pleasure in his. But this is inconsistent with attitudes' always having the same fraction of their objects' values, since *A*'s good objects are so much better than *B*'s. (In fact, it is possible that *A*'s pleasures have less value than their objects, whereas *B*'s pleasures have more.) So given the first modal condition, the simple (CP) requires a partly externalist view of virtue.

9. Moore, *Principia Ethica,* p. 219 (emphasis in original).

pain nor any attitude to it. But this claim is still intuitively attractive. If we had a choice between creating a world containing only pain and compassion and creating nothing, it would surely be best to create nothing. But then the compassion must be less good than the pain is evil.

Or consider the combination of an evil attitude and a higher-level hatred of it, for example, a malicious desire and shame at that desire. Since malice is evil, feeling pained by or ashamed of one's malice is good. But it would not be plausible to hold that feeling malice and shame at it is better than feeling neither malice nor shame. This conclusion would follow if the value of an attitude were greater than its object's value, but it does not given (CP).[10]

Compassion and shame are virtues, but a similar argument can be constructed for some vices. If one person enjoys pleasure and another wishes enviously that the first were not doing so, the second person's malicious envy is evil but not so evil as to outweigh the first's pleasure. Just as it would be wrong to inflict pain on one person so another could feel compassion, so it would be wrong to deny one person pleasure to prevent another from feeling envy. But then the envy must be less evil than the pleasure is good.

This first argument concerns only attitudes whose values are the opposite of their objects' values, namely, hating evil and loving good. It is therefore possible to accept it while holding that the remaining attitudes of loving good and loving evil have more value than their objects. But it is simplest if the relation between attitudes and their objects is uniform, so a conclusion like Moore's generalizes to all of (CP). And there are further arguments for (CP).

One such argument concerns the value of very high-level attitudes. Given their recursive form, both clauses (LG) and (HE) generate infinite hierarchies of virtuous attitudes. Thus, (LG) values not only the desire for pleasure, but also the desire for the desire for

---

10. This application of (CP) may seem to threaten the virtues of self-control. If the desire to control an evil desire is less good than the latter desire is evil, how can the combination of those desires be on balance virtuous? This objection forgets that when self-control is successful, what is present in a person is only a weakend evil desire, whereas the object of his controlling desire is a stronger evil desire that no longer exists. His controlling desire can therefore have less value than the stronger desire that is its object but more value than the weaker desire that remains. Nonetheless, it is true that the exact formulation of (CP) and the exact fraction of the value of the original evil desire it assigns to the controlling desire determine which instances of self-control are on balance virtuous and which are just lesser vices.

pleasure, the desire for the desire for the desire for pleasure, and so on. These clauses' recursive form is one of their attractive features, giving them more generality and unifying power than any non-recursive principle. It is also plausible in itself to hold that very high-level attitudes can be good, and it is a merit in, say, God that he can have them without detracting from his lower-level attitudes. But it would not be plausible to hold that these attitudes are very good, or that beings with merely human capacities should spend much time trying to form them. Our comparative principle avoids these implications. If the value of an attitude is always less than that of its object, say, by one-half, the values of progressively higher-level attitudes get progressively smaller and in fact diminish toward zero. Though B's desire for A's pleasure may have significant value, C's desire for B's desire has less value, and D's desire for C's even less. And this argument, again, has an analogue for vicious attitudes. Though D's taking depraved pleasure in C's pleasure in B's pleasure in A's pain is evil, it is not as evil as if D took direct pleasure in A's pain.[11]

A third argument for the principle trades on the proportionality view about the best divisions of love. In chapter 3 we used this view to move from the premise that x is better than y to the conclusion that it is best to love x more intensely than y. But we can equally well argue in the opposite direction, saying that if it is best to love x more, x must be better. There are several instances of this argument for (CP).

Imagine that a teacher works to develop knowledge in a student from a benevolent desire for the student's knowledge, and that as a result the student acquires knowledge. If you learn of these facts, which should you be more pleased by, the student's knowledge or the teacher's virtuous pursuit of knowledge? Surely you should be more pleased by the student's knowledge; it is the point of the exercise. Or imagine that you can produce only one of these types of good but not both. Right now an uncaring teacher is teaching using ineffective methods, so her student is not acquiring knowledge. You can either change the teacher's attitude while leaving her methods

---

11. Note that if the lexical view derived its claim about the comparative value of virtue from the more general claim that the values of attitudes are always infinitely greater than the values of their objects, it would require an infinite hierarchy of orders of infinity to capture the values of all the recursively generated virtues. If it recoiled from this implication, it could not derive its comparative claim from any more general claim about attitudes and their objects.

unchanged or change her methods but not her attitude. Surely in this case it is best to change the teacher's methods, so the student acquires knowledge. Or consider an example involving evils. If a torturer is causing a victim intense pain and also taking pleasure in that pain, surely you should be most pained by the victim's pain. If you can either interfere with the torturer's pleasure while leaving his torture machine running or secretly disconnect the machine, you should disconnect the machine. If so, however, the evil of the torturer's pleasure in pain must be less than that of the pain.

Or consider attitudes to one's own virtue. Which should the teacher in the example above have as her main motive for teaching, that she will thereby act virtuously or that through her teaching her student will gain knowledge? Which should she be most pleased by afterwards, her own good action or its effect? Many writers hold that there is a moral failing or even vice, called, variously, moral self-indulgence, narcissism, or priggishness, that consists in caring too much about one's own virtue. Williams says an agent is morally self-indulgent when "what the agent cares about is not so much other people, as himself caring about other people . . . [A] person may act from generosity or loyalty . . . and not attract the charge of moral self-indulgence, but that charge will be attracted if the suspicion is that his act is motivated by a concern for his own generosity or loyalty, the enhancement or preservation of his own self-image as a generous or loyal person."[12] Williams does not say that *any* concern for one's virtue is a failing; self-indulgence consists only in caring "disproportionately" about one's virtue, or having it be "more important" in one's motivation than a concern for other people.[13] He therefore allows that some concern for one's virtue, provided it is a lesser concern, can be part of complete virtue. His view therefore fits perfectly with (CP). Because the teacher's virtuous action is good, it is appropriate for her to desire and be pleased by it. But if her action is less good than the knowledge it produces, what is best is for her to care about her virtue less than about the knowledge. If

12. Williams, "Utilitarianism and Moral Self-Indulgence," p. 45. Williams's reference at the end of this passage to the agent's "self-image" introduces a different and extraneous consideration. Someone motivated by an *image* of himself as virtuous wants to believe he is virtuous, perhaps because of the comfort that belief affords. But a desire for the comfort that comes from believing oneself virtuous is different from a desire actually to be virtuous, and it is an excess of the latter that makes for moral self-indulgence in the philosophically most interesting sense.

13. Williams, "Utilitarianism and Moral Self-Indulgence," pp. 47, 45; see also Lemos, "High-Minded Egoism and the Problem of Priggishness," p. 550.

she cares more about her virtue, she divides her love disproportionately, which is at least a shortfall in virtue and in extreme cases a vice.

Similarly, (CP) can explain the failing of sentimentality or kitsch as defined by Milan Kundera: "Kitsch causes two tears to flow in quick succession. The first tear says: How nice to see children running on the grass! The second tear says: How nice to be moved, together with all mankind, by children running on the grass! It is the second tear that makes kitsch kitsch."[14] Kundera's "second tear" involves, again, an excessive concern with one's own attitude rather than, through that attitude, with an object in the world. Kitsch also usually involves a lower-level disproportion, an overvaluing of some trite object such as children running on the grass.[15] But this lower-level disproportion often originates in the higher-level self-indulgence: it is because one is so eager to have a fine attitude that one does not notice the banality of its object.

Not all theorists of virtue join in this condemnation of moral self-indulgence. Aristotle says a virtuous person chooses his actions "for their own sakes" or because they are "noble" rather than for any consequences they will produce. He also says a virtuous person is pleased by his virtuous actions, but he never says this person is pleased by their result.[16] Though other interpretations have been suggested, these remarks strongly suggest that Aristotle's virtuous person is motivated solely or primarily by concern that he himself act virtuously, that is, in a self-indulgent way. This is certainly evident in Aristotle's description of the proud person (*megalopsychos*), which Ross says "betrays somewhat nakedly the self-absorption which is the bad side of Aristotle's ethics."[17]

Aristotle's proud person, to give him his due, has every virtue and is good to the highest degree, which on the recursive account makes it appropriate for him to take some pleasure in his virtue. What is

---

14. Kundera, *The Unbearable Lightness of Being*, p. 251.

15. See Kekes, *Facing Evil*, pp. 218–21.

16. Aristotle, *Nicomachean Ethics*, 1105a32, 1144a20; 1116a11–14, 1116b2, 1120a23–29, 1140b6–7; 1099a10–15, 1104b4–6, 1104b30–33, 1175b24–1176a3, 1176b26–27.

17. Ross, *Aristotle*, p.208. Some commentators argue that to be motivated by the "noble," as Aristotle understands it, is to be motivated by concern for what benefits others or contributes to a common good; see, e.g., Irwin, *Aristotle's First Principles*, pp. 439–44. I find this interpretation, which relies heavily on passages outside the *Nicomachean Ethics*, difficult to square with important aspects of the *Ethics*. If accurate, however, it saves Aristotle at least partly from the charge of approving self-indulgence.

objectionable is only the kind of pleasure he takes. First, the proud person cares very much about being more virtuous than other people. He is competitive about virtue, liking to confer benefits but not to receive them, "for the one is the mark of a superior, the other of an inferior." When done a favour, he does a greater one in return, to place the other person in his debt.[18] But this concern for his rank in virtue can make him jealous about virtue, hoping that others who are less virtuous than himself will not increase their virtue to a level where it surpasses his own, and this higher-level jealousy is a vice. Even if he is not jealous about virtue, his competitiveness shows that he cares more about his own virtue than about other people's; this moral selfishness is likewise a vice. Most important, the proud person cares more about his virtue than about any benefits it can bring to other people. This is reflected most clearly in his tendency "to be sluggish and to hold back except where great honour or a great work is at stake, and to be a man of few deeds, but of great and notable ones."[19] Aristotle's proud person will not do small favours for other people, such as opening a door or helping start a car, because they are too commonplace for his outstanding virtue. His main concern is how an action will reflect on his standing in virtue rather than any good it will do others, and he therefore manifests in extreme form the self-indulgence rightly condemned by (CP).

Not all philosophers who reject (CP) join Aristotle in embracing preoccupation with one's virtue. Ross, for example, holds that virtue is infinitely better than other goods while also recognizing the "self-absorption" of an excessive concern with one's character. The question, however, is whether a position like Ross's is consistent. It is overwhelmingly plausible that given two goods, one greater than the other, it is best to care more about the greater; this is the minimal claim about division. If we accept this claim, however, and if virtue is even a finitely greater good, it follows that it is best to care more about one's virtue than about its effects; and this is unacceptable. It is a commonplace of contemporary writing about virtue that moral self-indulgence is a failing and that truly virtuous agents are not motivated primarily by thoughts of their own virtue. What is less

---

18. Aristotle, *Nicomachean Ethics*, 1249b9–12. Aristotle also discusses competition in virtue at 1168b28–1169b12. There he argues that such competition is instrumentally good (1169a7–11), but he never considers whether the desire to be more virtuous than others is in itself objectionable.

19. Aristotle, *Nicomachean Ethics*, 1124b25–27. On the self-indulgence this expresses, see Sherman, "Common Sense and Uncommon Virtue."

often noticed is the tension between these claims and the still widely held view that virtue is the greatest good. In fact, the best way to explain why self-indulgence is a failing is to hold, with our comparative principle, that virtue is a lesser good.

These initial arguments for (CP) concern its implications for particular cases, but there is also a more abstract argument. On the recursive account, virtue is a dependent intrinsic good, one that cannot be good unless other, base-level states are good or evil. It does not follow, as Sidgwick believed, that virtue can only be instrumentally good, but a weaker conclusion does seem appropriate. If virtue involves a relation to other goods and evils, it is fitting that it should be a lesser good, one whose value cannot exceed that of its object. Something secondary in the origin of its value should likewise have secondary weight. There is no logical compulsion about this argument; it is perfectly consistent to hold that virtue is a response to other goods but, as that response, has infinitely greater value. Nonetheless, it does seem in a looser way appropriate that a good defined by relation to other values should also be subordinate in its comparative worth.

I have given several arguments for the comparative principle's claim that virtue and vice are lesser values: about certain combinations of an object and an attitude, such as pain and compassion for it; about very high-level attitudes; about division and self-indulgence; and about virtue's status as a dependent good. Together, these arguments strongly support (CP), but there are also difficulties about the principle that a full discussion must address. These difficulties are not grounds for rejecting (CP), but they do make the issue of virtue's comparative value somewhat more complex.

2. *Difficulties*

The first difficulty concerns Moore's argument about pain and compassion. The comparative principle implies that a combination of pain and one person's compassion for it is always on balance evil, but what if two, twenty, or a hundred people feel compassion? Are the resulting combinations still on balance evil? I think our initial response is that they are. Our verdict may not be as confident here as in the case involving just one person's compassion, but I think many of us will say that given a choice between creating pain plus a hundred people's compassion for it and creating nothing, it is best to create nothing. But it is hard to see how the recursive account even with (CP) can endorse this judgment. If each of the hundred people's compassion is good, then even if each is less good than the pain is evil, can the sum of their goodness not outweigh the evil of the pain? Can enough virtuous attitudes to pain not make for on-balance goodness? This conclusion would not follow if the value of extra people's compassion diminished, but there seems no reason to believe it does. That others are sympathizing with someone's pain makes it no less appropriate for me to do so and should make it no less good. We may think the value of extra compassion diminishes if we consider compassion instrumentally, as helping to console the victim. (If ninety-nine people are already sympathizing with him, he will not take much more comfort from a hundredth.) But we do not think this way if we consider the compassion by itself. Then the value of each person's compassion seems the same, which implies that enough people's compassion can outweigh any pain.

This difficulty weakens the Moorean argument for (CP). That argument claims that if the recursive account includes (CP), it can capture our intuitive judgments about combinations of pain and compassion; if some such judgments are not captured, the support given (CP) is less. But it is not clear what direction the difficulty points in. It is certainly not a reason to hold, with Rashdall, that virtue is a greater good; that would only compound the difficulty. And if we cannot hold that the value of extra compassion diminishes, we may have to accept the conclusion about numbers, difficult though that may seem. We want to hold that virtue is intrinsically good; we also want to hold that in some cases, like that of the two worlds discussed in chapter 2, virtue can outweigh base-level values such as pleasure and pain. Given these assumptions, and adding that the value of extra people's compassion is constant, it seems unavoidable that some number of people's compassion can outweigh any pain. Though initially unsettling, the conclusion seems to be one we are forced to accept.[20]

The second difficulty concerns the comparative principle's scope. As originally formulated, (CP) applies indiscriminately to all atti-

20. We may also have to accept a parallel conclusion about times, namely, that a sufficiently long-lasting compassion can outweigh any pain. This conclusion might be mitigated to some extent if we accepted the second modal condition, which makes the appropriateness and therefore the value of compassion for a pain diminish as the pain recedes into the past. But this modal condition faces difficulties (see chapter 4, section 3) and in any case may not avoid the conclusion entirely. It is again unsettling to allow that the combination of a pain and long-lasting compassion for it can be on balance good, but it is hard to see how to avoid this.

tudes, making them all less good or evil than their objects. This claim is most compelling for attitudes whose objects are great goods or evils—for example, intense pleasures or pains. But it is less so for attitudes whose objects are trivial goods or evils. Imagine that one person goes out of his way to provide a small pleasure for another, say, by doing her a small favour. In this case, may the first person's benevolence not have more value than the pleasure it produces? (Of gift giving we say, "It's the thought that counts.") Or imagine that one person takes special trouble to cause another a small annoyance or pain. May his petty malice not be worse than its effect?

If we were persuaded by these examples, we would have to restrict (CP) so that it applies only to attitudes with objects of significant value. More generally, we could revise (CP) so the ratio between the maximum value of an attitude and the value of its object is not constant, as in the simple version discussed above, but changes continuously. When the value of the object is high, the maximum value of the attitude is just a small fraction of it. But as the value of the object declines, this fraction gets larger, and when the object is trivial, the attitude's value can be greater. Instead of a constant ratio between the maximum value of an attitude and that of its object, such as one-half, there are different ratios for objects of different values.

This revised principle implies that a combination of a trivial pain and one person's compassion for it can be on balance good. If we accepted this implication, as is not unimaginable, we might find it easier to accept that combinations involving a greater pain and several people's compassion can be good. But the revised principle has more troubling implications for the proportionality view about division.

The proportionality view holds that it is best to divide one's love proportionally among good objects. It is expressed not only in the holistic proportionality principle, but also in the asymptotic view of individual attitudes, at least if that view satisfies the proportionality constraint on slopes (see chapter 3, section 2). This constraint can be satisfied if the maximum value of an attitude is a constant fraction of its object's value, as in the simple (CP), but it is inconsistent with the revised (CP), which makes this fraction different for objects of different values.[21] To accept the revised (CP), therefore, is to deny that the best divisions of love are strictly proportioned to their objects' values. If x is twice as good as y, it is still best to love x

---

21. The proportionality constraint requires the asymptotes for attitudes to different objects to be linearly spaced, which is impossible given the revised (CP).

more—loving greater goods is still always better—but the ideal proportion is less than 2:1. One should love greater goods more than lesser goods, but not by as much as their degree of greater goodness suggests.[22]

I am not sure how objectionable this feature of the revised (CP) is. On the one hand, our intuitions may not be sufficiently precise to distinguish in particular cases between strictly proportional division and some slight departure from it. On the other hand, the general ideal of proportionality, when stated abstractly, has considerable intuitive appeal. My own preference is to retain the strict proportionality view by holding that the maximum value of an attitude is always the same fraction of its object's value, as in the simple version of (CP). This requires accepting what some may find counterintuitive: that even attitudes to trivial goods and evils have less value than their objects. (In gift giving, it's the gift that counts.) But it is also possible to prefer the revised (CP), which gives attitudes such as minor benevolence and petty malice more value than their objects. Either way, the recursive account retains the core claim of (CP): for objects above a threshold of goodness or evil, the value of any attitude to them is less than their own.

The most important difficulty for the comparative principle concerns the value on balance of some forms of loving evil, such as a torturer's sadistic pleasure in his victim's intense pain. According to recursion-clause (LE), this pleasure is intrinsically evil as an instance of loving evil. But according to base-clause (BG), it is also intrinsically good as an instance of pleasure, or as having the pleasantness that makes all pleasure sensations in that respect desirable. So is the torturer's pleasure on balance intrinsically good or evil? We surely want it to be on balance evil, so its presence makes a situation worse. But whether sadistic pleasure is on balance evil depends on the comparative values of its properties of vice and pleasantness. Only if the pleasure's evil as vice always outweighs its goodness as pleasure will it always be on balance evil. How can this be, given (CP)? Imagine that (CP) makes the maximum value of an attitude one-half that of its object, and that equal units of intensity of pleasure and pain have equal value. Then if the torturer takes 5 units of pleasure in his victim's 30 units of pain, his pleasure may indeed

---

22. The resulting overall departure from strict proportionality is mitigated if (PP) is retained in its original form. But having revised (CP), we may also want to revise (PP) to favour the not-quite-proportional divisions now preferred by the revised asymptotic view.

be on balance evil. It can have more than 5 units of disvalue as vice and make the overall situation worse. But if he takes 20 units of pleasure in his victim's 30 units of pain, his pleasure has more goodness as pleasure than its maximum 15 units of vice and makes the situation better. With sufficient intensity, a sadistic pleasure can be on balance good.[23]

This difficulty would not arise given the lexical view, which makes virtue and vice infinitely more valuable than pleasure or pain. Ross cites this very fact in arguing for the view: "It seems clear that when we consider such a pleasure [i.e., a pleasure of cruelty] we are able to say at once that it is bad, that it would have been better that it should not have existed. If the goodness of pleasure were commensurable with the goodness or badness of moral disposition, it would be possible that such a pleasure if sufficiently intense should be good on the whole. But in fact its intensity is a measure of its badness."[24] There are, however, compelling reasons to reject the lexical view. And once virtue and vice have just finite value compared to their objects, let alone lesser value, it seems that some instances of pleasure in intense pain can be on balance good.

This difficulty about pleasure in evil does not arise for the related vice of desiring evil, since desiring on its own has no intrinsic value. But it does arise for the vice of pursuing evil. Base-clause (BG) finds value in achievement, which consists in bringing about a goal that is extended across times and objects and has many other goals subordinate to it (see chapter 1, section 2). Imagine, therefore, that a torturer uses highly complex means to inflict intense pain on a large number of people. Though evil as a pursuit of evil, his action can be good as an achievement and therefore, given (CP), good on balance. There may seem to be a parallel difficulty about some virtues of hating evil, such as being pained by another's pain. Compassionate pain is good as an attitude to its object but evil as a pain. Given (CP), therefore, it can, if sufficiently intense, be on balance evil. But this last implication does not seem counterintuitive. We sometimes do not tell friends of hurts we have suffered, to spare them the pain of sympathizing with us. Even if we recognize that their compassion

---

23. This difficulty is nicely illustrated in Frankena's *Ethics*. Frankena claims both that malicious pleasure is always on balance evil and that every pleasure has some value as pleasure (pp. 89–90). But he does not explain why, as this combination of claims assumes, the moral evil of malicious pleasure must always outweigh its hedonic goodness.

24. Ross, *The Right and the Good*, p. 151.

would be morally good, we view the pain it involves as a greater evil. Compassionate pain therefore does not pose a serious difficulty for (CP), but sadistic pleasure does.

Can the recursive account avoid holding that sadistic pleasure can be on balance good? One way is to deny that pleasure is as such intrinsically good, or belongs among the base-level values identified by (BG). This anti-hedonist view can allow that pleasures with good objects are good; they are virtues as valued by (LG). But it denies that pleasure considered independently of any object, or in itself, is good. And a similar view denies that achievement considered independently of its object is good. Though pursuing good goals is good and achieving them perhaps better, achieving goals that are not good has no value at all.

These views certainly avoid implying that loving evil can be on balance good; if doing so were a necessity, we might have to adopt them. But they have other counterintuitive implications. For example, the anti-hedonist view denies that non-intentional pleasures such as those of suntanning are good. Though not completely unimaginable, this is an extreme claim. Surely most of us believe that simple bodily pleasures have some intrinsic worth. A less sweeping anti-hedonism denies only that intentional pleasures are good as pleasures: unstructured pleasure sensations have value, and only pleasures that something is the case do not. But this view still denies, implausibly, that pleasures with neutral objects are good. Consider a sports fan's pleasure, which may be very intense, that his local team has won a championship. If his feeling involves the same quality of pleasantness as the pleasure of suntanning, should it not likewise be good?[25] Nor do only pleasures with neutral objects seem good as pleasures; those with good objects do as well. Imagine that A lives in a world with many very good objects in which he takes appropriate pleasures, whereas B lives in an evil world by which he is appropriately pained. Do we not think A's state, though no more virtuous than B's, is on balance better because his virtue takes the form of pleasure? Or, if this example trades improperly on the evil of B's pain, imagine that A lives in a better world than B and can therefore

---

25. A similar point holds for the denial that achievements with neutral objects are good, since these achievements are central to sports and games. A mountain climber pursues a goal, that of standing atop a mountain, that is intrinsically trivial. But because achieving this goal by climbing is so complex and difficult, his doing so is widely thought to be of considerable value. On the intrinsic value of games see my *Perfectionism*, chap. 9; and Suits, *The Grasshopper*.

take more intense pleasure in its contents. Is *A*'s state not on balance preferable because it is more pleasant?[26]

It may seem that the solution to these difficulties is obvious: deny only that pleasures and achievements with evil objects are good as pleasures or achievements. Non-intentional pleasures are good as pleasures, as are pleasures with neutral or good objects, and only pleasures with evil objects, such as sadistic pleasures, lack value as pleasures. Attractive though it may seem, however, this conditionality view, as I will call it, would require major changes in the recursive account and even then cannot be captured in its entirety.

In the original recursive account, the base-clauses (BG) and (BE) are prior to and independent of the recursion-clauses (LG)–(HE), identifying their non-moral goods and evils without reference to any subsequent claims about good and evil attitudes. The base-clauses are also independent of each other, with neither restricted by the other's claims. But these structural features exclude the conditionality view just proposed. To say that sadistic pleasure has no value as pleasure is to make a claim about base-level values. To say it has no value because it is directed at evil is to ground that claim in something recursive. And in the original account, no base-level claim can depend on any recursive claim.

Because of this, capturing the conditionality view would require changing the account's structure, first by abandoning the independence of (BG) from (BE). A revised recursive account starts with an unchanged (BE), one saying as before that all pain, false belief, and failure are evil. This clause implies that compassionate pain is always evil as pain, but this is a plausible claim.[27] The revised account then follows (BE) with a version of (BG) that is restricted by (BE), one saying that pleasure and achievement are good *except when* directed at the evils identified by (BE), that is, except when directed at pain, false belief, or failure. This revised clause implies, as desired, that sadistic pleasure has no value as pleasure; when the recursion-clause (LE) is added, such pleasure will always be on balance evil. The re-

---

26. To be consistent with the asymptotic view and the first modal condition, this example must assume that *B* has significantly good objects in close possible worlds, so he can desire goods intensely but not take intense pleasure in them.

27. It is also a claim the account cannot deny without circularity. The denial would have to say that pain is evil except when it is pain at pain. But assuming the latter pain must be pain that is on balance evil, this generates an infinite series of further exceptions: pain is evil except when it is pain at pain, except when the second pain is pain at pain, except when the third pain is pain at pain, and so on. This circularity prefigures the one about sadistic pleasure discussed later.

vised (BG) also allows that pleasures with no, neutral, or good objects are good, so it has at least initially the right kind of implications. But it does not capture all the proposed conditionality view, since it does not imply that pleasures with higher-level evil objects lack value as pleasures. Imagine that while *B* takes sadistic pleasure in *A*'s pain, *C* takes a higher-level pleasure in *B*'s sadistic pleasure, enjoying the latter as sadistic. Surely if *B*'s pleasure lacks value as pleasure, *C*'s should too; it, too, is directed at evil. But a (BG) restricted only by (BE) cannot endorse this claim, since it denies value only to pleasures in base-level evils. If the recursive account is to yield the claim, it must be revised further to abandon the priority of all base-level over all recursive claims. More specifically, it must interpose the recursion-clause (LE) about hating evils between base-clauses (BE) and (BG). Then (BG) can be doubly restricted, saying that pleasure and achievement are good *except when* directed at the evils identified by either (BE) or (LE). This second revision makes *C*'s pleasure in *B*'s sadistic pleasure lack value as pleasure, as desired, but it still does not capture all the proposed conditionality view. Imagine that *B* hates a good of *A*'s—for example, is enviously pained by *A*'s pleasure—and that *C* takes a higher-level pleasure in *B*'s envious pain, delighting in it as envious. Here *C* loves an evil attitude of *B*'s, as in the previous example, but this attitude is now one of hating good rather than loving evil. Since the envious pain that *C* loves is evil, *C*'s pleasure in it should on our current proposal again not have value as pleasure. But this last claim cannot be captured by any changes in the recursive account. The recursion-clause that makes *B*'s envious pain evil, (HG), concerns the hatred of goods, and unlike (LE), which presupposes only base-level evils, (HG) requires a prior identification of base-level *goods*. But this identification is supposed to be given by the very base-clause (BG) we are now trying to restrict! Capturing the desired claim about pleasure in envious pain therefore involves a circularity: (BG) is to be restricted by a recursion-clause (HG) that in turn requires a completed (BG) before its own claims have substance. Changing the structure of the recursive account can capture some of the view that pleasures with evil objects lack value as pleasures, but it cannot capture all of it.

This problem of circularity does not arise for all claims about the merely conditional value of pleasure. Kant holds that pleasure has value as pleasure only when it is that of someone with a morally good will, and he can do so without circularity because he characterizes the good will not in terms of base-level goods and evils but as involving a willing for themselves of duties independent of goods and evils. The question, however, is whether an approach like Kant's is applicable to the specific attitudes before us—pleasures in pain, in sadism, and in envy. I do not believe it is. If we ask why these pleasures are evil, the answer is surely that they are directed at something evil. (If they also involve indifference to a duty, this duty is, *pace* Kant, a duty not to promote evil.) And any view that gives this explanation, as the recursive account does, cannot without circularity deny that all such pleasures lack value as pleasures.

The original structure of the recursive account, with independent base-clauses prior to all recursion-clauses, is attractive in its simplicity. Because of this, any revision that complicates the account's structure is in that respect unattractive, and it is especially so if the revision does not result in a fully motivated or principled view. Surely what is plausible in this area is only the fully general view that all pleasures with evil objects lack value as pleasures; any more partial view is unacceptably ad hoc. So if the recursive account cannot capture all the proposed conditionality view, because it cannot say that pleasures whose objects are made evil by clause (HG) lack value as pleasures, that view should be abandoned.

Where does this leave us? In my view there is only one principled way for the recursive account to hold that all pleasure in pain is on balance evil, and that is to deny that pleasure as such is a base-level good. This is not an unimaginable claim, but it has the extreme implication that innocent pleasures such as those of suntanning or supporting a sports team have no intrinsic worth. If we cannot accept this implication, we must grant that even pleasures in pain have value as pleasures and can therefore sometimes be on balance good. But this may not in the end be unacceptable.

First, the claim parallels one that is positively attractive. The recursive account holds that compassionate pain is always evil as pain; given (CP), it also holds that compassionate pain can sometimes be on balance evil. But we have seen that this last claim is attractive, fitting our practice of sometimes not revealing our hurts to friends. And if in this case the moral goodness of an attitude can be outweighed by its hedonic evil, why cannot the moral evil of pleasure in pain sometimes be outweighed by its hedonic goodness?

Second, there are cases where it seems right to hold that pleasure in pain is on balance good. Imagine that one person takes pleasure in another's minor mishap, such as her slipping on a banana peel, or laughs at a slightly pointed joke at her expense. (A great many jokes, including most political jokes, turn in a slightly malicious way on someone's failings.) On the recursive view, there is something morally objectionable about the first person's pleasure; it would be better if he got the same enjoyment from a neutral or, better, a good object. But what if he cannot do so? What if the only options, given his character, are his getting pleasure from slight evils for others and his getting no pleasure at all? Is it then best if he gets no pleasure? This seems an excessively prudish view.[28] It is, to repeat, unfortunate that the first person can get pleasure only in this way; it would be better if he had non-malicious sources of enjoyment. But to say that his pleasure is on balance evil is to condemn all things considered what is for many people one of their readiest sources of enjoyment. The issue here is not the value of pleasures in great evils, such as a torturer's pleasure in his victim's intense pain. It is only that of pleasures in small evils, ones the love of which (CP) makes an even smaller evil. It does not seem wrong to hold that these pleasures' small evil as vices can be outweighed by their greater goodness as pleasures. On the contrary, on all but a prudish view it seems right.

Pleasures in small evils, then, can be on balance good. But what about pleasures in great evils? Is it not still counterintuitive to hold that they can be on balance good? The recursive account can avoid this implication by revising its treatment of pleasure as a base-level good and in particular by denying that equal units of intensity of pleasure and pain always have equal value. As originally formulated, (BG) and (BE) say that pleasures and pains are, respectively, better and worse when they are more intense, but they do not say by how much. The simplest view makes these relationships linear: the value of an additional unit of intensity of pleasure or pain is always the same, so pleasures and pains that are twice as intense are always twice as good or evil. This linear view is attractive as applied to pains, for which I will initially assume it, but it is considerably less attractive for pleasures. Imagine that A has a choice between the certainty of a pleasure of 10 units of intensity and a gamble with a .51 probability of giving him a pleasure of 20 units of intensity and a .49 probability of giving him no pleasure. The linear view says he should prefer the gamble, but I think many of us would say he should not. Or imagine that C can give either A a pleasure of 21 units of intensity or each of A and B a pleasure of 10 units. The linear view says C should give A

---

28. For a discussion of jokes that seems to assume this prudish view, see de Sousa, *The Rationality of Emotion,* chap. 11.

the 21 units, but again, many would disagree. To capture the judgments these examples suggest, the recursive account can abandon a linear treatment of pleasure and hold that the value of an extra unit of intensity in a pleasure gets smaller as the pleasure's intensity increases, diminishing asymptotically toward zero. On this asymptotic view, the second 10 units of intensity in a pleasure have less value than the first, so *A* should not take his gamble, and *C* should give the equal pleasures to *A* and *B*. Assuming these are attractive implications, we have independent reasons to adopt an asymptotic view of pleasure. And doing so can avoid the implication that pleasures in great evils can be on balance good.

If the recursive account retains a linear view of pain and holds that the maximum value of an attitude is always the same fraction of its object's value, it holds that the moral evil of loving a pain that is considerably more intense is always considerably greater. On any view, this implies that the intensity of pleasure required to outweigh this moral evil is also considerably greater. But given an asymptotic view of pleasure, the value of increases in the intensity of a pleasure gets progressively less and eventually becomes quite small. This implies, initially, that many fewer cases of pleasure in pain are on balance good than is the case given a linear view of pleasure. More important, it implies that some pleasures in pain can never be on balance good. Since the asymptotic view makes the value of increases in the intensity of pleasure diminish toward zero, it places an upper bound on the value of any pleasure, whatever its intensity. This implies that if the moral evil of a pleasure in pain is above that bound, its moral evil cannot be outweighed by its hedonic goodness. Imagine that the upper bound on the value of a pleasure is 10 units, and that the value of an attitude of intensity i is one-half that of its object. Then, if *B* takes sadistic pleasure of intensity i in *A*'s 30 units of pain, the value of his pleasure must on balance be negative. Its moral evil as an attitude to its object is 15 units, which is greater than the maximum 10 units of goodness it can have as a pleasure, so his sadistic pleasure makes the situation worse. By combining a linear view of pain with an asymptotic view of pleasure, the recursive account can allow that some pleasures in mild pains are on balance good. This, I have claimed, is plausible. But it can also hold that pleasures in more intense pains, ones above a certain threshold, are always on balance evil. By treating pleasure and pain asymmetrically, it can consistently hold that pleasure in all forms is a base-level good, that attitudes always have less value than their objects, and that pleasures in intense pains are never on balance good.

The more specific implications of this approach depend on exactly how fast the value of extra units of pleasure diminishes, or exactly what the upper bound on a pleasure's value is. If this bound is low, comparatively few cases of pleasure in pain are on balance good, but intense innocent pleasures have only limited value compared to other goods. If the bound is higher, innocent pleasures have more value, but more pleasures in pain are good. It may be that no precise version of the view is attractive in every respect: either it gives too little value to innocent pleasures, such as those of suntanning, or it allows too many vicious pleasures to be good. This dilemma may be relieved to some degree if the recursive account extends its asymmetrical treatment of pleasure and pain by adopting a non-linear view of pain contrary to the one adopted for pleasure. On this second view, the value of an additional unit of intensity in a pain becomes greater as the pain's intensity increases, so pains that are twice as intense are more than twice as evil.[29] This view makes intense pain more evil, which, given (CP), makes sadistic pleasure in it also more evil as an attitude, and this allows the upper bound on the value of a pleasure as pleasure to be higher while pleasures in intense pains are still always on balance evil. This doubly non-linear approach may not entirely resolve the dilemma about innocent versus vicious pleasures. Nonetheless, either it or the simpler asymmetrical view seems to offer the best response to the difficulty about the value on balance of sadistic pleasure, allowing the recursive account to retain both its original structure and the comparative principle while denying that the worst pleasures in evil can ever be on balance good.

I have considered three difficulties for the comparative principle: the case where many people sympathize with a pain, attitudes to trivial goods and evils, and some vices of loving evil. Though these difficulties make (CP)'s adoption less straightforward, none calls for the abandonment of its central claims. The most attractive versions of the recursive account still hold that the value of an attitude to a significant good or evil is always less than that of its object, and that virtue and vice are in that sense lesser intrinsic values.

---

29. This view is defended in Mayerfeld, "The Moral Asymmetry of Happiness and Suffering." It implies, for example, that if D can relieve either a pain of A's of 19 units of intensity or pains of 10 units of intensity for each of B and C, D should relieve the pain of A.

3. *Applications*

Having defended (CP), I will now apply it to some more specific philosophical issues. The first of these, introduced in chapter 2, concerns the relationship between acting rightly and achieving one's own good, or between the "moral life" and the "good life."

Any view that makes virtue intrinsically good allows some overlap between acting rightly and achieving one's good. When what is right is what results in the most good, as in standard consequentialisms it always is, a person who acts rightly from a desire for that good performs the most virtuous action he can and so maximizes one aspect of his good. Whether he maximizes his good on balance, however, depends on how the value of the virtue he gains compares to that of the non-moral goods his action may require him to forgo.

Given the lexical view, which gives virtue infinite value compared to other goods, a person who acts rightly from virtuous motives does always maximize his good, but the same is not true if virtue has only finite value, and especially not if, as (CP) claims, it has lesser value. Imagine, first, that a person forgoes a base-level good of his own in favour of a much greater good of other people, say, 10 units of his own pleasure in favour of 100 units of others'. If the value of his attitude is one-half that of its object, the value of his virtuous action is $\frac{1}{2} \times 100 = 50$, a gain of 45 over the $\frac{1}{2} \times 10 = 5$ units involved in pursuing his own pleasure. Since these 45 units of virtue outweigh the 10 he loses in pleasure, his acting rightly does maximize his good; equivalently, his preferring his pleasure would fail to maximize his good because it would involve such extreme selfishness. But now imagine that the person forgoes the same 10 units of his pleasure for an only slightly greater good of others, say, 20 units of their pleasure. Here the additional value of his virtuous action is only $(\frac{1}{2} \times 20) - (\frac{1}{2} \times 10) = 5$; since this does not outweigh the loss of 10, his action is not best for him overall. His moral gain, though real, is smaller than his non-moral loss. Given our comparative principle, therefore, the moral and good lives do not always coincide. Preferring a much greater good of others can maximize one's own good all things considered, but preferring an only slightly greater good of others does not. This result is intuitively plausible. If virtue is intrinsically good, there must be cases where it makes an otherwise self-sacrificing action best in self-interested terms, but it would be going too far to say this is always so. Even if virtuous action is always a good, its goodness is not always sufficient to prevent right action, even from the best motives, from involving sacrifice by the agent.

The second application of (CP) is to an argument about private charity and welfare. Aristotle's *Politics* gives as one objection to the system of communal ownership proposed in Plato's *Republic* that it will prevent citizens from making generous use of private property.[30] Similarly, some contemporary conservatives argue that preserving the value of private charity requires dismantling the welfare state. Murray Rothbard writes, "It is hardly 'charity' to take wealth by force and hand it over to someone else. Indeed, this is the direct opposite of charity, which can only be an unbought, voluntary act of grace."[31] Milton and Rose Friedman concur: "We believe that one of the greatest costs of our present welfare system is that it not only undermines and destroys the family, but also poisons the springs of charitable action."[32]

This critique of public welfare comes from the political right, but related arguments are made on the left. Richard M. Titmuss argues that allowing a free market in blood is objectionable in part because it discourages voluntary blood donation.[33] This is but one instance of a more general argument that capitalism, with its incentives to competitiveness and self-seeking, undermines the virtues of benevolence and other-concern.[34] But let us concentrate on the conservative argument against public welfare.

This argument's central claim—that people will live less virtuously if they are forced to contribute to welfare—can take either a moral or an empirical form. Its moral version says that even if people have the best attitudes possible in a welfare state, their attitudes cannot for at least three reasons be as good as those expressed through private charity. Though they can want their government to relieve poverty and be pleased when it does, they cannot themselves act against poverty, which is a higher form of virtue; even if they do act to relieve poverty, say, by remitting their own tax to the government, they cannot do so freely; and because welfare benefits a large mass

---

30. Aristotle, *Politics*, 1263b11–14; for internal criticism of this argument, see Irwin, "Generosity and Property in Aristotle's *Politics.*" Edmund Burke writes similarly: "It is better to cherish virtue and humanity by leaving much to free will, even with some loss to the object, than to attempt to make men mere machines and instruments of a political benevolence" (*Reflections on the Revolution in France*, p. 91).

31. Rothbard, *Power and Market*, p. 63.

32. Friedman and Friedman, *Free to Choose*, p. 154. A more moderate version of this argument is given in Brody, "The Role of Private Philanthropy in a Free and Democratic State."

33, Titmuss, *The Gift Relationship*.

34. See, e.g., Tawney, *Equality*.

of people, their action cannot have the special value of "caring" for personally known individuals.[35] The empirical version of the claim says that even if attitudes could in principle be as good in a welfare state, they will not in fact be so. Though people could want and be pleased by their government's relieving poverty, their attitudes will not be seriously engaged if they cannot themselves act against poverty; and many who would respond benevolently to the needs of known individuals if left free to do so will be indifferent or resentful if forced to contribute to a mass.

These moral and empirical claims have limitations. Even if people cannot perform some virtuous actions in a welfare state, they can perform others: they can freely campaign and vote for political parties that support welfare and can make charitable contributions of time and effort if not so much of money. As for the contrast with "caring," it does not apply to the many charitable contributions routed through large agencies such as the United Way, whose operations are just as impersonal as welfare's. Nonetheless, the claims taken together may have some force. It is arguable that the virtuous actions possible in a welfare state, such as voting and contributing time, are usually of lesser moral value. If a voter knows that a majority of other voters support welfare, he cannot vote with the belief, which on a plausible view is necessary for the special value of virtuous action, that his doing so will make a difference in promoting what is good. And if a large part of his income has gone in tax to the state, he cannot aim at as great goods in his charitable actions as if he still had that income to contribute.

Let us therefore ignore their limitations and assume that some combination of moral and empirical claims establishes that some people will live more virtuously outside a welfare state. Even so, the conservative anti-welfare argument is seriously incomplete.

As formulated by Aristotle, Rothbard, and others, this argument considers the effects of welfare only on those who will be wealthy enough to contribute to charity in a free market, and not at all on those who will be poor enough to need it. Since the poor cannot be encouraged or inhibited in charitable actions, the argument essentially ignores their good, in effect treating them as means to the virtue of the rich. This feature of the argument is objectionable on

---

35. For the superiority of caring in this sense to any impersonal benevolence, see, e.g., Noddings, *Caring*, pp. 47, 151–53. The impersonality of the welfare state is also seen as troubling, though not as a reason to dismantle it, in Ignatieff, *The Needs of Strangers*.

any view, but even more so given (CP). This principle implies that although the virtue expressed in charitable action is good, it is less good than the non-moral benefits for others that it aims to produce. Faced with the benevolence of the rich and the pleasure and other base-level goods it can give the poor, we should care more about the latter; as objects of the benevolence in question, they have the greater moral weight. So in considering only effects on virtue, the conservative argument ignores not only some goods but the most important ones. A serious assessment of public welfare must take the opposite tack, caring most about the non-moral good of the poor and only secondarily about the moral achievements of the rich.[36]

It is not that effects on virtue can never provide a reason for choosing among social arrangements. If the poor were only slightly less well off in a free market with private charity and everyone else acted much more virtuously, the free market could be on balance preferable. So even given (CP), the conservative argument can in principle succeed, as can left-wing arguments such as Titmuss's against the sale of blood. But how persuasive the argument is in practice depends on the force of the moral and empirical claims at its core, and here there are reasons to be skeptical. The non-moral superiority of public welfare is surely substantial, if only because welfare is so much better at benefiting all the needy rather than just a few among them. And given their many limitations, it is hard to see how the moral and empirical claims can overcome this superiority. Even if some expressions of virtue are not possible in a welfare state, others that are almost as good are, and this makes it hard to see how the small gain in virtue for some can be enough to make the free market on balance better. This conclusion is not guaranteed by (CP) alone, which allows gains in virtue in principle to outweigh losses in other goods. But it is certainly supported by (CP), which makes that outweighing much less likely.

The final application of the comparative principle is to the theological problem of evil, the problem of how the existence of evil is consistent with the hypothesis of the world's creation by an all-

---

36. A complete assessment must also consider the virtue of the poor. As it happens, arguments on this topic are made at both ends of the political spectrum. Those on the right say the welfare state encourages dependence and with it a lack of self-reliance and self-respect in its beneficiaries. Those on the left say these harmful effects come more from the arbitrary provisions of private charity and are less common when the poor can regard a minimum level of assistance as their right.

powerful and perfectly virtuous God. One aspect of this problem concerns the moral evils of sin and vice. It is commonly addressed by arguing that free will, which is necessary for the highest moral goods, brings with it the possibility of moral evil.[37] But I am interested in a second aspect of the problem, which concerns non-moral evils such as pain. More specifically, I am interested in a proposed "virtue solution" to this aspect of the problem, one saying that non-moral evils were created by God because they are necessary conditions for moral goods such as compassion, courage, and endurance. A. C. Ewing writes that "some goods, and these by no means the lowest but among the highest, are such that they necessarily involve some evil as the condition of their attainment. Courage, unselfishness and the highest forms of love are of very great intrinsic and not only instrumental value but one could hardly have them if there were no such thing as suffering."[38] John Hick concurs, saying that "men and women often act in true compassion and massive generosity in the face of unmerited suffering, especially when it comes in such dramatic forms as an earthquake or a mining disaster. It seems, then, that in a world that is to be the scene of compassionate love and self-giving for others, suffering must fall upon mankind with something of the haphazardousness and inequity that we now experience."[39] According to this virtue solution, God's creation of non-moral evils such as pain is justified as a means to higher moral goods of hating pain.

An initial objection to this solution is that it cannot account for all the non-moral evil in the world. Though some pains are the objects of compassionate or courageous attitudes, many others, such as the pains of people dying alone and almost all those of animals, are not. How could a perfectly virtuous God allow so much unnoticed and therefore unredeemed suffering? This difficulty is often recognized by the solution's proponents, who respond by invoking an afterlife in which all past evils, both non-moral and moral, will be made good.[40] But aside from forcing this desperate response, the first objection allows that non-moral evils can in principle be justified by moral goods. Some more far-reaching objections deny this.

37. This free-will solution may work for sin, which is necessarily voluntary, but not for vice, which can involve evil attitudes beyond a person's control.

38. Ewing, *Value and Reality*, p. 215; see also pp. 216–17.

39. Hick, *Evil and the God of Love*, p. 334.

40. Ewing, *Value and Reality*, pp. 225–35; and Hick, *Evil and the God of Love*, p. 336.

The simplest such objection appeals to (CP), claiming that the moral good of hating an evil is always smaller than the evil in question. Moore makes this objection immediately after arguing that compassion is less good than its object is evil:

> we have no reason to maintain the paradox that an ideal world would be one in which vice and suffering must exist in order that it may contain the goods consisting in the appropriate emotion towards them. It is not a positive good that suffering should exist, in order that we may compassionate it; or wickedness, that we may hate it. There is no reason to think that any actual evil whatsoever would be contained in the Ideal. It follows that we cannot admit the actual validity of any of the arguments commonly used in Theodicies.[41]

As we have seen, (CP) and Moore's argument for it are plausible only for the combination of a pain and one person's compassion for it; if many people feel compassion, their virtue can outweigh the pain. So, consistently with (CP), a pain could be justified on balance if enough people felt compassion for it. But this only strengthens the first objection about unredeemed pains. If all that is needed for the good of compassion is one person's pain, which everyone else can hate, why does the world contain so many pains?

A different objection appeals to an internalist view of virtue, on which the value of an attitude cannot be affected by its external circumstances. In a world without real pain there can still be virtuous hatreds of pain, since people can be glad their world does not contain pain and hope it never does. (How can they know what pain is if they have never experienced it? An all-powerful God can give them this knowledge.) On an internalist view, these attitudes are just as good as hatred of real pain. So what, from the point of view of virtue, is the justification for real pain? I have defended a partly externalist view of virtue, but those drawn to internalism have a further objection to the virtue solution: it makes the value of people's attitudes depend unacceptably on their external circumstances. This objection is especially relevant to Christian versions of the solution, since the Christian view of virtue is in other respects internalist. As the story of the widow and her two mites indicates, Christian ethics usually treats virtue as a purely inner state of the soul, independent of environment. So how can it hold that attitudes would be less good in an environment without real pain?

41. Moore, *Principia Ethica*, p. 220.

Nor is it only pure internalism that underwrites this kind of objection. Let us assume a partly externalist view on which people's attitudes are better when they respond to real evils, and better still when they respond to greater real evils. This view will also hold that attitudes are better when they respond to real goods and better still when they respond to greater goods. Why, then, is the ideal world not one with only very great non-moral goods, such as pleasure and knowledge, for people to love, and no non-moral evils at all? On a partly externalist view, this world is better in terms of virtue than one with neither non-moral goods nor evils; it is also better than one with only lesser non-moral goods. Why is it not also just as good in terms of virtue as one containing great non-moral evils and therefore, given the absence of those evils, better all things considered? The virtue solution to the problem of evil assumes that people's attitudes can only be the best possible in the right environment. Why must that environment contain non-moral evils rather than, instead, just great non-moral goods?

One possible answer is that hating non-moral evils is intrinsically better, or a higher form of virtue, than loving non-moral goods. But this claim is implausible. All the versions of the recursive account we have considered make the value of a virtuous attitude the same regardless of whether its object is good or evil, so loving a good of a given magnitude is just as good as hating an evil of the same magnitude. And a claim of intrinsic superiority for the virtues of hating evil would have to be very strong to play the role envisaged here. Imagine that the value of hating an evil of magnitude m is greater, but only finitely so, than the value of loving a good of magnitude m. In that case, there should be some greater magnitude n such that the value of loving a good of magnitude n is greater still. Only if hating evil or some instances of hating evil are infinitely better than any loving of good can the contribution of real evils to overall value not always be equalled by very great real goods. But that lexical claim— for example, that compassion for another's pain is infinitely better than pleasure at her pleasure—is not credible.[42]

---

42. It may seem that a relevant priority claim was implicit in our earlier discussion of sadistic pleasure. If the value of pleasure has an upper bound whereas the evil of pain does not, there are some virtues of hating a pain of intensity m that are greater than any possible virtue of loving a pleasure of intensity m. But this implication follows not from a view about the values of the virtues as such, but from a view about the greater evil of the pain. Given (CP), therefore, the greater moral good of hating pain can only be had at the cost of the even greater non-moral evil in the pain itself, so the pain is still not on balance justified.

A different answer is that an ideal world must contain not just some but all moral goods or virtues. Though a world with only very great non-moral goods might appear to contain as much virtue as any other, it cannot contain the full range of virtues and therefore cannot on a proper accounting be as good. Ewing gives this answer, saying, "[T]he more different kinds of good there are the better the world, provided they are not purchased at too high a price in evil." Or, "[T]he best universe would not be confined to any one kind of good but should presumably include all sorts unless a particular kind were unattainable without a degree of evil that outweighed the good attained."[43] On this view, the value of variety in forms of virtue is what justifies the existence of non-moral evils, since without those evils, and assuming externalism, there could only be a truncated list of virtues.[44]

One can challenge the value this view places on variety; Moore, for one, is happy to accept that an ideal world may not contain certain moral goods.[45] But even granting this value, note the condition Ewing attaches to it: to contribute to the value of variety, a virtue of hating an evil must not be "outweighed" by, or smaller than, that evil. This is, in fact, a very weak condition. Imagine that the positive value of compassion for a pain of 10 units of disvalue is only slightly greater—say, 11 units. Is this enough to make a world with no other non-moral evils better, on grounds of variety, if it contains the pain and compassion than if it contained a pleasure of 10 units of value and a benevolent pleasure in that pleasure whose value as a virtue was likewise 11 units? Many, I suspect, will say not. But even Ewing's weak condition is not satisfied given our comparative principle. That principle claims that the value of a hatred of evil is always less than the disvalue of that evil, so the outweighing Ewing fears always occurs when only one person hates an evil. Even if variety in virtues could be a significant good, the condition for its being so is never satisfied in this kind of case. Since (CP) does not yield a similar conclusion when many people hate an evil, Ewing's condition could be satisfied in a world with just a limited amount of non-moral evil—for example, just one pain that everyone else feels compassion for. But

---

43. Ewing, *Value and Reality*, pp. 216, 219.
44. A world without non-moral evils could still contain the virtues of hating real moral evils. People could hate the vices of hating good, being indifferent to good, and loving lesser goods more than greater ones. So not all virtues of hating real evil would be absent in a world without pain, only some.
45. Moore, *Principia Ethica*, pp. 184, 216–22.

it is hard to see his condition satisfied in the actual world, which contains so much non-moral evil. Given (CP), the virtues of hating real evil that add to the variety of moral goods in that world are almost always less good, even when taken together, than their objects are evil.

Even assuming a partly externalist view, the virtue solution to the problem of evil must explain why the best world requires the conditions for virtues of hating real evils rather than just for those of loving real goods. It can only do so, it seems, by valuing variety in moral goods, or by insisting that an ideal world must contain all forms of virtue. But this insistence, at least in Ewing's version, carries with it a condition that our comparative principle says is not satisfied in our world. Though this principle does not by itself refute the virtue solution, it again makes a commonly advanced argument much harder to sustain.

6

Attitudes, Beliefs, and Love as a Condition of Value

In this chapter I will explore some further issues about the recursive account. They include the effect on the values of attitudes of beliefs about the existence of their objects, the difference between two forms of virtuous love, and the difference between the recursive account and a rival view that gives attitudes greater importance in relation to the values of their objects.

1. *False Belief and Fantasy*

Attitudes are often accompanied by beliefs about the existence of their objects. In fact, for each main type of attitude there is a standard such belief. Someone who desires an object usually believes that it does not exist; someone who pursues an object believes (and must believe) that he can make it exist; and someone who takes pleasure in an object usually believes that it does exist. In the simplest cases these beliefs are true, and the object has the ontological status attributed to it. But they can also be false, as when a person takes pleasure in what he falsely believes is an existing good or evil. Does this falsity affect an attitude's value?

I do not believe it does. Consider pleasure in what someone falsely believes is knowledge—for example, Aristotle's pleasure in what he believed was his explanatory knowledge of biology. Assuming that Aristotle's overestimation of his biological beliefs did not result from self-deception or thoughtlessness, his pleasure in them seems just as good as pleasure in real knowledge of the same value. The overall state of someone who takes pleasure in real knowledge is better than Aristotle's, given the extra value of her knowledge, but in itself her pleasure in knowledge seems of exactly equal worth. The same seems true of pleasure in what is falsely believed to be an existing evil. Imagine that, in a psychological experiment of the kind conducted by Stanley Milgram, a subject inflicts what he falsely believes is intense pain on a victim and takes sadistic pleasure in doing so. His sadistic pleasure seems just as evil as if its object were real pain. Pleasure in what is believed to be a real good or evil involves an emotional commitment to that good or evil whose moral value seems unaffected by whether the belief is true.

In other cases, attitudes are not accompanied by their standard ontological beliefs. To take the central example, someone can take pleasure in a good or evil that he knows is not real but is self-consciously imagining or fantasizing about.[1] This kind of attitude is often stimulated by literature: a novel or drama portrays certain occurrences, and we respond to them emotionally even though we know they are the author's invention. Such attitudes also occur in daydreams, where we invent the imagined occurrences ourselves and, again, respond emotionally to them. Taking these different cases together, we can speak generally of *fantasies*, or self-conscious imaginings involving pleasure in what is imagined, and *horrors*, involving pain. Can fantasies and horrors have intrinsic value, and if so, how much?

The object of a fantasy or horror is often something that would be good or evil if it existed; in this it is just like the object of a desire. Pleasure or pain in the object can therefore be appropriate or inappropriate and on that basis intrinsically good or evil. Compassion for the suffering of King Lear, even though it is only stage suffering, is fitting to that suffering and therefore good. Pleasure in what is known to be fictional pain, such as that of a rape victim in a pornographic video, can likewise be evil. Of course, fantasies and horrors can also have instrumental qualities, and these can be what is most important about them. If rape fantasies encourage men to commit real rape, this causal fact can be more significant morally than the fantasies' intrinsic viciousness; but that viciousness still remains. To confirm this, imagine that rape fantasies discouraged real rapes, by siphoning off the hostile energies that lead to them. The fantasies might then be on balance good, but it would surely be disturbing if men could only avoid committing rape by such intrinsically odious means. Like attitudes to objects believed to be real, attitudes to

---

1. This kind of case is discussed in Cherry, "The Inward and the Outward"; Stocker, "Emotional Thoughts"; and Greenspan, *Emotions and Reasons*.

merely imagined objects can have intrinsic value and should be held to do so by the recursive account.

It may be objected that we do not need to posit separate values in fantasies and horrors. Someone who takes pleasure in imagining an object does so only because he desires the object in reality, and any goodness or evil in his fantasy is already accounted for by that in the desire from which it springs.

This argument can be persuasive only for what Christopher Cherry calls "surrogate fantasies," where a person desires an object in reality, cannot have it in reality, and indulges in fantasies about it as a kind of substitute.[2] But even here the argument is not compelling. Surely desiring an evil such as the pain of a rape victim and also fantasizing about it is worse than merely desiring it. (I assume that whether a person fantasizes about an object does not depend solely on the intensity of his desire for it.) And the argument does not apply at all to what Cherry calls "autonomous fantasies." These are fantasies disconnected from any attitudes to their objects as real, ones where a person enjoys an object as imagined but would not enjoy it if it were actual and does not desire it to be actual. Cherry quotes the feminist Lynne Segal's description of masochistic sexual fantasies in which "I am always passive, objectified, humiliated and whatever abuse I can imagine to be happening at the time also contains the threat of even worse to follow." Despite enjoying this type of fantasy, Segal resents it and wishes she were free of it, but her reason "is *not at all* that it encourages real submissiveness, and most certainly *not* any desire for real pain, hurt or humiliation."[3] She has no desire that her fantasy-object be real and therefore fantasizes independently of desire. Similarly, I would argue, at least some men who enjoy the rapes in pornographic videos would not take pleasure in a real rape if they saw one—they would be repelled—and have no desire to commit rape.[4] But if some fantasies are in this way autonomous from desires, their moral value cannot be reduced to that of desires. The fantasies must be, independently, intrinsically good or evil.

2. Cherry, "The Inward and the Outward," pp. 179–81.
3. Cartlege and Ryan, *Sensual Uncertainty in Sex and Love*, p. 42; quoted in Cherry, "The Inward and the Outward," p. 182.
4. It may be objected that the men's enjoyment must indicate some desire to rape, even if that desire is too weak to overcome their inhibitions or lead them actually to rape. But what is the evidence for this claim, other than an ungrounded assumption that fantasies must reflect desires? In any case, a very weak desire to rape would not be as intrinsically evil as an intensely enjoyed rape fantasy intuitively is.

Though fantasies and horrors can be good or evil, they seem to have less intrinsic value than attitudes to objects believed to be real. Moore writes that "a conscious compassion for real suffering seems to be better, *as a whole*, than a compassion for sufferings merely imaginary," and this claim is intuitively plausible.[5] Compassion for the stage pain of Lear, though good, seems less good than an otherwise identical compassion for what is believed to be real pain of the same intensity. Surely someone who sympathizes with stage pain but not with that of real people has worse attitudes than if he did the opposite, and the same holds for vicious attitudes. Someone who takes pleasure in a merely fantasized rape has a less vicious attitude than if he took an equally intense pleasure in a real rape. I have said that pleasure in an object believed to be real involves an emotional commitment to that object, but the same degree of commitment does not seem to be present in a mere fantasy about the object. It is therefore appropriate that the fantasy should count as less virtuous or vicious, so that whatever the value is of pleasure in a good or evil believed to exist, the value of pleasure in the same good or evil as merely imagined is less. There may be confirmation for this idea in the very autonomy of some vicious fantasies. That some men who could not enjoy a real rape do enjoy fantasized rape may reflect their recognition, even if subconscious, of the greater evil of the former enjoyment. Though their inhibitions prevent the more vicious pleasure, they allow the less vicious one.

According to Moore, the claim that pleasures in goods and evils have less value when their objects are not believed to be real involves an application of the principle of organic unities. Moore assumes that the attitudes present in pleasures in real and in self-consciously imagined objects are the same; the only difference is that the former are accompanied by a belief in their object's reality. But this belief by itself has no intrinsic value. (Remember that it makes no difference to the value of an attitude whether its accompanying ontological belief is true.) If the pleasure in a real object has more value, Moore concludes, it must be because the combination of pleasure and belief has value as a combination, and therefore more value on balance, than if the belief were absent.[6]

---

5. Moore, *Principia Ethica*, p. 219. By speaking of the value only "as a whole" of the compassion, Moore means to exclude from consideration the disvalue of the real pain. (For a remark possibly in tension with this one, see Moore, *Principia Ethica*, p. 210.)

6. Moore, *Principia Ethica*, pp. 194, 219.

This is certainly one explanation of the greater value of attitudes involving ontological beliefs, but it is not the only one, nor, in my view, the best one. A different explanation says that ontological beliefs not only accompany but enter into the contents of attitudes, so the latter are directed at objects *as existing* or *as merely imagined.*[7] This certainly seems true of compassion for real pain. Surely the object of this compassion is another's pain *as really existing*, not just pain independently of whether it is real. It is an internal feature of the compassion, not just an addition to it, that the other person is seen as actually suffering. The same explanation can be given for fantasies and horrors. Especially when someone takes pleasure only in imagined and not in real rapes, it is plausible to see the object of his pleasure as not just rape but rape as merely imagined, so his belief again enters into his attitude's content. This explanation may not be forced on us in the latter case. Perhaps we can equally well see the pleasure's object as just rape, with a belief in the rape's nonreality as a necessary but separately existing condition for the pleasure's being felt. But the explanation does seem plausible and enables us to avoid complicating the recursive account in Moore's way. We can see the contents of attitudes as always ontologically qualified, so one takes pleasure in an object either as believed real or as self-consciously imagined, with the former pleasure being either better or worse than the latter.

Its application to fantasies and horrors brings the recursive account into contact with traditional Christian views about "sins of thought" or "sins of the heart." Even if a person does not sin outwardly, these views say, he can sin inwardly if he engages in the wrong kind of imagining, for example, by fantasizing about adulterous sex. But there is an important difference between these two types of view. To call a fantasy sinful is to evaluate it as morally wrong, and judgments about wrongness presuppose voluntariness, so something can be wrong only if a person could have chosen to avoid it. Voluntariness may seem to be present in some vicious fantasies, as when a person rents a pornographic video in order to stimulate a rape fantasy. But even here it is usually only the renting and playing of the video and not the resulting pleasure that is voluntary. Once the video is running, the person's enjoyment of it is automatic and unchosen. And often nothing about a fantasy is voluntary: both an imagining and a person's pleasure in it come unbidden into his mind. This is especially common with autonomous fantasies that

---

7. This seems to be Greenspan's view; see *Emotions and Reasons,* p. 145.

their subject resents, such as Segal's masochistic fantasies. If she does not choose these fantasies but in fact wishes she were free of them, how can her having them involve sin?

Faced with this difficulty, proponents of the Christian view resort to desperate measures. Aquinas describes the sin in vicious fantasies as that of "consent to delectation," as if there were in every such fantasy a specific choice to take pleasure in its object.[8] This is the right kind of claim to sustain the Christian view, since it attaches voluntariness to the pleasure itself rather than just to causal antecedents such as renting a video. But it is fanciful to hold that we always or even ever have such direct control over our emotions. Defenders of Aquinas may reply that even when a person cannot now control a vicious fantasy, he could in the past have avoided developing the evil character that now makes the fantasy irresistible.[9] But it is hard to see the relevance of this point. How does the fact that a person could once have voluntarily prevented a response from becoming involuntary make that response any less involuntary now? And surely there are many cases of vicious fantasy that do not derive in this way from past choices and therefore cannot even in a derivative way be considered sinful.

Other defenders of the Christian view deny that wrongness requires voluntariness. Robert M. Adams calls for recognition of a category of "involuntary sins," of which sins of thought are one instance.[10] But these manoeuvres are all unnecessary if fantasies can be evaluated, as in the recursive account, as intrinsically good or evil. Pain and false belief are evil even when they are not voluntary, and the same can be true of vicious fantasies. They can be something it is appropriate to be pained by and something a person should struggle against, even if they are not now under his control. Voluntary fantasies may be intrinsically worse, if they originate in a desire for evil feelings, and they may also be the result of a morally wrong choice. But even involuntary fantasies can be evil in the sense of making a life intrinsically less good.

The recursive account makes the degree of value of a fantasy or horror, like that of any attitude, depend on the degree of value of its object, so that fantasizing about intense pain is worse than fantasiz-

---

8. Aquinas, *Summa Theologica*, I–II, qu. 74, a. 8.

9. See, e.g., Grisez, *The Way of the Lord Jesus*, vol. 1, pp. 372–73; Sankowski, "Responsibility of Persons for Their Emotions," pp. 833–35; Oakley, *Morality and the Emotions*, chap. 4; and Sherman, *Making a Necessity of Virtue*, p. 78.

10. Adams, "Involuntary Sins."

ing about mild pain. But there may be other factors that affect these attitudes' values.

For example, the account may hold, as an extension of the view that fantasies and horrors have less value than attitudes to objects believed real, that the degree of value of an imagining depends on the degree to which its content is close to reality, or realistic. Taking pleasure in a graphic film depiction of intense pain is worse than taking a similar pleasure in a depiction that clearly is contrived, such as in a cartoon, and taking pleasure in the evil motives of a realistically portrayed villain is worse than taking pleasure in the caricature malice of, say, the Joker in the movie *Batman*. Some imaginings, such as those stimulated by highly realistic films, have contents that are closer to reality, while the contents of others are more improbable. One possible extension of the recursive account holds that, other things equal, attitudes to the former imaginings have greater intrinsic value.

It may be objected that unrealistically imagined goods and evils are already imagined as lesser goods and evils. The pain of a cartoon character may be preceded by what is normally a cause of intense pain and may produce the short-term response characteristic of intense pain. But its victim recovers so quickly and completely that it is not presented even in the cartoon world as serious pain. Similarly, the character of a realistic fictional villain has many more facets than that of a simple caricature such as the Joker. This means the realistic character contains many more moral evils that a fantasizer can viciously take pleasure in, and many more traits associated with moral evil that he can take pleasure in for that association.

Though there is much to these points, I do not think they fully explain the intuitive appeal of the view that realistic fantasies and horrors are morally more serious. And there are several possible bases for this view. If we believe that fantasy involves a "willing suspension of disbelief" and that this suspension can never be complete, we can hold that realistic imaginings involve a degree of belief, or of something close to belief, in their objects, and that a greater degree of belief or quasi-belief makes for greater intrinsic value. Alternatively, we can ground the degree-of-realism view in the first modal condition discussed in chapter 4. As applied to desires, that condition says the degree of value of a desire for a nonexistent object depends on the degree to which the object's existing is a close possibility. As extended to feelings, the same condition can say the value of pleasure in an object known not to be real depends on how close the object is to reality.[11] Whatever its basis, however, the degree-of- realism view again is confirmed by facts about the kinds of fantasies people actually have. When they take pleasure in fictional pain or vice, it is usually of precisely the unrealistic kind, such as cartoon pain or the vice of cardboard villains. Even many rape videos, though in one sense highly graphic, contain other features, for example of plot, that are decidedly unrealistic. Once again, it seems that people's moral inhibitions prevent them from indulging in worse attitudes but allow them ones that are less bad.

Another possibly relevant factor is the fantasizer's own presence in his fantasy. Someone who indulges in a rape fantasy can imagine a rape being committed by someone else, whose actions he views as a spectator. Though taking pleasure in the imagined rape, he is not in this case a participant in it. Alternatively, he can imagine himself committing the rape, and that in either of two ways. He can again observe from the outside as a person identified as himself commits a rape. The person he observes will have various of his distinguishing traits, such as his name and appearance, but he will view the rapist's action from a spectator's point of view. Or he can imagine his committing a rape from the inside, from the rapist's point of view, with all the thoughts and sensations that experience would involve. In this case he is doubly present in the fantasy, both as a participant and in the point of view from which its content is imagined.[12]

---

11. There is an important apparent difference between the modal condition and the degree-of-realism view about fantasies. As formulated in chapter 4, the modal condition says that desires for objects very close to reality have as much value as desires for real objects, so concern after a choice between goods should be divided in strict proportion to their values. But we have just said that any pleasure in a self-consciously imagined object has less value than a similar pleasure involving belief in the object's reality. Perhaps this difference is not entirely unbridgeable. Even the most realistic fictions, assuming they involve merely fictional characters, are for that reason far from being actual and so do not satisfy the modal condition to any significant degree. (There is no close possible world in which King Lear exists.) And if we imagine a fantasy involving real people in a situation that could easily have been real—for example, a first-person rape fantasy involving a person one could have attacked a moment ago—it is not so implausible that its value is equal to that of the same feeling with a real object. At the very least, given the content of this fantasy, it is hard to treat the fantasy as entirely autonomous and therefore unconnected to seriously vicious desires.

12. On these types of fantasy, see Williams, "Imagination and the Self," pp. 38–39; and Wollheim, *The Thread of Life*, pp. 71–76. Wollheim argues that a fourth type of fantasy is possible in which one imagines certain actions from the inside but does not imagine oneself as the person performing them; I leave it open whether this fourth type of fantasy is possible.

These types of fantasy seem intuitively to differ in value. Even given otherwise identical contents and reactions to them, the first rape fantasy seems less vicious than the second, where the rapist the person imagines from the outside is himself. And the second seems less evil than the third, where he imagines his act of raping from the inside. The second of these moral differences can be partly explained by some points made earlier. In imagining his rape from the inside, the person imagines both additional moral evils, such as the rapist's pleasure in his raping, and additional items associated with moral evil. On both counts his fantasy provides more scope for morally vicious pleasure. But it is not clear that these points explain all of the second difference, and they are not relevant to the first. To affirm the differences clearly, we must introduce an asymmetry into the recursive account, one making it intrinsically worse to love one's own moral evil or causing of evil than to love the similar evil of others. Even where two imagined rapes are equally evil, a person's fantasizing his own act of raping is worse because the act is his own. These and other asymmetries will be discussed more fully in chapter 7. Here we need only note that in the intuitive difference between wholly external fantasies and ones imagined from the inside, we have one possible support for the view that love of one's own moral evil is worse than a similar love of other people's.

To conclude this section, let me apply its claims to the virtue solution to the theological problem of evil, the solution claiming that the existence of pain is justified because it is a condition for virtues such as compassion (see chapter 5, section 3). We can now give two further objections to this argument.

First, it is not true that even the full value of compassion requires the existence of real pain. It is enough if people falsely believe there is pain, for example, if everyone falsely believes that one person is suffering. Since the value of an attitude involving belief in its object's existence is unaffected by whether that belief is true, a world free of pain can still contain the most valuable compassion for pain. This world will not be free of all non-moral evil, since it will contain the evil of false belief. But surely this evil, especially if the false belief concerns only one person's pain, will be smaller than that of all the pain the actual world contains.

Second, even a world free of all non-moral evil can contain some compassion, since it can contain compassion for self-consciously imagined pain. Moore makes this point, saying that a world without pain can still contain compassion for the pain of a fictional character such as Lear.[13] This compassion may be less good than compassion for pain believed to be real, but the loss of value this involves is surely outweighed by the gain from having no pain. Given the comparative principle, even compassion for real pain is less good than that pain is evil. If compassion for imaginary pain has even some positive value, the difference in value between the two forms of compassion can be smaller than that between the pain's existing and its not existing. In Ewing's version of the virtue solution, it is not the value of compassion alone that justifies the existence of real pain; there is also the value of a full variety of virtues. But this argument, too, is undercut by the possibility of compassion for imaginary pain. A world free of all non-moral evil cannot contain the form of compassion involving belief that the pain is real. But since it can still contain some compassion, its shortfall in variety of virtues is not very great. Surely that shortfall, which consists only in the difference between compassion with and without ontological belief, is not sufficient to justify the existence of all the pain in the world.

2. *Virtue and Moral Beliefs*

In chapter 1, I distinguished two different ways of loving something good. One can believe that an object is intrinsically good and love it because of that belief, or love it *as* something good. This is *intellectualized* love, which derives from a judgment of value. Alternatively, without relying on any belief about goodness, one can feel a direct emotional attraction to an object, desiring or pursuing it for its own sake independently of its evaluative qualities. This is *simple emotional* love, which, though often directed at something good, is not directed at it for its goodness. I take it as evident that both forms of love occur. It is not the case, as some philosophers claim, that all desire is for objects thought of as good, so that what I call simple emotional love is not possible.[14] Physical appetites such as hunger and thirst are independent of evaluation, and the same is true of some desires with more sophisticated objects. Simple curiosity, for example, is a desire for knowledge just as knowledge, without any belief about its good-

---

13. Moore, *Principia Ethica*, p. 219.
14. See, e.g., Anscombe, *Intention*, pp. 70–72, 76–78; and Sherman, *Making a Necessity of Virtue*, p. 57.

ness. Nor, as other philosophers claim, do desires always precede evaluation, so we call things good only when we already desire them, and intellectualized love is not possible;[15] sometimes beliefs about goodness do shape our attitudes. So both forms of love occur and can even be directed at the same object. A person can simultaneously desire knowledge from simple curiosity and because he believes it to be good. But the forms of love are distinct, and questions therefore arise about their comparative values. Does only one form have value, or are both good to some degree? If both are good, is one better? Is there an ideal mix of the two for a given good object?

Unlike most questions about the recursive account, these turn partly on an issue in metaethics, that between cognitivist and noncognitivist views of moral judgment. On a cognitivist view, the judgment that an object is intrinsically good expresses a proposition that can be objectively true or false and can therefore be the object of a full-blooded belief. On a noncognitivist view, that judgment expresses not a belief but an attitude—more specifically, a positive attitude to the object—and cannot be true or false. If we accept cognitivism, the questions I have raised about the two forms of love arise in a very forceful way. Intellectualized love of a good involves a mental state, a belief about the object's goodness, that is not present in simple attraction to the object, and we can ask whether the presence and influence of this belief makes the resulting attitude better or less good. But the questions do not arise so forcefully given noncognitivism, which makes what is expressed in a moral judgment just another kind of attitude, not essentially different from ones such as desires. The attitudes expressed in moral judgments may be distinctive in various ways. They may be qualitatively sui generis, as different introspectively from pleasures and desires as the latter are from each other, and they may have special formal properties such as universality. But however they differ, attitudes to objects as good are less distinctive given noncognitivism than if they involved full-blooded beliefs, and questions about their comparative value are therefore less pressing.

To make these questions more interesting, let us assume a cognitivist view of moral judgment. We can then consider three main views about the two forms of love, paralleling views about the more frequently discussed topic of the comparative values of action from the motive of duty, or from belief that an action is right, and action from emotions such as love and compassion.

15. Gauthier, *Morals by Agreement*, pp. 46–59.

The first view holds that only love of a good as good has value, while simple emotional love does not. This *intellectualist* view parallels Kant's view that only action from the motive of duty has moral worth.[16] In a strong version it can hold, as Kant is sometimes taken to, that the presence of simpler emotions makes a person's attitudes morally less good, either intrinsically or by limiting his capacity for more valuable attitudes. A contrary *emotionalist* view holds that only emotional love has value, while love derived from judgments of goodness does not. It parallels the view of Stocker, Williams, and others that in certain situations, thoughts of one's duty are positively inappropriate. Of a man who chooses to save his wife's life rather than a stranger's, Williams says that if his motivating thought is partly that in situations like this, one is permitted to save one's wife, he has "one thought too many."[17] Similarly, an emotionalist view can say that thoughts about intrinsic goodness detract from what should be a direct emotional attraction to an object such as pleasure or knowledge. A final *mixed* view gives value to both forms of love, as Ross and Blum give value to actions done both from duty and from emotion.[18] This last view has further variants. One holds that loving a good as good is better than loving it simply emotionally, a second that loving it emotionally is better, and a third that the two have roughly equal worth. These are moderate intellectualist, moderate emotionalist, and fully mixed views.

Unfortunately, our assessment of these views may be affected by another issue in metaethics. Assuming a cognitivist view of moral judgment, what is the connection between the belief that an object is good and a positive attitude to it, such as a desire for it? Metaethical internalism holds that the evaluative belief is itself motivating, independently of pre-existing desires. To believe that an object is good is already and in a distinctive way to be oriented toward it. Metaethical externalism, by contrast, denies that a belief about goodness is intrinsically motivating. To issue in action, or indeed in any positive attitude, the belief must be combined with an independent attraction to goodness as good. One first has a general

---

16. Kant, *Foundations of the Metaphysics of Morals*, p. 11. For recent defences of the Kantian view, see Herman, "On the Value of Acting from the Motive of Duty"; and Baron, "The Alleged Moral Repugnance of Acting from Duty."
17. Williams, "Persons, Character, and Morality," p. 18; see also Stocker, "The Schizophrenia of Modern Ethical Theories."
18. Ross, *The Right and the Good*, pp. 160–73; and Blum, *Friendship, Altruism, and Morality*, p. 8.

desire for whatever is good, then believes that a particular object is good; only given both these mental states does one desire that object.

Of these two metaethical views, internalism seems more favourable to an intellectualist ranking of the two forms of love. By making love of a good as good involve a distinct kind of motivation, it allows and even encourages the thought that such love is higher and more virtuous. But this ranking is not so compelling given externalism, which makes intellectualized love rest at bottom on a simple desire, and externalism may even support emotionalist views. Emotionalism objects to the indirectness of intellectualized attitudes, to their relating to an object only via an intervening belief. This objection seems especially germane when both forms of love start from the same type of mental state: some simple desire.[19]

At the risk of oversimplifying, let us ignore this metaethical issue and consider the three views about love in the abstract. The arguments for pure intellectualism, which parallel those for the Kantian view that only action from the motive of duty has worth, claim that emotions such as compassion are objectionably contingent in two respects. First, they are contingent in their origin. Whether a person feels them at all can depend on accidents of his temperament and upbringing; whether he feels them in a particular situation depends on whether something in the situation elicits them. Second, these emotions are only contingently and therefore unreliably related to right action. Because they are not always present, they will not always lead a person to act as he should, and even when they are present they can just as easily lead him astray. Love for a particular person can make one care too much about that person's interests, preferring small benefits for her to much larger ones for others.

But these arguments do not successfully distinguish emotional attitudes from ones based on beliefs about goodness.[20] The latter, too, are contingent in their origin, since whether a person has a given moral belief depends on his innate moral sensitivity, his upbringing, and so on. Nor should contingency of origin matter if we are assessing an attitude's *intrinsic* value. Why should the fact that a form of love is not always present mean that it is not fully and properly good

19. This is not to say that all metaethical externalists endorse emotionalism. Ross denies that moral beliefs are themselves motivating (*The Foundations of Ethics*, pp. 226–28) but still holds that the desire to do one's duty and the desire for an object as good are better than any merely emotional desire (*The Right and the Good*, pp. 164, 165–66).

20. For a parallel discussion, see Blum, *Friendship, Altruism, and Morality*, chap. 1.

when it is present? As for the connection with right action, that, too, fail to distinguish emotional from intellectualized attitudes. If an intellectualized attitude involves a false belief about goodness, as it easily can, it can lead a person to pursue what does not have value or to prefer what has less value. Nor should this second contingency matter if we are assessing an attitude's intrinsic rather than its instrumental goodness. An intellectualized attitude that leads to wrong action can still be to some degree good in itself, and the same holds of emotional love of a somewhat inappropriate intensity. Though perhaps evil because of its effects, such love can still, given its appropriate orientation, be to some degree intrinsically good.

There seem, then, to be no persuasive arguments for the view that only love of a good as good is good, and there is likewise little plausibility in the contrary view that only emotional love is good. The principal objection to intellectualized love is that it relates indirectly to its object, given its dependence on a moral belief. But this is at most a reason for giving such love less value, not for giving it no value at all. The credible view, then, is a mixed one according to which both forms of love have some intrinsic worth. Neither form is valueless; each is good to some degree. But if we accept this mixed view, we face the further question of how the values of the two forms compare. We may want to answer this question differently for different types of goods. For a perfectionist good such as knowledge, there is some intuitive appeal to the claim that loving it as good is intrinsically better than loving it from a simple emotion such as curiosity. Some irrelevant factors may seem to support this claim. Given a cognitivist view of moral judgments, someone who loves knowledge as good has a kind of knowledge about it—that it is good—that someone motivated only by curiosity may not have, and this additional knowledge is a base-level good. In addition, the term "curiosity" often suggests an interest in more trivial facts than are the objects of the most valuable knowledge. But we can set aside these factors by considering the values only as attitudes of the two forms of love for the same kind of knowledge, say, scientific knowledge. Even in this restricted comparison, some may hold that love of the knowledge as good, which responds to the moral quality of the knowledge, is for that reason better.[21] But the opposite claim may be plausible for welfarist goods such as pleasure and even more so

---

21. For this preference for intellectualized love, see Ross, *The Right and the Good*, pp. 165–66; and Lomasky, *Persons, Rights, and the Moral Community*, p. 253.

for the welfarist evil of pain. It is for pain in particular that Stocker's and Williams's preference for a direct emotional concern not dependent on moral beliefs seems most attractive. So perhaps we should refuse to compare the two forms of love in the abstract, saying only that for some goods love of them as good is better, while for others the opposite is true.

If we do compare the forms in the abstract, I see no reason to judge either as superior. Intellectualized love responds appropriately to an object's moral properties, which is a positive feature. But simple emotional love is more direct, which is likewise a positive feature. These respective merits seem roughly to cancel each other out. Because we cannot assign numerical values to instances of virtue, we cannot speak meaningfully of precise equality between the two forms of love. But if we are forced to compare them in the abstract, the most reasonable conclusion seems to be that neither is determinately better than the other. Given the same intensity and the same object, love of that object as good is neither better nor worse than love of it from simple emotion.

This leaves a final question about how, if at all, the two forms of love should be combined. Imagine that a person has a total of 10 units of love for a given good. A neutral view says it is a matter of indifference how these units are divided between the two forms. If she has 10 units of intellectualized love and none of emotional love, this is neither better nor worse than if she had the opposite 0–10 split or a 5–5 split. A different, proportionality, view says that the ideal is to divide one's love in proportion to the two forms' values, so a 5–5 split is better than either a 10–0 or a 0–10 split. The difference between these views turns on how the asymptotic view of individual attitudes, which makes the values of additional units of love diminish (see chapter 3, section 2), applies to the two forms of love. The neutral view applies diminishing marginal value only to a person's total love for an object as compounded from the two forms. Since a unit of either form always makes the same contribution to this total, there are no distributive preferences between them. But the proportionality view applies diminishing value to each form separately. It holds that an additional unit of each form adds less value the more of that form there is, so the best combinations of love are compounded roughly equally from each.

Of these two, I find the proportionality view more attractive. Someone who loves a good only intellectually or only emotionally seems to respond less adequately to it than if she loved it in both ways. And if the two forms have roughly equal value, the ideal should be to mix them roughly equally. (If for some good objects, such as knowledge, one form of love is better, then the best mix for those objects favours the better form by as much as it is better.) This mixed ideal need involve no preference about how a person arrives at its favoured state. One possibility is that she first loves a good only emotionally, and then from repeated exposure to it comes to appreciate it as good and to love it for that reason. This is an Aristotelian model of the development of virtue, starting from non-rational attitudes, either innate or trained, and intellectualizing them. Alternatively, she can first love a good only as good and then develop an emotional attachment to it; this is an anti-Aristotelian model. Given their identical endpoints, these processes can be equally morally desirable. What matters is that each results in the overall attitude to a good that is best, combining love for it as good and from simple emotion, and in roughly equal proportion.

So far I have discussed the role of moral beliefs in virtuous attitudes. Similar questions arise, though with an added complexity, about some moral vices. I have in mind the pure vices and vices of indifference, those involving hatred of good, love of evil, or indifference to good or evil. Merely emotional forms of these vices are clearly possible. One can know another is in pain and be indifferent to her pain as pain, and one can also desire another's pain as pain. But what about intellectualized forms of these vices? Can one think of another's pain as evil and be indifferent to or desire it *as* evil?

The answer depends on our choice between metaethical internalism and externalism. Assuming internalism, intellectualized forms of these vices cannot occur. If to believe that an object is evil is already to be motivated against it, one cannot combine that belief with no or the opposite motivation. Unlike the virtues, which come in both intellectualized and emotional forms, the vices on this view occur only as simple emotions.[22] Assuming externalism, however, intellectualized vices are possible. If the belief that an object is evil is not intrinsically motivating, it can coexist with indifference or even attraction to its object as evil. In fact, given externalism, there is no logical reason why belief that an object is evil should lead to hatred rather than love of it.

22. This claim is slightly exaggerated for vices of indifference. A very mild internalism requires only some, and possibly a very weak, motivation as a condition of accepting a moral belief. If this motivation can be below the threshold intensity for positive value in appropriately oriented attitudes (see chapter 3, section 1), there can be some intellectualized vices of indifference.

The issue about intellectualized vice is therefore a test case for internalism and externalism. Unfortunately, the test seems to give conflicting results. Some philosophers argue that intellectualized indifference, where one knows an object is good or evil but remains unconcerned about it, exists and is evidence for externalism.[23] But it is much harder to conceive of intellectualized pure vice, where one desires a state such as another's pain precisely as evil or because it is evil. Loving evil for that very quality seems a dubious phenomenon, and its being so supports internalism. At least one externalist, Milo, seems to allow for such vice under the heading of "Satanic wickedness." (Recall the motto of Milton's Satan: "Evil, be thou my good.") But even Milo allows that the existence of such wickedness is "especially problematic," and he ends up understanding it as involving a desire for evils for the properties that make them evil, that is, as involving only emotional desire.[24] One would expect the two forms of intellectualized vice to be either both possible or both not. Intuitively, however, their status is very different.

If intellectualized vice is possible, a view parallel to the one defended above regarding the two forms of virtue seems plausible. Both intellectualized and merely emotional vice are evil, and to a roughly equal degree. And what is morally worst is combining the two forms equally, so that one desires another's pain just as pain and as evil with equal intensity. The height of vice is being inappropriately oriented to an object in both of the two possible ways.

One question remains, about the case where a moral belief is false. Imagine that a person believes an object to be good and desires it as good, but in fact the object is evil. Is his desire intrinsically good or evil? I think the recursive account has to say that, considered in itself, his desire is good. Just as a false belief about an object's existence does not on its own affect the value of an attitude based upon it, so a false moral belief should not by itself undermine the value of any resulting intellectualized love. When a person's attitudes are appropriate given his moral beliefs, they should normally, like other appropriate attitudes, be good.[25] But this may seem a

23. Milo, *Immorality*, chap. 6; and Brink, *Moral Realism and the Foundations of Ethics*, pp. 46–50.

24. Milo, *Immorality*, pp. 7–8, 236–37; see also Ross, *The Right and the Good*, p. 163. The impossibility of intellectualized pure vice is also argued for in McNaughton, *Moral Vision*, pp. 140–44.

25. For a parallel view about false beliefs about rightness, see Milo, *Immorality*, pp. 54, 251–52.

counterintuitive implication. Imagine that a Nazi believes the extermination of the Jews is good and desires it as good. Is it not highly counterintuitive to call his attitude virtuous?

In almost any imaginable case, the account's approval of the Nazi's attitude will be highly qualified. First, alongside his intellectualized desire for the Jews' destruction, he will often have a simple emotional desire for that end, involving simple hatred of Jews. This emotional desire will be intrinsically evil and, if sufficiently intense, will make his attitudes on balance evil. Second, the Nazi's moral belief will often have a morally evil origin. It will result from his emotional hatred by rationalization or self-deception: he will desire emotionally to destroy the Jews, as well as desiring to desire what is good, and will reconcile these desires by persuading himself that destroying the Jews is good. Here his moral belief, like the factual beliefs of a cynic or a blindly charitable person (see chapter 4, sections 1 and 2), reflects the moral quality of its originating desire, which in his case is evil. There may remain a small element of good in his character, namely, his desire to desire what is good. But this goodness is surely outweighed by the much greater evil in the emotional hatred that gives his belief its content. Nor does this outweighing occur only when the false belief results directly from an evil desire, by rationalization. A belief can also be evil if its origins reflect indifference to goodness and evil. If the Nazi retains his belief about the goodness of destroying the Jews because he has not critically examined it, either because of his emotional desire or from simple thoughtlessness, he shows an indifference to intrinsic values that is likewise evil. If we held that people can always know what is good and evil by a little effort, we could hold that all false moral beliefs reflect some vice of indifference.[26] Then in any possible case, the Nazi's false belief would involve some moral evil. But even without this strong claim, we can say that in many cases of moral error, including most imaginable Nazi cases, there is at least a lack of serious attention to questions of value that involves some vice of moral indifference.

Given these points, a case where the Nazi's desire was intrinsically only good would have to be very unusual. First, the Nazi would have to desire the destruction of the Jews only as good and not at all from emotional hatred. Second, his moral belief could not originate by

---

26. Aquinas defends this view at least about general moral beliefs; see *Summa Theologica*, I–II, q. 19, a. 6.

rationalization from hatred or by any process involving moral indifference. This last condition might be satisfied if he was taught as a
child to believe that Jews are evil by parents whose treatment of him
in other respects gave him reason to trust their teaching. In addition, he could not later in life have been exposed to any evidence
that would undermine his belief, which at the least would require
his not encountering any Jews. If these various conditions were all
satisfied—and some may deny they could be—it would be possible
for a Nazi to have a sincere and innocent desire for something in
fact evil because he believed it to be good. In this highly unusual
case, I think it would be right to call his desire morally good. The
desire might be immensely evil instrumentally and therefore evil all
things considered. But considered on its own, as an attitude to an
object, it would have positive moral worth.

3. *Love as a Condition of Value*

I have said that the recursive account makes virtue a dependent intrinsic good, one that cannot be good unless other, base-level states
are good or evil. But given what has just been said about false moral
beliefs, this is not strictly true. Imagine that there are no base-level
goods or evils, so nothing that is not an attitude has any intrinsic
value. A person can falsely believe that, say, pleasure is good and desire it as good. If so, the recursive account makes his desire good
even though its intentional object is not, so his virtue can be the
only intrinsic good.[27] But this circumstance is highly unusual. Simple emotional love cannot be good unless its object is good, and the
same holds for intellectualized love on the assumption that its originating moral belief is true. For the vast majority of forms of virtue,
their having value on the recursive account presupposes an independent value in their object. That object is, for example, already
good in itself, and the goodness of loving it is only an addition to
that independent and prior goodness.

This feature of the recursive account is not shared by a rival view
most clearly stated by Moore. One of Moore's central intrinsic
goods is the admiring contemplation of beauty, which is a form of
the love of beauty. Early in *Principia Ethica* he argues that the exis-

27. This possibility is noted in McTaggart, *The Nature of Existence,* vol. 2,
pp. 422–23.

tence of beauty is good apart from any appreciation of it,[28] but he later allows that this may not be so,[29] and in *Ethics* he implicitly denies that beauty is good.[30] But he never abandons his belief that the admiring contemplation of beauty is good. Moore therefore envisages a case where the love of an object is good even though the object is not. More important, he holds that when beauty is the object of admiring contemplation, its real existence makes the overall situation significantly better than if the beauty did not exist.[31] Given an admiring contemplation of a beauty that is falsely believed to exist and an otherwise similar admiration of real beauty, the latter is better in a way that cannot be attributed to any value in the beauty on its own. An object with little or no value when it is not the object of virtuous love contributes significant value when it is.

Moore's formulation of this view uses his doctrine of organic unities. He does not say that when beauty is the object of admiration, it is itself intrinsically good. Given his strict view of intrinsic goodness, he cannot say this. Instead, he says that when beauty is the object of admiration, its existence makes for a whole composed of the beauty, the admiration, and the relation between them, and that this whole is good as a whole or in addition to any goodness in its parts. But essentially the same view can be expressed in terms of conditional values. Given the looser view of intrinsic goodness as just the goodness in a given object, we can say that when beauty is the object of admiration it is itself intrinsically good, though only conditionally. The presence of admiration still allows the existence of beauty to contribute value that it would not contribute on its own, but this value is now located in the beauty itself.

I will use this second formulation of Moore's view, if only because it seems simpler. I will therefore speak of a rival to the recursive view called the *conditionality* view, on which the love of x is in some cases not an additional good to x but a condition of x's having value. This view can be applied not only to beauty, as it is by Moore, but also to perfectionist states such as knowledge, achievement, and perhaps virtue. One can hold that if a person has knowledge but no love of knowledge, that is, no desire for, pursuit of, or pleasure in knowledge for its own sake, his knowledge has no value. But if he does love knowledge, his actually having knowledge makes his state bet-

28. Moore, *Principia Ethica*, pp. 83–85.
29. Moore, *Principia Ethica*, pp. 202, 203.
30. Moore, *Ethics*, p. 107.
31. Moore, *Principia Ethica*, pp. 197–200.

ter than if he had the love but no knowledge. (This is possible if he desires knowledge he does not have or takes pleasure in what he falsely believes is knowledge.) A similar view is possible about achievement, so that, for example, athletic or business achievement has value only when accompanied by love of such achievement for itself. Such a view is even possible, though in my view less plausible, about virtue. If a person cares benevolently about others' pleasure but not also about his own benevolence, it can be said, his benevolence has no value. But if he does love that benevolence, it is an additional moral good.

Versions of this conditionality view are affirmed by several philosophers. Aristotle sometimes takes the recursive line that if an activity is good, pleasure in it is an additional good,[32] but at other times he says that for an action to be virtuous, a person must choose it and enjoy it for its own sake.[33] Here, quite differently, an attitude to an action is necessary for the action to have value. The conditionality view also represents the best interpretation of Mill's doctrine of higher and lower pleasures.[34] Mill holds that the only candidates for intrinsic goodness are "pleasures," which are best understood as states or activities accompanied by pleasure. If a person reads poetry without pleasure, on this view, his doing so is not a pleasure and has no intrinsic worth. But if he does take pleasure in his reading, the value in his activity is not a function just of the quantity or intensity of his pleasure. Pleasure in a "higher" activity such as poetry makes for more value than a similar pleasure in a "lower" activity such as pushpin. Something that would not have value on its own does have value when it is the object of accompanying pleasure.

A view similar to Mill's is defended by Frankena,[35] and a more complex view is proposed by Parfit:

> What is good for someone is neither just what Hedonists claim, nor just what is claimed by Objective List Theorists. We might believe that if we had *either* of these, *without the other*, what we had would have little or no value. We might claim, for example, that what is good or bad for someone is to have knowledge, to be engaged in rational activity, to experience mutual love, and to be aware of beauty, while strongly wanting just these things . . . Pleasure with many other kinds of object has no value. And, if they are entirely devoid of pleasure, there is no

---

32. Aristotle, *Nicomachean Ethics*, 1174a4–9, b23–33.
33. Aristotle, *Nicomachean Ethics*, 1099a16–21, 1105a32, 1144a20.
34. Mill, *Utilitarianism*, pp. 210–14.
35. Frankena, *Ethics*, pp. 89–92.

value in knowledge, rational activity, love, or the awareness of beauty. What is of value, or is good for someone, is to have both.[36]

Parfit claims not only that objectively worthy states such as knowledge are valueless if unaccompanied by pleasure, but also that pleasure is valueless if unaccompanied by something of objective worth. The second claim is not made by other defenders of the conditionality view. Mill allows that even lower pleasures have some value; Frankena holds that every pleasure is as a pleasure to some degree good. Parfit therefore proposes an extension of their view involving a second conditionality. On one side are attitudes such as pleasure, on the other perfectionist states such as knowledge. Just as pleasure is necessary for the states to have value, so the states are necessary for value in the pleasure.[37]

But Parfit's extension rests on a confusion between intentional directedness and conditionality. Let us grant that pleasure as such and on its own has no value. (In chapter 5 I called this is an extreme view, but let us grant it.) The pleasure that is given value by the presence of knowledge cannot be just any pleasure simultaneous with the knowledge, such as the pleasure of suntanning by someone who happens at the time to have knowledge. It must be a pleasure intentionally directed at knowledge, that is, a pleasure in knowledge. (In the same way, the pleasure whose presence gives knowledge value cannot be just any simultaneous pleasure, such as that of suntanning; it, too, must be a pleasure in knowledge.) But pleasure in knowledge is an intentional attitude that, like all such attitudes, can exist when its object does not, as when a person takes pleasure in what he falsely believes is knowledge. It can therefore be found good by any view that, like the recursive view, evaluates attitudes by their intentional objects and independently of any external accompaniment. If Parfit's second claim is truly to concern conditionality, it must hold that even pleasure in knowledge, that is, even pleasure as intentionally characterized, has no value when not accompanied by knowledge. But this claim is not intuitively plausible: Aristotle's pleasure in what he falsely believed was his biological knowledge seems just as good, as an attitude, as pleasure in real knowledge. Its value, contrary to Parfit, seems unaffected by the presence or absence of the knowledge. To summarize: a view denying that pleasure

---

36. Parfit, *Reasons and Persons*, p. 502.
37. For a similarly symmetrical view, though about "meaningfulness" rather than just goodness, see Wolf, "Happiness and Meaning."

as such has value can hold that pleasures with objects such as knowledge have value. But this last is not a conditionality claim parallel to the one found in Mill's and Frankena's views; it ascribes a purely internal value to certain intentional attitudes such as intentional pleasures. And although a conditionality claim about these attitudes is possible, it is not, when properly understood, credible.

The plausible version of the conditionality view, then, makes just the one claim that perfectionist states such as knowledge have value only when accompanied by love of them for their own sake. In this form, the view is an important rival to the recursive account, making the values of attitudes prior to rather than derivative from their objects' values. But there are several respects in which this view is problematic. We can approach the first of these through a technical question about the view's formulation.

As in the recursive account, the love this view makes a condition of value can be either intellectualized, involving a moral belief, or simply emotional. The view is easy to state if it requires only simple emotional love, but I do not think many will find this attractive. For perfectionist states such as knowledge, intellectualized love seems if anything the more appropriate form, and I think the view's proponents will want such love to provide at least one source of these states' value. But it is not clear that intellectualized love can coherently play this role.

Consider first a pure intellectualist version of the conditionality view, one holding that knowledge has value only when accompanied by love of it based on a moral belief. What, we need to ask, is the content of this moral belief? What do people believe about knowledge when they have the required attitude to it? The simplest answer is that they believe that knowledge is simply or unconditionally good, so the love that gives knowledge value is love for it as simply good. But this belief is, by the conditionality view's own lights, false. According to that view, knowledge is not good simply but only when accompanied by certain attitudes. (This falsity is especially clear on a Moorean formulation. Then it is never true that knowledge itself is good; what can be good is only a whole composed of knowledge and love of it.) But it is implausible to make value in the knowledge require an accompanying evaluative belief that is always and necessarily false. Surely a belief playing that role must at least sometimes be true.

The intellectualist view may try to meet this condition by complicating its required belief, so it is now the belief that knowledge is good when and only when accompanied by love of it based on the belief that knowledge is good. But this does not remove the difficulty. The belief embedded in this more complex one, that knowledge is simply good, is still by the conditionality view's lights false, and if we agree that the value of knowledge cannot require the presence of a belief that is always false, this makes the more complex belief also false. In fact, trying to complicate the required belief in this way only generates an infinite regress. To avoid being false, the belief must hold that knowledge is good when and only when accompanied by love of it based on the belief that knowledge is good when and only when accompanied by love of it based on the belief, and so on. At no point is there a completed belief that can be true.

This difficulty would not arise if the conditionality view used two distinct concepts in its central claim, as Kant does when he says that actions have moral worth only when done from the motive of duty. If Kant holds that actions have moral worth (one concept) only when done from the belief that they are right (a different concept), his conditionality claim poses no threat to the latter belief's truth.[38] But our conditionality view takes the same property of goodness to be both what knowledge conditionally has and what the conditioning belief ascribes to it. And this creates the difficulty that the relevant belief is, by the view's lights, always false.

The difficulty may be solvable if the required belief can involve self-reference of a kind found in other mental states such as intentions. The content of an intention to raise one's arm cannot be just that one perform the action of raising one's arm, since that could happen independently of one's presently intending it. The intention's content must be that one perform the action of raising one's arm by way of carrying out *this very intention,* so the intention refers internally to itself.[39] Similarly, the intellectualist conditionality view could make its required belief hold that knowledge is good when and only when accompanied by love of it based on a moral belief with the same content as *this very belief.* If this self-reference is possible, it both allows the belief in question to be true and avoids a regress. But there is an important difference between this self-reference and the kind found in an ordinary intention. The latter is

38. If Kant held that an action is *right* only when done from the belief that it is right, as he is sometimes taken to do, he would face a difficulty about that belief's truth. Ross, who interprets Kant this way, raises essentially this objection in *The Right and the Good,* pp. 5–6.
39. Searle, *Intentionality,* pp. 85–86; see also Harman, "Practical Reasoning," pp. 438–46. Searle finds a similar self-reference in perceptions and memories.

to the intention as an individual mental state, as had by a particular person at a particular time. But someone who believes that knowledge is good only conditionally cannot believe that its being good requires his present individual belief; any belief with the same content would do. His belief's self-reference must therefore run through the belief to its content, so he believes that any belief *with the same content as this one* can generate the love that gives knowledge value. And this more generic self-reference may be problematic in a way that the individual self-reference of intentions is not. Even if a mental state can refer to itself as an individual state, how can it refer to its content if that content is not fixed before the self-reference occurs?

If the more generic self-reference is not possible, I do not see how there can be a conditioning intellectualized love whose constituent belief is not false. But let us waive this difficulty and assume that a self-referring belief can supply the conditionality view's central case of intellectualized love. Once it has this case, the view can go on to allow that intellectualized love based on a false belief can also give its object value. (What was objectionable was only the strong claim that the love required for value *must* involve a false belief; once a true belief is possible, others can play a derivative role.) For example, the view can hold that if a person loves knowledge from the false belief that knowledge is simply good, that, too, gives his knowledge value. Though not the central case of intellectualized love, this can now be a derivative one. But if the view liberalizes its condition in this way, it will have to complicate its true belief further. That belief must now be that knowledge is good when and only when accompanied by love of it based either on a belief with the same content as this one or on the false belief that knowledge is simply good. And a further complication is needed if simple emotional love can also give an object value, as in a mixed version of the conditionality view. Then the belief present in the central case of intellectualized love must be that knowledge is good when and only when accompanied by either love of it based on a belief with the same content as this one, love based on the belief that knowledge is simply good, or simple emotional love.

In my view, these complications diminish the intuitive appeal of the conditionality view. That view has a certain plausibility when the attitudes it requires for value in an object are comparatively simple, such as simple emotional love of an object or love based on the simple belief that the object is good. But when the belief present in the central case of intellectualized love becomes as complex as the self-referring disjunctions just formulated, some of that appeal dissipates. The complications also have the unfortunate implication that almost no one has ever loved a state such as knowledge with a true belief about its value. Since the self-referring disjunctions will occur only to those few philosophers who think systematically about the conditionality view, the vast majority of people with an intellectualized love for knowledge will base that love on a false evaluative belief.[40]

This first is a technical difficulty for the conditionality view, but a second difficulty concerns its central distinguishing claim. The recursive account says it is best if perfectionist states such as knowledge and achievement are accompanied by love of them for themselves; then there are two intrinsic goods present in a person rather than only one. But the account insists that the knowledge and achievement without the love still have worth. This, of course, the conditionality view denies, and its doing so is its defining feature. But that denial seems in many cases counterintuitive.

This is most obviously true of pure intellectualist versions of the view, which require love of a perfectionist state based on the belief that it is good. (I again waive the technical difficulty for this view.) Though defended by some political philosophers under the heading of the "endorsement constraint,"[41] this view seems impossibly high-minded, making necessary a type of attitude many clearly admirable activities lack. So I will assume that the more plausible conditionality view is a mixed one, allowing that knowledge and achievement have value when accompanied by love of them based either on a moral belief or on simple emotion. But even this more generous view is too restrictive.

Imagine an artist who creates exceptionally fine works of art. It may be a necessary condition for her doing so that she set extremely high standards for herself, ones even her best work cannot meet. Only if her reach in this sense exceeds her grasp will she devote herself fully to her art. But a side effect of her adopting these standards may be that she is perpetually dissatisfied with her work and the

---

40. Could many of these people not have a true belief if they believed only that knowledge is good when, but not only when, accompanied by love of it based on the belief that knowledge is simply good? This less ambitious belief, which gives only a sufficient condition for the value of knowledge, can indeed be true. But how many people other than philosophers will formulate a belief that is explicitly restricted in this way?

41. See Dworkin, "Foundations of Liberal Equality," pp. 237–38, 262–67; and Kmylicka, *Contemporary Political Philosophy*, pp. 203–4.

process of producing it, taking no pleasure, either intellectualized or emotional, in either. If so, the conditionality view says her artistic activity has no value whatsoever, so her engaging in it is no better than if from similar motives she counted blades of grass. This surely is absurd. It is uncontroversial that her inability to value her work for itself is a loss, but to say it deprives her highly skilful activity of all worth is going too far.

It may be objected that this example is unfair. Though the artist takes no pleasure in her particular works of art, she still loves art for its own sake because she desires to create works of great quality and is driven by this desire. This response abandons something strongly suggested in many presentations of the conditionality view: that value in a particular state x requires an accompanying love directed at x itself. It is now enough if there is a more generic love directed at the type of good of which x is an instance. But even this weaker requirement is too strong. Imagine that after years of never meeting her exacting standards, the artist becomes disillusioned with art and ceases to desire artistic achievement for its own sake. But she still keeps creating art, either from inertia or because others want her to, and her art is still of high quality. Does her achievement then have no more value than counting blades of grass? That still seems counterintuitive.

Nor do only examples of disillusionment illustrate this point; so do ones where a person pursues perfectionist states only as a means to some other end. Imagine that the artist creates her works only as a means to providing pleasure and enlightenment to those who will view them, or that a scientist pursues medical research only as a means to the relief of suffering his discoveries may make possible. If these individuals do not care about their art or research for themselves, the conditionality view says their skilful activities are valueless, and that again is absurd. The same holds if the artist and scientist pursue their activities only as means to neutral goals such as fame and money. Here, too, the view says their activities have no more value than if they counted blades of grass, but surely doing something demanding in pursuit of fame is better than doing something mindless. Some may object that people who value perfectionist activities only as means cannot in fact achieve excellence in them. This objection seems to me sentimental about the power of good motives in art and even more so science, where less noble aspirations are far more prevalent than we may like to imagine. And in other fields it does not apply at all. In sports of aggression such as boxing, football, and sprinting, it seems to be a necessary condition for the highest levels of achievement that one be motivated primarily by the desire to win and even to crush an opponent. Only so can one generate the power and explosiveness that success in these sports demands. Such sports therefore raise very starkly a conflict between the ideals of the amateur and the professional. The amateur plays for love and therefore plays less well; the professional plays to win and therefore plays better. We may regret this conflict; we may wish that in all fields the best attitudes could accompany the best achievements, and the recursive account explains our view. But it is going too far to say, as the conditionality view does, that the achievements of the professional focused on winning count for nothing. On the contrary, they can be extremely impressive.

The conditionality view, then, is implausible in its central claim that perfectionist states lack value apart from love of them for themselves. And the view faces a further difficulty. To be most plausible, it should not only make certain attitudes necessary for value in their objects but also hold that those attitudes are good in themselves. Thus, it should hold that Aristotle's pleasure in what he falsely believed was his biological knowledge was good in itself, as is any similar pleasure in real knowledge. When a person has knowledge and loves it for itself, two goods are present: the love, which is good unconditionally, and the knowledge, which is good when accompanied by the love. But the attitudes that confer value also have value themselves.

If it takes this line, the conditionality view faces the question of what makes good attitudes good. The recursive account gives a uniform answer to this question in terms of the value of an attitude's object: if an attitude is one of loving, it is good because its object is good; if it is one of hating, it is good because its object is evil. But the conditionality view cannot give a uniform answer because it cannot apply its conditionality claim to all objects of attitudes. This claim may be initially plausible for perfectionist states such as knowledge and achievement, but it is not so for evils. It is not plausible to hold that false belief and failure are evil only when accompanied by certain attitudes, nor is it plausible to hold this about pain. The conditionality claim is also not plausible for welfarist goods such as pleasure; if pleasure is good, it is so unconditionally. Nor, finally, is this kind of claim plausible for one person's attitude to another's knowledge or achievement. If one person has knowledge and loves that knowledge for itself, another person's being pleased by these facts cannot be a condition for value in the first person. It can only be, in the familiar recursive way, an additional good in the second person.

The conditionality view must therefore be supplemented by recursive claims about many attitudes. But then it cannot give a uniform explanation of the goodness of all good attitudes, since it cannot give a recursive explanation of the goodness of attitudes whose objects are not on their own good, as it claims knowledge is not. This is already to some extent a defect, since it is, other things equal, preferable to have a single explanation of a single kind of good. But there is a greater difficulty when we ask why, by the view's lights, the love of a state such as knowledge is good.

The answer cannot be that the object of this love is simply good, since the view denies this is so. It can only be that the object is one that is good when accompanied by love of it for its own sake. But this is a far less satisfying explanation, in part because it is much more complex. There is something immediately persuasive in the claim that love of a good is good because its object is good, but rather less appeal in the claim that love of an object is good because the object when accompanied by that love is good. The latter claim seems to involve an illicit kind of bootstrapping, an attitude's being made good by something involving itself. And even if it does not involve bootstrapping, the explanation only raises a further question: why is the good attitude to knowledge one of loving the knowledge for itself rather than, say, hating it? Why is the desirable response to knowledge positive rather than negative? The obvious answer is that love is the appropriate response to knowledge, but what is the basis for this claim? The recursive account says attitudes are appropriate when they respond to the goodness or evil of their objects, but the conditionality view cannot take this line. So on what ground can it make love in particular the desirable attitude to knowledge? It seems that the conditionality view can give no answer to this question. At a crucial point, it must rest on an ungrounded assertion that an attitude is appropriate and therefore good even though nothing in its object makes it so. And that leaves it unable to explain something the recursive account explains in a simple and satisfying way.

The conditionality view is similar to the recursive account in giving a central place in value theory to attitudes evaluated in relation to their objects. It differs from that account in making the values of attitudes not always derivative from the values of their objects, but in some cases determinative of them. The conditionality view is historically important and for at least some goods has some initial intuitive appeal. But I do not believe that, examined carefully, it has the overall credibility of the simpler recursive account.

7

Extending the Account

To this point I have developed the recursive account using a comparatively simple set of base-level values. The goods and evils in base-clauses (BG) and (BE) are all single states of individuals, and they are also all agent-neutral, or good or evil to the same degree from all persons' points of view. But the recursion-clauses that follow can equally well be combined with more complex base-level values; the result is to extend the range of virtues and vices the recursive account captures. In this chapter I will consider three possible extensions to the base-clauses (BG) and (BE) and the additional traits they bring into the recursive fold. The first extension is to distributive and other holistic values involving combinations of states, for example, of all members of a society, that have intrinsic value as combinations. The second is to agent-relative values, which are good or evil only or to a greater degree from some people's points of view than from others'. The final extension takes us beyond consequentialism to address those moral considerations other than intrinsic goodness that are recognized by deontological theories. Here we will see how the recursive account, even if not a complete account of virtue and vice, nonetheless provides a model for other, more inclusive accounts.

1. Holistic Virtues

Pleasure and pain are single states of individuals, as are the beliefs and intentions whose successful match with the world makes for knowledge and achievement. But some theories also find value in certain distributions of these states or of the means to them among individuals. Thus, some hold that *equal distributions* of pleasure, knowledge, or money are intrinsically good as equal, and unequal distributions intrinsically evil. These distributive values are often described in the language of justice, so equal distributions are "just" and unequal ones "unjust." Then the specific reason a more equal distribution of pleasure is better is that it is closer to distributive justice. Since equality and inequality involve states of an entire group—for example, a society—they are holistic values, located in combinations of states as combinations. These values are usually not the only ones a theory recognizes; they merely supplement individual values such as pleasure and pain. In Moore's terminology, they are additional values in a whole "as a whole" that must be added to the values in its parts to determine its value "on the whole."[1] But their holistic character sets them apart from the atomistic values in our original base-clauses.

The recursive account can extend these clauses to include equality in distribution as a base-level good and inequality as a base-level evil. If it does, it can use these values to define a virtue of holistic justice distinct from the proportional justice discussed in chapter 4. The latter form of justice is a virtue of proportion that involves dividing one's concern proportionally between the goods of different people. Holistic justice, by contrast, involves having appropriate attitudes to the single values of equality and inequality. More specifically, it involves desiring, pursuing, and taking pleasure in equal distributions as equal and having the opposite attitudes to unequal ones, namely, desiring and seeking to prevent them and being pained by them. It is a simple virtue, involving an appropriately oriented attitude to a single good or evil. Holistic justice still concerns distribution, as proportional justice does, but in a different way. Instead of turning on the distribution of a virtuous person's own concern, it is directed at an intrinsically distributive object, namely, equality or its opposite. As a simple virtue, holistic justice has a contrary pure vice that consists in hating equal distributions and loving unequal ones. But this pure vice is rare; the more common holistic injustice involves indifference to equality or insufficient concern for it.[2] A holistically unjust person acts on motives such as greed when a just person would be restrained

---

1. Moore, *Principia Ethica*, p. 214f; and chapter 3, section 3 here.
2. Williams, "Justice as a Virtue," p. 197. Williams identifies the virtue of justice by reference to a prior value of just distribution, or, as in my terminology, a holistic simple virtue.

by the desire to avoid inequality. But his injustice, like holistic justice, is identified by its relation to a single distributive good or evil.

Equality and inequality are not the only possible distributive values. Some theories hold that what is intrinsically good in distribution is not an equal division of intrinsic or instrumental goods but one that is *proportioned to desert*, so that, for example, the more virtuous receive more and the less virtuous less. Such theories likewise describe this good in the language of justice. Aristotle calls distributive justice "a species of the proportionate" and says its demands are satisfied when the ratio between two people's awards is the same as the ratio between their merits.[3] Ross agrees, identifying as an additional good to pleasure and virtue "the proportionment of happiness to virtue" and identifying the duty to pursue this good as one of justice.[4] Aristotle's and Ross's view is like the egalitarian one in valuing a pattern of distribution across individuals, but the pattern is now one of dividing a good such as pleasure in proportion to people's differing degrees of virtue. The view therefore grounds an alternative virtue of holistic justice, one that involves desiring, pursuing, and taking pleasure in distributions that match desert and being pained by ones that do not. If desert merely supplements equality as a distributive good, so that there are two such goods, a fully just person will want distributions to be both equal and proportioned to virtue, which requires everyone to be equal in virtue. If desert supplants equality, he will care only about proportioning pleasure to virtue.

This proportional desert view values only a pattern of distribution across individuals and says nothing about what anyone on his own deserves. Its demands are just as well satisfied when two equally virtuous people enjoy the same low level of pleasure as when they enjoy the same high level. A second desert view, which is holistic but in a different way, does address individual desert. It holds that for each individual, given his degree of virtue or vice, there is a specific quantity of pleasure or pain that he ideally deserves or should receive. Whatever happens to other people, his having just this pleasure or pain is best from the point of view of desert, and his having either more or less is less good and can in extreme cases be evil. If he is virtuous to degree m, a pleasure of some specific degree n is called for as a reward; if he is vicious, a specific pain is deserved as

3. Aristotle, *Nicomachean Ethics*, 1131a26–b24.
4. Ross, *The Right and the Good*, p. 27. See also pp. 21, 72, 138; and Ross, *The Foundations of Ethics*, p. 286.

punishment. (The latter is specifically retributive desert.) This *individual desert view* has implications for distribution, since if each person gets what he deserves the more virtuous will receive more than the less virtuous. But its focus is not this distributive pattern as such; it is the fit or lack of it between virtue and pleasure in each person's life. The view therefore makes a different kind of holistic addition to (BG) and (BE). It holds that the combination of virtue and pleasure in a single life has additional value as a combination that must be added to the values of its parts, as does the combination of vice and pain. If we label the good combinations of this type "just" and the evil ones "unjust," as is commonly done, the view grounds a third virtue of holistic justice, which involves desiring, pursuing, and taking pleasure in situations where a virtuous person is rewarded or a vicious one punished, and being pained by their opposites. The virtue's focus is still a combination of states, but now in one person's life rather than across lives.

This individual desert view gives rise to issues parallel to ones discussed above about compassionate pain and malicious pleasure. Consider first deserved pain, where a vicious person suffers a fitting intensity of pain as punishment for his vice. His pain is good as an instance of desert but evil as pain, so mixed attitudes are appropriate to it as they are to compassionate pain. We should be pleased that retribution is being done but pained at the infliction of pain. If the punishment is on balance worth inflicting, the goodness of the desert must outweigh the evil of the pain, so our ideal attitude to the situation is on balance positive. But this attitude still contains an element of pain, and its positive element is internally limited. If we are fully virtuous, we will be pleased by the infliction of only so much pain as is deserved and no more. A more intense pain would be both less good as retribution and more evil as pain, so there are two moral reasons to be pained by it. We should have a positive attitude only to pain of the deserved intensity as deserved, and that with pain at its painfulness, and a negative attitude to any greater pain.

As Nozick notes, these features distinguish the virtue of retributive justice from the superficially similar vice of vengefulness, or the desire for revenge.[5] A person can desire revenge for any harm or injury done him and not just for one involving a wrong or vice on another's part. (Consider a criminal seeking revenge against the

---

5. Nozick, *Philosophical Explanations,* pp. 366–68.

detective who put him in jail.) Revenge therefore need not rest, as retribution does, on any belief about justice or desert. In addition, the desire for revenge is not internally limited, as the desire for retribution is. Even if a vengeful person does not in fact inflict unlimited pain, there is nothing in his motivation that requires him not to do so; this is why feuds based on revenge so often escalate. Finally, revenge is accompanied by a different emotional tone than retribution. As Nozick puts it, revenge involves "pleasure in the suffering of another, while retribution either need involve no emotional tone, or involves another one, namely, pleasure at justice being done."[6] Whereas vengefulness is a form of malice, involving delight in another's evil, retributive justice has a different, and good, intentional object. In fact, the contrast here is even greater. A fully virtuous response to just retribution has a sombre tone, one suffused with regret. While feeling pleasure that justice is being done, we are pained by the infliction of pain, with the latter emotion limiting and qualifying the first. So, far from being a form of malice, retributive justice at its best involves the virtue of compassion. Interestingly, this last claim is denied by Aquinas. Discussing whether the blessed in heaven will take pleasure in the suffering of the damned, he says they will not take pleasure in that suffering as such but will do so indirectly, "by considering therein the order of Divine justice."[7] Here Aquinas distinguishes, as we have, between the intentional objects of malice and retributive justice. But he also denies that the blessed will pity the suffering of the damned, since this would require them to want the suffering to end, which they will not do.[8] But this second argument fails to distinguish between hating pain as pain and hating it on balance, where only the latter requires wanting on balance that it end. If we draw this distinction, we can separate the emotional tone of retributive justice in two ways from that of vengefulness: it takes pleasure in a good rather than an evil, and in its best form is accompanied by pain at that evil as evil rather than by glee.

A related vice, which I will call vindictiveness, differs more subtly from retributive justice. Unlike pure vengefulness, vindictiveness does involve a just desire that a vicious person suffer deserved pain. But instead of supplementing this desire with hatred of the pain as pain, vindictiveness involves a malicious desire for that pain for it-

6. Nozick, *Philosophical Explanations,* p. 367.
7. Aquinas, *Summa Theologica,* Supp., q. 94, a. 3.
8. Aquinas, *Summa Theologica,* Supp., q. 94, a. 2.

self. In many cases this malicious desire ends up stronger than the desire for justice, so it becomes the dominant element in the person's motivation. This is often shown in his seeking excessive punishment, which he does in a punitive or vindictive way. (If he believes this excessive punishment is justified, this may be because of self-deception originating in his malicious desire.) This is a constant danger with retributive justice: when we seek it, our attitudes may slip from the appropriate object of deserved retribution to the inappropriate one of pain. The two objects are sufficiently close that it can be hard to be certain whether in pursuing what we think is justice we are not also or even mainly motivated by malice. Vindictiveness is a less serious vice than pure vengefulness, since it involves some concern for the good of retributive justice, but this concern may show itself only in a weak occurrent attitude and in more extreme cases may not even do that. It is possible for a person to be psychologically such that he cannot take pleasure in another's pain unless he believes that pain is deserved, but when he has this belief the object of his pleasure is the pain only as pain and not as deserved. His belief, though causally necessary for the pleasure, does not enter into its intentional content. This is a worse form of vindictiveness, closer in its occurrent manifestations to pure vengefulness. And we may wonder whether it is not encouraged by some forms of popular entertainment, including some Hollywood movies. The conclusions of these movies feature the elaborate and gruesome death of the movie's villain at the hands of its hero. Within the movie's plot, the death of the villain is deserved, and the audience knows this. But their reaction to his death is not the sombre one associated with retributive justice; it is typically glee. May it not be that many in the audience need a plot making the villain's death deserved in order to take full pleasure in it but, given that plot, take pleasure only in the death and its gruesomeness and not in its being deserved? If so, the movie's plot provides the causal condition for what is essentially a form of malice.

Now consider undeserved pleasure, where a vicious person who should suffer pain instead enjoys delight. This pleasure is, again, evil as undeserved but good as pleasure, with mixed attitudes appropriate to it as they are to malicious pleasure. Some may resist the second half of this claim, holding that whereas deserved pain remains evil as pain, undeserved pleasure loses its goodness as pleasure. There is nothing good in a vicious person's enjoying pleasure, and the only attitude appropriate to it is pain at the undesert. Attractive though it may seem, this view involves the same circularity as the view that malicious pleasure lacks value as pleasure (see chapter 5, section 2). Since what makes a pleasure undeserved is its being that of a vicious person, an account of undesert presupposes one of virtue and vice. And if the latter account is given even partly in recursive terms, its base-clauses must either hold that all pleasure is good as pleasure or deny value to innocent pleasures such as those of eating ice cream. The intermediate view that only pleasures not associated with a higher-level evil of vice are good as pleasures introduces a circular dependence of what must come first in the recursive account on what must come later.

If a theory of desert includes both the proportional and the individual desert views, its structure is very close to that of the recursive account. Consider first the individual desert view. When fully elaborated, it shows how the degree of desert value of a pleasure or pain varies with its intensity, given a fixed degree of virtue or vice in its subject. This is similar to how the recursive account calculates the degree of value of an individual attitude given its intensity and the value of its object, though the desert view uses an optimality rather than an asymptotic approach (see chapter 3, section 2). As for the proportional desert view, it makes a holistic addition to the individual desert view that parallels that of the proportionality principle in the recursive account and is needed for similar reasons. It makes very disproportionate distributions evil and all reductions in disproportion in one respect good. Both the concept of virtue and that of desert turn on the idea of fittingness, either of an attitude to an object or of a reward to a state of character, and it should be no surprise that they are captured by formally similar principles.[9] But within the recursive account the importance of desert is that it provides objects for additional virtues and vices of holistic justice and injustice.

Equality and desert are not the only possible holistic additions to base-clauses (BG) and (BE). To give just one more example, some writers on environmental ethics hold that in addition to the values in individual organisms' lives, there are further intrinsic values in wholes combining these organisms in certain ways, such as species and ecosystems. Perhaps the best-known expression of this *deep ecological* view is Aldo Leopold's claim that what is right is whatever tends to preserve "the integrity, stability, and beauty of the biotic

9. For an account of desert paralleling the recursive account of virtue, see Kagan, "Equality and Desert."

community."[10] If the recursive account affirms these ecological values, it will recognize a further holistic virtue of desiring and seeking to preserve environmental wholes for themselves, feeling pleasure and even awe at them, and being pained by their destruction. It will also recognize a contrary vice of desiring to destroy environmental wholes or, more commonly, being indifferent to or insufficiently concerned about them. But this virtue and vice will again result, like the various versions of holistic justice and injustice, from applying the same recursive structure to an extended set of base-level goods and evils. Once holistic values are added to the base-clauses (BG) and (BE), the same recursion-clauses (LG)–(HE) identify a wider, because now partly holistic, set of virtues and vices.

2. *Agent-Relative Virtues*

The values in our original base-clauses are not only single states of individuals; they are also all agent-neutral, or good or evil in the same way and to the same degree from all persons' points of view. If one person's pleasure is good, it is just as good from others' point of view as from his own, and from strangers' as from his children's or closest friends'. It is good simply or full stop, with the same significance for all agents everywhere.

This agent-neutrality about base-level values implies a strict *impartialism* about both right action and virtue. Given a standard consequentialist principle, what is right is always what will result in the greatest total good for all persons, with each person's good counting equally in this calculation. Likewise, what is most virtuous is caring equally or impartially about all persons' goods, with no preferences among them. A fully virtuous person, and especially one with the virtue of proportional justice, cares neither more nor less about her own good than about other people's, or about any one person's than about another's.

Though some with traditional consequentialist leanings may welcome this impartialism, others will reject it. They will say that if, for example, one can prevent an equivalent harm to a stranger or to one's father, one should prefer protecting one's father. Here it would be not right but wrong to weigh the threatened harms equally. One should likewise have more intense feelings about one's

---

10. Leopold, *A Sand County Almanac*, pp. 224–25.

father, with failure to do so not a virtue but its opposite. As Stocker puts it, strict impartialism implies that a fully virtuous person will be just as pained by each death in a faraway massacre as by the death of her father, and therefore, given the much greater numbers involved, much more pained by the massacre as a whole.[11] But this, many will say, is absurd. Not only is strict impartiality toward everyone not required by virtue, it is positively disproportionate and therefore contrary to virtue. It fails to respond properly to the greater importance from each person's point of view of a parent or other intimate as against someone with no special relation to her.

The recursive account can accommodate this *partialist* view if it extends its base-clauses to include agent-relative values, ones that are good or evil only or to a greater degree from some people's points of view than from others'. A father's pleasure, for example, though good to some degree for all people, can be a greater good from his children's point of view than from strangers'. This can make it right for his children to pursue his pleasure rather than a stranger's and also makes it virtuous of them to prefer his pleasure. It is now intrinsically better for them to care about their father's pleasure than a stranger's equal pleasure, and what proportionality demands is no longer strict impartiality but as much more concern for their father's pleasure as the extended base-clauses make it, from their point of view, more important. Children need not care about their father's pleasure *as* a greater good for them. Though their love certainly can take this intellectualized form, it need not and in family relations usually does not. Children usually have just a simple emotional preference for their parents' good, one not based on any beliefs about its comparative value. But if that good is in fact from their point of view greater, their preferring it makes their attitudes proportionally divided and virtuous.

Whether this type of agent-relative extension is possible depends on how the recursive account understands its central properties of intrinsic goodness and evil (see chapter 1, section 1). If it holds, with Moore, that goodness is a simple, unanalyzable property, it is hard to see how it can allow agent-relativity, since it is hard to see how an object can have this kind of property from one point of view but not another. But the two alternative views of goodness do allow agent-relativity. They analyze intrinsic goodness as what it is appro-

---

11. Stocker, *Valuing Emotions,* p. 319; Stocker attributes this example to Frances Kamm.

priate to love for its own sake or as what people have reason to desire and pursue. And there is no reason why what is appropriate or rational for different people cannot be different, so that, for example, each person has more reason to care about the pleasure of people who stand in certain relations to her. These two views make goodness a complex property, and the particular complexity they involve allows relativity. Since I want to explore the effect of including agent-relative values in the recursive account, I will assume one of these views in what follows.[12]

An important application of these values is the one just discussed, to family and other personal relations. An account with partly agent-relative base-clauses can say that from each person's point of view, the pleasure, pain, and knowledge of her parents, spouse, and other family members have more value than those of strangers. Within the family there can be further gradations of value, with the pleasure of a father or a sister counting more than that of a grandfather or a second cousin. This makes it virtuous and proportionate to care more about some family members than about others, just as it is to care more about family in general than about strangers. A similar treatment can be extended to others with whom one has intimate relationships, such as friends, and even to members of larger groups, such as schools, professions, and nations. On a nationalist view, for example, the good of each person's fellow citizens counts more from his point of view than that of foreigners. When deciding political issues about, say, trade and immigration, he should give more weight to his co-nationals' interests, and he should likewise care more about those interests. Though having some impartial concern for people everywhere, he should have extra concern for members of his own national group.

This first application of agent-relativity enriches the explanation of the value of personal relationships given in chapter 2. There I argued that, given the recursive account, love and friendship involve not only base-level goods such as pleasure, mutual understanding, and shared achievements, but also the higher-level goods of desire for and pleasure in each other's goods and virtues for their own sakes. Now we can add that the partiality of these relationships, their involving more concern for loved ones than for strangers, is a fur-

---

12. Agent-relative values also require the looser view of intrinsic goodness, on which such goodness can depend on a state's relational properties. But I have already allowed this view in formulating the recursive account (see chapter 1, section 1).

ther aspect of their value. It is not just that we have to a higher degree toward friends and family attitudes that are equally good when directed at anyone, but that our special concern for our intimates is itself good, as responding appropriately to the special value their goods and virtues have from our point of view.

The virtues generated by this first type of agent-relativity can be gathered together under the heading of loyalty.[13] There is loyalty to family members or friends, loyalty to a school or profession, and patriotism, or loyalty to one's nation, and opposed to these are the vices of disloyalty and betrayal. Sometimes disloyalty stems from selfish motives, as when a person betrays a friend for money. Here her attitude would also count as vicious by agent-neutral standards, but there is an additional ground of condemnation if the friend was someone to whom she owed special concern; betraying a friend for money is worse than doing the same to a stranger. There are also cases of disloyalty from impartial motives, as when someone lets her father suffer harm to prevent an only slightly greater harm to a stranger or shows no more concern for her own nation than for others. These are the more distinctive vices of disloyalty that only agent-relative values let our account capture. Since loyalty is a virtue of proportion, there are contrary vices of caring too much about specially related individuals. In the family there is nepotism, or excessive concern for one's children; in the nation there are chauvinism and xenophobia. Since the value of an attitude depends, as always, on the value of its object, what is most virtuous is caring only as much more about family and co-nationals as the extended base-clauses make their goods from one's point of view more important.

Sometimes the objects of loyal attitudes are partly holistic. The members of a nation or culture, for example, typically care and think it important to care that it survive and flourish into the future; for example, many Quebecois view the survival of French culture in Quebec as a central political goal.[14] In so doing, they need not believe their culture's survival will be better for individual persons, in the sense of making their individual lives better. They can and should allow that their descendants will live just as well if, the culture in question having disappeared, they are raised as fully participating members of a different culture. But the members of a culture can still care about its survival if they value a holistic state of it: that

13. See Oldenquist, "Loyalties"; and Fletcher, *Loyalty.*
14. C. Taylor, *Multiculturalism and "The Politics of Recognition,"* p. 58.

it have members at many times in the future. They can likewise value other holistic states, such as that their culture achieve full self-expression through sovereignty or political statehood, that it flourish in the arts and sciences, and even that it become internationally powerful and dominate its neighbours. These holistic states are common objects of patriotic attitudes, which focus on them as much as on the goods of individual members. But they are also valued in a highly partial way. People care much more about their own culture's survival and flourishing than about that of other cultures, and they take this disproportionate concern to be an important part of loyalty to their culture. The recursive account can explain their view if it says that from each person's point of view, certain holistic states of his own culture have greater value and call for greater love than similar states of distant cultures. Holistic attitudes of this type seem less important in more intimate relationships such as those of the family, where the primary focus is the goods of individuals. But even here, a person can care that her family persist as a lineage into the future or succeed in ways not reducible to the success of its members. And wherever holistic concern is present, the virtues of loyalty have a dual focus, responding to two different agent-relative values. They involve caring more about the goods of a group's individual members than about the similar goods of non-members and also more about the group's holistic states. Their doing so is appropriate if, from the points of view of members, both these states have greater intrinsic value.[15]

In all their forms, the virtues of loyalty are a response to facts about the past. The members of a person's family, profession, and even nation are people with whom she has shared a history that is not shared with non-members. She has lived, worked, or shared a language and government with them as she has not with outsiders.[16] To ground demands of loyalty, a history must have a certain moral character. It must be a history of jointly doing good, either to each other or to outsiders, or of jointly suffering evil, but it cannot be one of jointly doing evil. Guards who together ran a Nazi labour camp should not on that basis care more about each other's good or want their association to persist into the future. If anything, they should now dissociate, to separate themselves from this aspect of their past.

---

15. On this dual focus of national loyalty, see my "Justification of National Partiality," pp. 144–48.

16. On the historical basis of loyalty, see Nozick, *Anarchy, State, and Utopia,* pp. 167–68; and Fletcher, *Loyalty,* chap. 1.

The moral quality of a shared history also determines how strong the resulting demands of loyalty are. Other things equal, a history that involved closer and more frequent interaction calls for more intense loyalty, or a stronger preference for those who participated in it. Also, other things equal, a history that was morally better or produced greater goods calls for greater loyalty. These two points explain why family loyalty is on most views the paradigm virtue of loyalty. Family members have both interacted intimately over a long period and produced enormous benefits for each other; think of those resulting from child rearing. They are therefore the people toward whom the most intense partiality is appropriate. In other groups, such as professions and nations, the degree of interaction has been less, but significant benefits have still been produced, such as the security that results when a society is governed by the rule of law. These groups' histories therefore still make significant demands of loyalty, if not as strong as those of families. And in groups where both the interaction and the good produced have been less, the partiality due to members is again less.[17]

This historical account of the basis of loyalty is not reductive. It does not explain the agent-relativity of familial and patriotic concern in non-agent-relative terms but assumes relativity, saying that each person should give preference to the good of those who participated *with her* in a certain history. But the account does unify the virtues of loyalty, showing how in each of them partiality is in the present an appropriate response to a shared history of a morally significant kind. This history gives states of participants in it greater value from each other's points of view, which in turn makes their preferring those states proportionate and virtuous.

The agent-relativities that ground the virtues of loyalty are reciprocal, with states of all participants in a history having greater value from all others' points of view. This befits the history's character as one of jointly producing goods or jointly suffering evils. But there can also be unilateral relativities based on unilateral histories. If one person has significantly and continuously benefited another who has not been able to reciprocate, an extended recursive account can say that the first person's states have greater value from the second person's point of view but not vice versa. This agent-relativity will then ground a unilateral virtue of gratitude, which involves the second person's caring specially about the pleasure and other goods of

17. See my "Justification of National Partiality," pp. 148–55.

the first. This virtue is not the restricted form of gratitude that gives a specific benefit a specific acknowledgment, such as a thank you or a reciprocal birthday present. It is a more encompassing virtue that gives continuing special concern to those who have provided continuing benefits, but it is again an agent-relative virtue based on a morally significant history.

A different application of agent-relativity concerns evils that resulted from a person's own agency. It makes pain, death, and other harms that he caused worse from his point of view than similar states for which he is not responsible. Imagine that a person causes a serious evil in a way that involves no moral failing on his part, as when, to borrow an example of Williams's, a truck driver kills a child who suddenly runs into the road. If the driver was driving safely, his action was not wrong and involved no vicious attitude, so he has no ground for guilt or shame. But he will surely feel deeply pained by the child's death—more so than by a similar death he did not cause. He will also feel pained by his action of killing the child, wishing intensely that he could somehow have avoided it. He will feel what Williams calls "agent-regret," regret based on the connection of a bad outcome to his agency, and many will find it morally vital for him to do so.[18]

The recursive account can explain the appropriateness of agent-regret if it extends its base-clauses to hold that evils a person causes are from his point of view worse. Then the recursion-clauses will imply that he should be more pained by these evils and also that he should be more pained by the actions that caused them. The instrumental clauses make it intrinsically good to hate what causes intrinsic evil, and intrinsically better to hate what causes greater evil. But then the same agent-relativity that makes the products of his agency intrinsically worse from his point of view makes that agency itself instrumentally worse, so he should feel more pained by actions of his that caused evil than by actions of others with identical results.

The same agent-relativity can explain distinctive features of the virtue of remorse. As Taylor emphasizes, remorse differs from shame and guilt in being focused not just on inner states such as a person's attitudes and feelings, but also and even primarily on his actions and their outer effects.[19] If I feel shame, I am pained by an

18. Williams, "Moral Luck," pp. 27–28. See also his *Shame and Necessity*, pp. 69–70; and Baron, "Remorse and Agent-Regret."
19. G. Taylor, *Pride, Shame, and Guilt*, pp. 97–107.

attitude of mine considered in itself. If I feel remorse, I am in addition and more centrally pained by what that attitude caused for others. This dual focus is captured to some extent by the original recursive account, which sees remorse as combining pain at one's own moral evil with a further pain at the evil it caused. But this treatment ignores the internal connection between the elements of remorse, the fact that we care as much as we do about the second evil because it resulted from our vice. The second agent-relativity remedies this lack, making an origin in our own agency a special ground for pain at evil in the world.

The same agent-relativity can also illuminate certain vices. In chapter 5, we discussed the value on balance of sadistic pleasure, such as a torturer's pleasure in his victim's pain. The original recursive account finds this pleasure evil in the same way as any pleasure in evil, and thus in the same way as a spectator's pleasure in the victim's pain. But I think many will say that however evil a spectator's pleasure at witnessing a torturing, the torturer's pleasure is even worse; this is reflected in our reserving the word "sadistic" for the latter pleasure. This view can be explained if the same pain is worse from the torturer's point of view than from anyone else's, because he caused it. Or consider the suggestion in chapter 6 that first-person rape fantasies, especially ones imagined from the inside, are worse than otherwise identical fantasies from a spectator's point of view. Part of the explanation can be, again, that first-person fantasies involve pleasure in evils that, because they originate in one's imagined agency, are from one's own point of view worse.

The recursive account could in principle endorse a similar agent-relativity about goods a person causes, so that pleasure, knowledge, and other benefits are better from his point of view when they result from his agency. But this parallel extension is not nearly so plausible. Imagine that a person causes some benefit accidentally, in a way that reflects no merit on his part. I see no reason why he should be specially pleased by this benefit, as against others he did not cause; such pleasure seems even morally suspect. If so, a plausible recursive account will apply this type of agent-relativity only to evils and not to goods, giving the former but not the latter greater value from a person's point of view when they result from his agency.

The most difficult issue about agent-relativity concerns goods and evils in a person's own life. How good from her point of view are her own pleasure, knowledge, and virtue, and how evil are her pain and vice? How much should she care about these states of herself as against similar states of other people?

Reflection on personal relationships may suggest that she should care most about her own states. The degree of value, from her point of view, of states of another person depends on how closely she has interacted with that other person, and to whom has she been closer than herself? If there is a continuum of intensity of appropriate concern running from strangers through friends to family members, she herself should be at the most intense end, so her own states count more from her point of view than those of anyone else.

A self-favouring agent-relativity of this kind may be plausible for one value: moral vice. I think many will find it appealing to hold that each person should care more about her own vices, working harder to prevent them and being more pained by their presence. She should feel more intense shame at her own malice or cowardice than regret at the similar failings of others, as is suggested by our reserving the term "shame" for such self-directed pain. The idea is not that she should care only about her own vice, as some have thought;[20] she should still have some concern for other people's. Imagine that she can help amend others' characters by working as a moral tutor or counsellor, but that doing so threatens to undermine her own character, either by diverting energy from her own self-improvement or, more seriously, by encouraging her in smugness or moral pride. If the resulting reductions in others' vice are sufficiently great, she should still accept this work, even considering the risks for herself, so others' vice still has weight against her own. It is just that, given the agent-relativity, the reductions in others' vice must be significantly and not just marginally greater to make this preference right.

But a similar self-favouring agent-relativity does not seem plausible for other values, starting with moral virtue. Taking more pleasure in one's own benevolence or courage seems disproportionate and an objectionable form of moral pride. The same holds for nonmoral values such as pleasure and pain. Several philosophers argue that the theory of right action should grant each person an agent-relative permission to attach some more weight to his own good, so he does not act wrongly if, for example, he pursues a lesser pleasure of his own rather than a somewhat greater pleasure of another. This agent-relative permission helps explain how supererogation is possible, since a person who does not use the permission but instead pursues another's somewhat greater good does more than his duty re-

20. See, e.g., Sidgwick, *The Methods of Ethics,* p. 11.

quires.[21] But however plausible this permission is in the theory of the right, I do not believe a parallel permission should be adopted in the theory of the moral good or of virtue. The attitudes of a person who acts as the agent-relative permission allows and who prefers his own, somewhat lesser pleasure are surely not as virtuous as those of someone who weighs others' pleasures impartially against his own. The first person is at least somewhat selfish, and even if his selfish action is permitted in the theory of right action, it still involves, if not a vice, then at least a shortfall in virtue. In fact, its involving a shortfall in virtue is needed to explain how supererogatory action, though not required, is morally preferable (see chapter 2, section 3). In the most plausible recursive account, it is still most virtuous to give as much weight to others' pleasure as to one's own, so what an agent-relative permission about the right allows is precisely action from less than the best motives.[22]

If anything seems plausible for values other than vice, it is an opposite, self-denying agent-relativity. Return to the example of the teacher who successfully develops knowledge in a student from a virtuous desire for the student's knowledge. The original recursive account says she should be most pleased by the knowledge she has produced but should also be pleased, if to a lesser degree, by her own virtue in pursuing it. This does seem an ideal combination of attitudes; nothing can be better than caring proportionally about one's virtue and its results. But now imagine that, though aware of her virtue, the teacher does not take any pleasure in it, concentrating all her delight on the student's knowledge. Instead of reserving some love for the virtue inside herself, she directs all her joy at that virtue's external object. In some conditions, this indifference to her own virtue could involve an objectionable form of self-abnegation, but in others it surely does not. In these conditions, which I will specify below, directing all one's love at goods outside the self seems no less good than reserving a portion for one's virtue. It is not that caring only about external goods is better than caring proportion-

---

21. Scheffler, *The Rejection of Consequentialism;* Davis, "Abortion and Self-Defense"; and chapter 1, section 3 here.

22. Is it inconsistent for judgments about the right and the morally good to diverge in this way? I do not believe it is. A theory of right action that includes the agent-relative permission already holds that an action it is permissible to perform can have less good consequences than some alternative. Why can it not likewise hold that the first action can issue from less good motives? In each case, the permissive claim about right action is partly independent of claims about the good.

ally about one's virtue; nothing is better than that. But it does seem that a person who does not delight in her virtue because she is focused entirely on goods outside her can have attitudes that are morally good to an equal extent. If so, the plausible agent-relative permission in the theory of virtue must be self-denying. It must imply that though a person can be ideally morally good while caring in the appropriately limited way about her virtue, she can be equally good while ignoring it.

A similar point applies to non-moral goods. As Slote notes, the commonsense theory of right action permits people to give not only more but also less weight to their own good, so that a person who pursues a lesser pleasure of another rather than a somewhat greater pleasure of his own does not act wrongly.[23] But this second permission does seem to have an intuitive parallel in the theory of the moral good. Though a person who prefers another's lesser pleasure can be objectionably self-abnegating, he need not be. In some conditions, which I will again specify below, his attitudes can be as virtuous as those of someone who divides his love impartially. His attitudes are not better, because nothing is better than impartiality, but they are also not less good.[24] To confirm this suggestion, consider the values in themselves of pleasure at one's own pleasure and pain at one's pain. The claim that these attitudes are virtuous and morally good is not nearly so compelling as a similar claim about attitudes to other people's pleasures and pains. I suspect many will say that if a person takes pleasure in his own pleasure, that is good as giving him an extra pleasure but not in any other way, and especially not as virtuous. If he is pained by his pain, that is only evil as pain and in no way good. This view can be explained by the self-denying agent-relativity just proposed. If pleasure in one's pleasure is optional in the way I have suggested, so that a person who lacks this pleasure need not lack any virtue, the only moral difference its presence makes may turn on its value as pleasure.

Something like this view is defended by Ross. He takes a strictly agent-neutral view both of the values of knowledge and virtue and of the moral duties to pursue them. But he denies that there is any duty to pursue one's own pleasure, and he also denies that there is any virtue concerned with one's pleasure. Virtue consists in loving knowledge and virtue in anyone and loving pleasure in others, but

---

23. Slote, *Common-Sense Morality and Consequentialism*, chap. 1.
24. For a similar view, see Kamm, "The Noble Warrior," pp. 247–48.

not in loving pleasure in oneself.[25] In *The Foundations of Ethics,* he grounds this asymmetry in a self-denying agent-relative claim about value. Whereas knowledge and virtue are good simply or agent-neutrally, he claims, what is good from each person's point of view is only other people's pleasure, and not his own. That is why the duty to promote what is good includes a duty to promote others' pleasure but not one's own, and why a recursive account of virtue makes a desire for others' pleasure a virtue, but not a desire for his own.[26]

But Ross's agent-relativity is too crude to capture the intuitive claims we want. If each person's pleasure is from her point of view never good, as Ross claims, then self-abnegation is not only not always but never a moral failing, since it involves indifference to something that is from her point of view always neutral. This is not what we want to say. We still want to hold that in some conditions, caring less about one's own pleasure is a shortfall in virtue and even a vice. Similarly, if each person's pleasure is for her never good, self-abnegation is not only as good as but always better than impartiality between oneself and others. Impartiality now involves caring as much about something neutral as about something good, which is disproportionate and a form of fetishism. This is again not what we want to say. We want impartiality, while no longer the uniquely best combination of attitudes, to remain as good as any other. The intuitive claims we want to capture are permissive, making self-abnegation in some forms an equally virtuous option. But Ross's agent-relativity makes self-abnegation mandatory and any other attitude a failing.[27]

If it is to capture the desired claims, a self-denying agent-relativity must be more complex. It must hold that each person's virtue and pleasure are always good from other people's point of view and are good from his point of view *except when* he is indifferent to them in a specified way. If he does love his virtue or pleasure for itself, it is good and an appropriate object of his love. The same holds if he

25. Ross, *The Right and the Good,* pp. 24–26, 134–35, 160.

26. Ross, *The Foundations of Ethics,* pp. 282–84. Ross understands the agent-neutral goodness of knowledge and virtue in a Moorean way, as involving a simple, unanalyzable property. Recognizing that this understanding excludes agent-relativity, he takes pleasure to be good only in a secondary way, one making each person's pleasure appropriate for others, but not for him, to love.

27. Ross's agent-relativity has similarly unacceptable implications in the theory of right action. As Stocker points out, it implies that someone who pursues a much greater pleasure of himself rather than a lesser pleasure of another always acts wrongly; see Stocker, "Agent and Other: Against Ethical Universalism," p. 208.

does not love it and does not satisfy certain conditions. But if he is indifferent to his virtue or pleasure and does satisfy those conditions, it is not from his point of view good, and his indifference to it is not a flaw. The desired agent-relativity is biconditional, making each person's virtue and pleasure neutral from his point of view if and only if he is indifferent to them in the right way.[28] It can therefore explain why impartiality and the favoured form of self-abnegation are equally virtuous, since each responds equally proportionally to the values that are present when it is. It can also explain why pleasure at one's pleasure and pain at one's pain do not seem virtuous, since their presence need not make a person's overall attitudes better. In both cases there are two equally good attitudes to a state of oneself, since the relevant states both have value when one cares about them but need not when one does not.

The acceptability of this proposal depends on how it specifies the conditions that make self-abnegation not a failing in virtue. Let us start with the easiest case. Imagine that a person who does not care about his own pleasure but does care about other people's has the following moral beliefs: that his pleasure, though not good from his point of view, is good from others' point of view, so they ought to desire and pursue it; that his pleasure, though not now good from his point of view, would be good from his point of view if he did care about it; and that others' pleasure would not be good from their point of view if, like him, they were indifferent to it in the right way. Surely in this case his self-abnegation involves no lack of self-respect or failure to value the self equally with others. His beliefs give his own pleasure the same moral status as everyone else's, and his lesser concern for that pleasure is recognized by him as a free choice he might equally well not have made.

Other cases raise more difficult questions. What if a person has only some of these moral beliefs—for example, if he believes that his pleasure is good from others' points of view but does not realize that it would be good from his own if he cared about it? We may find it hard to decide whether this type of self-abnegation is a failing. Or what if a person has no relevant moral beliefs, his self-abnegation taking an entirely emotional form? Simple emotional self-abnegation can in my view be consistent with ideal virtue if its con-

---

28. A more sophisticated agent-relativity will take account of degrees of love, saying that if a person loves his virtue or pleasure less than is appropriate for that of others, his virtue or pleasure has for him correspondingly less value. Obviously, his loving it more than is appropriate for others' cannot give it more value.

stituent attitudes mimic those that follow from the moral beliefs listed above. Imagine that a person who does not care about his own pleasure is pleased in a simply emotional way when others care about it and pained when they do not; imagine also that when he contemplates a world in which he does care about his pleasure, he is pleased both by his pleasure and by his caring about it, and that when he sees others indifferent to their own pleasure, he is not pained. If it is accompanied by these attitudes, simple emotional self-abnegation can, I think, be ideally morally good. Without them, however, as in most actual cases of simple emotional indifference to one's good, such self-abnegation is indeed a failing. The final case is of someone whose self-abnegation rests on a false moral belief—for example, that his pleasure, unlike anyone else's, has no value from anyone's point of view. The treatment of this case is the same as that of any other involving false moral belief. If the formation of the belief involved a vice such as self-hatred or indifference to one's own worth, then any attitude based on the belief likewise involves a vice. Since this is almost always the case, self-abnegation based on a false belief about the self's lack of worth is almost always a failing in virtue. It is just conceivable, however, that a belief of this kind could arise innocently, in which case intellectualized self-abnegation based on the belief could be consistent with ideal virtue.

There are, then, difficult questions about the exact conditions in which indifference to one's own pleasure or virtue can be fully virtuous. But at least one case is clear: where a person's moral beliefs give his own states the same status as other people's, so his self-abnegation involves no failure of self-respect. The biconditional agent-relativity needed to support this conclusion is somewhat complex, but the complexity is needed to capture the permissive claims that seem most plausible in this area. Only if each person's virtue and pleasure are in some circumstances good from his point of view and in others not can we explain why both his caring impartially about them and his being in the right way indifferent to them can be equally morally good.

The various agent-relative extensions of (BG) and (BE) are important. If the recursive account could use only agent-neutral base-level values, it would be committed to a strict impartialist view of virtue and would be unacceptable to those who emphasize partialist virtues such as loyalty, gratitude, and agent-regret. But if the account analyzes intrinsic goodness in either of two possible ways, it can affirm agent-relative goods and evils and on that basis accommodate partialist virtues. In fact, it can explain these virtues' status in the same way as other virtues', by saying they involve appropriate attitudes to what from a person's point of view are greater and lesser values.

3. *Non-Consequentialist Virtues*

To this point, I have developed the recursive account as a consequentialist one characterizing virtue and vice entirely by their relation to the central consequentialist properties of intrinsic goodness and evil. The account captures a surprisingly wide range of virtues and vices, but there is at least one virtue that falls outside its ambit.

Imagine that a person performs an action because he believes it is morally right or, having failed to perform this action, feels guilt at having acted wrongly. His *conscientiousness*, to use that term for love of right actions as right and hatred of wrong ones, seems intuitively to be an important virtue; persons motivated by it are on that basis morally good. But conscientiousness is directed at rightness and wrongness rather than at intrinsic goodness and evil. Its value therefore cannot be captured by the recursive account, which is in that respect incomplete.

This incompleteness would not arise if, as Moore held, rightness were analyzable in terms of goodness, so the right action is always by definition the one that produces the most good.[29] But few even among consequentialists now accept this view. It implies that someone who believes an action is right even though it does not maximize the good is not just morally mistaken but conceptually confused, which is surely not credible. Against this, most contemporary philosophers treat the belief that an action is right as distinct from the belief that it will produce the most good, which implies that the desire to do what is right is likewise distinct from any desire concerned with goodness.

If so, capturing the virtue of conscientiousness requires a non-consequentialist extension to the recursive account, one saying that loving what is right and hating what is wrong as right and wrong are, like loving good and hating evil, themselves intrinsically good. The two forms of conscientiousness, like the other virtues we have discussed, are morally appropriate to their intentional objects and therefore good. This final extension to the account no longer con-

---

29. Moore, *Principia Ethica*, pp. 18, 25, 146–47, 208; the view is used to deny distinct value to conscientiousness on p. 218.

cerns only the account's base- or lowest-level claims; it makes an additional claim about attitudes. This latter claim cannot itself be recursive, since the property it ascribes to conscientiousness— intrinsic goodness—is not the same as that had by the object of con-scientiousness. Instead, it requires a principle saying that love of what is right as right has the different property of intrinsic good-ness. Once this latter goodness is established, however, it is subject to recursive principles, so that if acting from a conscientious motive is good, so are desiring to act from that motive and being pleased by someone else's doing so. A plausible treatment of conscientiousness may be partly agent-relative, making it appropriate for each person to care more about his own acting wrongly than about other peo-ple's doing so. Just as our having the separate term "shame" suggests that each person should be more pained by his own moral vice, so the term "guilt" suggests that he should be more pained by his own wrongdoing. Each person, we may believe, has a special responsi-bility to ensure that *he* does not act wrongly, and he should feel specially pained when he does. This non-consequentialist agent-relativity may be combined with a consequentialist one to ground a specific form of the virtue of remorse. Just as we care more about evils resulting from our own failures of character, so we may care more about evils resulting from our own wrongful actions and may express that caring in the heightened regret characteristic of remorse.

How does the value of conscientiousness compare to that of other, recursive virtues? Ross holds that conscientiousness is the highest virtue, higher even than intellectualized love of the good,[30] but I see no reason for this view. If a person acts simultaneously from a desire to do what is right and a desire to produce the most good, believing the two coincide, his two motives seem to me of equal value. Each involves an intellectualized attitude to a moral property, and I see no reason to rank either above the other; loving the right as right and the good as good seem to have equal moral worth. If so, then given our claims in chapter 6, conscientiousness is also equal in value to a simple emotional desire for the most good. If conscien-tiousness has the same value as intellectualized love of the good, which in turn has the same value as emotional love, then there are three virtuous desires from which a person can act—to do what is right, to produce certain results because they are good, and to pro-duce those results apart from their goodness—and these desires are

---

30. Ross, *The Right and the Good*, pp. 158, 164–65.

roughly equally good. If we apply the asymptotic view to the three desires together, it will not matter how a person divides his motivation between them (see chapter 6, section 2). But if we take the values of increases in the intensity of each to diminish separately, the ideal will be an equal mixture of all three. The ideal consequentialist agent will be motivated by conscientiousness, intellectualized love of the good, and simple emotional love, and in roughly equal proportion.[31]

This view about the comparative value of conscientiousness implies that this virtue has greater value when greater goods are at stake. If the desire to act rightly is equal in value to the desire for the goods such action will produce, and the latter desire is better when greater goods will be produced, then the former desire must be better too. Some may find this claim objectionable, arguing that the motive of duty must have the same value in all circumstances. But is this so? Imagine that one person cares about acting rightly when great goods are at stake but is indifferent in trivial cases, whereas another has the opposite motivations. Surely the first person's conscientiousness is better, because it responds to more significant moral duties. So our comparative view does seem attractive on this point. The view also implies that conscientiousness has less value than the results it can produce. If the desire to act rightly is equal in value to the desire for certain goods, which by the comparative principle (CP) has less value than those goods, then the desire to act rightly must likewise have less value. This, too, seems correct. A teacher who develops knowledge in a student should be motivated more by a desire that the student acquire that knowledge than by a desire herself to act rightly; after the fact, she should be more pleased that her student learned than that she did her duty. Like all forms of virtue, conscientiousness has less value, and should be less an object of concern, than its (in this case indirect) intentional object.

Given a consequentialist theory, the desire to act rightly can only supplement the desire to produce the most good, at least for someone with true moral beliefs. But the scope for non-consequentialist virtue expands if we abandon the assumption that right actions must be identified by the goodness of their outcomes. A deontological theory can hold that some actions—for example, telling the

---

31. Another possibility is to apply the asymptotic view to conscientiousness and intellectualized love of the good together, and to simple emotional love separately. If the two applications are given equal weight, the resulting ideal is a roughly equal mixture of intellectualized motives, however divided, and simple emotion.

truth—can be right even when they will not produce the best outcome. An adherent of this morality may therefore sometimes find that his desires to act rightly and to promote the good conflict, the one directing him to tell the truth, the other to lie. If he is in fact to act rightly, his conscientious desire must be stronger than his consequentialist one, so that he cares more about avoiding the wrong of lying than about promoting what is good. And if the former desire is indeed stronger, a deontologically extended account of virtue can say that his combination of attitudes is morally best. In his particular circumstances, an action's being a truth-telling does more to make it right than its having less than the best outcome does to make it wrong. In caring more about telling the truth, therefore, he prefers what has greater moral importance and in that sense divides his love proportionally. The object of his greater concern is not itself an intrinsic good; it is a deontological ground of rightness. But it can be compared to intrinsic goods and in this case outweighs them, making his greater concern for it intrinsically better and his division of love most virtuous.

A deontological theory can recognize as many types of conflict between conscientiousness and the desire to promote the good as it contains non-consequentialist principles of right. If, in addition to truth-telling, such actions as promise-keeping, not killing, and not stealing can be right despite not producing the best outcome, then for each of these types of action there can be cases where the desire to act rightly is morally better than the desire for the greatest attainable goods and where an ideal deontological agent will not be motivated primarily by a concern for outcomes. Since conscientiousness is an intellectualized virtue, its further analysis parallels that of intellectualized love of the good. If a person's desire to perform an action involves a belief about its rightness that is both true and the result of serious reflection, his desire is clearly intrinsically good. The same holds if his belief is false but was arrived at innocently. But if his false belief resulted from self-deception to satisfy a vicious desire or reflects indifference to issues of right and wrong, then his superficially conscientious motivation has little or no value. This analysis helps to answer a common objection to conscientiousness, one based on examples of rigid adherence to clearly mistaken moral principles.[32] A person who follows his "conscience" by upholding

---

32. Nowell-Smith, *Ethics,* chap. 17, 18; and Bennett, "The Conscience of Huckleberry Finn."

the slave laws of a racist society is not being truly conscientious if what he should be doing is scrutinizing those laws and realizing they are wrong. In his situation, violating the laws out of sympathy with the victims of slavery may be not a derogation from conscientiousness but a step toward discovering what it really requires. In no credible theory is conscientiousness the only virtue. Someone motivated only by the desire to act rightly and never by compassion or similar emotions clearly lacks important virtues. And if the content of his conscientious desire reflects other vices, that desire is not even significantly good. But if his conscientiousness involves strong desires both to do and to know what is right, as in the best cases it does, it is a non-consequentialist virtue.

An extended account of virtue can supplement conscientiousness with further deontological virtues, ones that do not rest on beliefs about rightness and are therefore emotional rather than intellectualized. If it is intrinsically good to desire pleasure or knowledge without thinking it good, it can surely be likewise good to desire truth-telling or promise-keeping without thinking it right. Or, since deontological duties are often expressed negatively, as prohibitions, it can surely be good to be averse to lying and breaking promises without thinking them wrong. Recoiling from these actions from simple emotion can be good just as avoiding them for their moral properties is. Given the crucially agent-relative structure of deontological theories, these simply emotional virtues must also be agent-relative. Since a deontological view makes it wrong for a person to lie even to prevent more lies by other people, his aversion should be directed especially at his own lying, so that he is more pained by one lie of his own than by several lies of others, and likewise for his own promise-breaking, killing, and so on. His own violation of a prohibition has greater moral weight from his point of view, so his hatred of it should be stronger. If it takes this line, a deontologically extended account of virtue can expand its list of virtues to include one for every distinct ground of rightness that is independent of good outcomes. And if it calculates the values of the two types of deontological virtue separately, it can hold that an ideal deontological agent is motivated both by conscientiousness and by simple emotional aversions to wrong-making properties of actions, and in roughly equal proportion. Such an agent avoids lying both because it is wrong and because, apart from its wrongness, he is repelled by lying. It may again be a matter of indifference in which order the two types of virtue develop. Perhaps a person is first trained to be averse to lying and promise-breaking in a simply emotional way and only later comes to think of them as wrong; perhaps he first avoids them as wrong and only later develops the simpler revulsion. Either way, his end state is ideally virtuous if it combines intellectualized and emotional aversions to wrong actions in roughly equal proportion.

This concludes my exploration of possible extensions to the recursive account. It is not essential that they all be accepted; a reader may find some but not others attractive. But the extensions do underscore the flexibility of the general type of account being developed in this book and its capacity to accommodate a wide range of virtues and vices. The first two extensions stay within a consequentialist framework, identifying additional virtues by reference to additional goods and evils. In the first extension, these goods and evils are no longer single states of individuals but combinations of states valued as combinations; the resulting virtues include the various forms of holistic justice. The second extension adds goods and evils that are agent-relative, with greater value from some people's points of view than from others'; here the resulting virtues include loyalty, gratitude, and agent-regret. The third extension moves beyond consequentialism to recognize virtues based on attitudes to rightness and wrongness or to the deontological properties that ground them, but even this extension shares basic features of the recursive account and in that sense is modelled on it. It still identifies the virtues and vices as appropriate and inappropriate attitudes to morally important properties and still holds that they are good and evil on that basis. The properties in question are no longer just intrinsic goodness and evil, so the resulting theory is no longer fully recursive. But as in our initial recursive account, properties other than virtue are specified first, and virtue is defined as an appropriate response to them. Even after the abandonment of consequentialism, the basic approach to virtue and vice remains.

The central feature of this approach is its treating virtue and vice as derivative moral properties, ones involving a relation to other, more fundamental properties. Virtue and vice are intrinsically good and evil, since they are good and evil apart from their consequences, but their being so rests on an intentional relation to properties whose moral status is independent of and prior to that relation. This feature of the approach contrasts sharply with that of the dominant view of virtue in recent years, virtue ethics. Though many versions of virtue ethics have been proposed, they all agree in giving virtue a more central place among moral properties, so that, far from presupposing a prior identification of the good or right, virtue serves to identify them. I do not believe that virtue ethics in any of its variations gives an adequate account of virtue and vice or their place in moral thinking. With the recursive account now fully developed, and using it as background, I will now examine this rival approach.

8

Against Virtue Ethics

Contemporary virtue ethics traces its origins to Elizabeth Anscombe's 1958 article "Modern Moral Philosophy." Anscombe argued that since the concept of duty used in modern moral theories is unintelligible apart from belief in a divine lawgiver, philosophers should return to an Aristotelian ethics focused on concepts tied to the virtues and vices, such as those of the untruthful, the unchaste, and the unjust. It took some time for Anscombe's recommendation to have much effect, but by the 1980s a number of philosophers were defending ethical theories centred on the virtues and intended as a fundamental alternative to consequentialism and deontology. This movement now has sufficient strength that most current writing on virtue is done under the banner of virtue ethics, which in some quarters is viewed as a third main "method of ethics."[1]

Much of the impetus for the virtue ethics movement has come from the assumption that other moral theories cannot treat virtue as more than instrumentally good. I have tried to show that this assumption is false: a consequentialism that includes the recursive account can value virtue intrinsically, as can a deontology that extends the account in the way suggested in chapter 7. And once these alternatives are clearly in view, it becomes evident that virtue ethics does not adequately explain either the nature of virtue or its moral importance. To show this will take some time, since there are many strands in the virtue ethics movement and many features that have been taken to be distinctive of it.

---

1. See, e.g., Baron, Pettit, and Slote, *Three Methods of Ethics*.

1. *Virtue and Right Action*

It is often said that virtue ethics is distinguished by its account of moral rightness.[2] Whereas consequentialism identifies right actions by the goodness of their outcomes and deontology by their relation to principles of duty, virtue ethics derives rightness from virtue, so right actions are those standing in some specified relation to virtuous motives, character traits, or persons. This gives virtue the same centrality that goodness and duty have in other moral theories and makes for a distinctive approach to ethics.

This suggestion fits many prominent versions of virtue ethics, such as those of Rosalind Hursthouse and Michael Slote. But it does not fit others, such as Anscombe's or the one ascribed to many ancient ethicists by Julia Annas. There are in fact two possible structures for a virtue-ethical theory, which lead to different accounts of rightness and virtue while masking a deeper similarity. To approach the differences and the similarity, let us compare Anscombe's proposed theory with Hursthouse's.

Though Anscombe's theory uses concepts tied to the particular virtues, such as those of the untruthful and the unjust, it applies these concepts directly to actions, with no reference to motives or character traits. Thus, Anscombe says that despite having no adequate concept of a virtue, we can recognize immediately that securing the judicial execution of the innocent, not paying debts, and similar actions are unjust.[3] If anything, she understands a just person in part as one who is habitually disposed to avoid unjust actions,[4] so the identification runs from actions to character traits rather than vice versa. And a similar identification is possible using only the simpler moral concept of rightness. A theory structurally similar to Anscombe's can identify actions as right independently of virtue and define the different virtues as dispositions to act rightly in different domains.[5]

It is not that virtue plays no role in Anscombe's theory. She seems

2. Some virtue ethicists, such as Anscombe and Slote, take it to be an important feature of their view that it eschews specifically moral concepts in favour of more broadly ethical ones; others, such as Annas, argue that virtue ethics does use moral concepts. I will side with Annas and treat virtue ethics as a moral view, making moral claims.

3. Anscombe, "Modern Moral Philosophy," pp. 40–41.

4. Anscombe, "Modern Moral Philosophy," pp. 41–42.

5. This is essentially Annas's line; see *The Morality of Happiness,* pp. 9, 48–49, 108–15.

to think that although an action's being unjust is a fact just about it, it does not by itself give a person a reason to avoid the action. To do so it must be supplemented by some other fact, such as that a divine lawgiver forbids unjust actions[6] or, more relevantly for our concerns, that unjust actions detract from the agent's flourishing. Anscombe holds that the virtues as she understands them are traits a person needs to flourish or live well.[7] She also assumes an egoistic theory of normative reasons, according to which all of a person's reasons for action derive from his own good or flourishing. This is why, in her proposed theory, a person has reason to act justly: to flourish he needs the virtue of justice, which will dispose him to avoid unjust actions. His ultimate reason to pursue his own flourishing entails, through the relation of virtue to flourishing, a further reason to act justly. And a similar implication can hold if the virtues involve, more simply, dispositions to act rightly.[8]

As so understood, Anscombe's theory distinguishes sharply between what we can call morality and rationality. Morality concerns the status of actions as just, right, and so on; rationality concerns a person's reasons to perform such actions. Though the virtues play no role in Anscombe's account of morality, they are vital to her account of rationality. I will therefore call hers a *rationality* version of virtue ethics, since it uses virtue to establish not moral claims but only claims about what people have reason to do.

Hursthouse's theory contains the same elements as Anscombe's but arranged in a different way. It takes what Anscombe holds to be true of the virtues to define them, so they just are those traits a person needs to flourish or live well. It then uses the virtues as so defined to identify right actions as those standing in some specified relation to virtuous motives, traits, or persons. Add the egoistic assumption that all a person's reasons for action derive from his own flourishing, and it follows that every person has reason to act rightly. The conclusion is the same as in Anscombe's theory, as are the premises from which it is derived, but the derivation follows a different route.[9]

---

6. Anscombe, "Modern Moral Philosophy," p. 43.

7. Anscombe, "Modern Moral Philosophy," p. 43.

8. This again seems to be Annas's line. She does not think a person's practical deliberations are complete when he has identified an action as right. He must connect the action to his final good, which Annas calls his happiness but which she understands in much the same way as Anscombe understands flourishing. And the connection runs, again, through the claim that virtue is not just one but the prime constituent of his good (see *The Morality of Happiness*).

9. Hursthouse, "Virtue Theory and Abortion."

Hursthouse's theory reverses the structure of Anscombe's, defining the virtues independently of rightness and deriving rightness from virtue. It is what I will call a *morality* version of virtue ethics, one that does use virtue to establish moral claims. But this difference between the theories, however striking, is in fact consistent with a more fundamental similarity.

Despite their structural opposition, Anscombe's and Hursthouse's theories both use claims about the place of virtue in a person's flourishing or good to explain why he has reason to act rightly. Both therefore derive, if not rightness itself, then at least the rationality of caring about it from claims about virtue.[10] Both also face the same fundamental challenge: to justify the close connection they assert between a person's good and the actions conventionally judged to be right. The precise form of this challenge differs slightly for the two theories. Anscombe's must show how the virtues, understood as involving dispositions to act justly, courageously, and so on, are in fact essential to each person's good. Hursthouse's must show how the virtues, defined as essential to each person's good, include traits such as justice and courage. But the core of this challenge to the theories is essentially the same.

Nor is this similarity found only between theories that relate the virtues to flourishing: any virtue ethics can be stated in either a morality or a rationality form. Its morality version will identify virtue by some property F independent of virtue and rightness by relation to virtue; its rationality version will define the virtues as dispositions to do what is independently right while asserting that the virtues also have F. But both versions will ground the rationality of right action in its connection, via virtue, to the same property F.

Given this fundamental similarity, it would be tedious to discuss morality and rationality versions of virtue ethics separately. And since morality versions seem more prominent in the current virtue-ethics literature, it is to them that I will direct the greater part of my attention. Many of my criticisms of these theories will apply with slight modifications to rationality theories, and I will sometimes mention when this is so. But I will mostly discuss theories that do use virtue to derive moral claims. The remainder of this section will con-

---

10. Crisp argues that this grounding of moral reasons in virtue is what centrally distinguishes virtue ethics from other views ("Modern Moral Philosophy and the Virtues," pp. 6–7). This suggestion has the merit of including both morality and rationality theories in virtue ethics, but it excludes anti-theoretical views such as McDowell's (see section 4 of this chapter).

sider the attempt these theories make to identify right actions by reference to virtue.

There are three main ways this identification can proceed. One view, proposed by Slote, identifies right actions as those actually done from virtuous motives; a second, defended in the nineteenth century by James Martineau, says they are those done from the most virtuous motives a person has available to act from; a third, defended by Hursthouse, says they are those that might be done from virtuous motives, or those a virtuous person might perform.[11]

The first of these views identifies right actions by the absolute value of their actual motives. Thus, Slote says his agent-based virtue ethics "understands rightness in terms of good motivations and wrongness in terms of the having of bad motives."[12] But I do not find this particular formulation most attractive. Slote's type of view makes a cut on the continuum from supremely vicious to supremely virtuous motives such that only actions from motives above the cut are right. And there are several places where this cut can come.

A very undemanding version of this first view says that only actions from supremely vicious motives, such as supreme malice, are wrong, and all other actions are right. But this is obviously unacceptable: it implies that someone who causes another significant avoidable pain from significant but not supreme malice acts rightly. A similar objection applies to the version of the view suggested in Slote's remark, which makes the cut at the neutral point between virtuous and vicious motives. It implies that a person who gives someone in dire need minimal aid from barely minimal compassion when he could easily give greater aid acts rightly; that, too, is unacceptable. We could go to the other extreme and count only actions from supremely virtuous motives as right, but that would be too demanding. Slote and others suggest that virtue ethics goes naturally with a satisficing approach, one satisfied with what is reasonably good rather than always demanding what is best, and that approach is at-

---

11. As it happens, the three views can also be included in a technically consequentialist theory. This theory will first identify the virtues using the recursive account and then identify right actions by one of the three relations to them. While it still makes goodness its central property, it will not have the parallel structure of the theory discussed in this book, but a sequential structure in which virtue is related directly to goodness and rightness only indirectly, via virtue. Though I cannot argue the point here, I do not think this sequential theory is as true to the core ideas of consequentialism as one with a parallel structure and the more familiar account of rightness in terms of outcomes.

12. Slote, "Agent-Based Virtue Ethics," p. 241.

tractive here.[13] It leads to a version of Slote's view that makes actions right when done from reasonably virtuous motives, ones reasonably far up the scale of virtue, and wrong otherwise. Slote himself takes just this line elsewhere. Considering a theory that equates the supremely virtuous motive with universal benevolence, he says it should identify right actions as those done either from this motive or from some other reasonably close in value to it.[14] So I will assume a satisficing formulation as best for this first virtue-ethical view of rightness.

However it is formulated, this view has several problematic features. First, it implies that there cannot be purely conscientious action, action just from the motive of duty, by any person with only true beliefs about the ground of rightness and her own motives. If such a person believes an action of hers would be right, she must believe it would be done from some other motive that is reasonably virtuous and must therefore have that other motive. But surely action just from the motive of duty is not restricted to people suffering from some delusion.

Second, the view directs the attention of a person who wants to act rightly self-indulgently inward, at her own motives rather than at states of the world. To determine what is right, she must examine the desires her actions would spring from rather than their objective qualities or likely effects. This, too, is counterintuitive. Surely conscientiousness, even when only part of a person's motivation, need not be so unattractively self-absorbed.

Most important, Slote's view threatens to collapse the distinction between rightness and moral goodness, or between evaluations of actions just as actions and in light of their motives. We normally think an action can be wrong but done from good motives or right but done from bad ones—one can do the wrong thing for a right reason or the right thing for a wrong one. But Slote's view, as stated, denies both these possibilities.

The simplest case of wrong action from a good motive is where a person has false beliefs about his action. For example, he sees another in pain, believes a drug will relieve her pain, and administers it, but in fact the drug kills her. If he acts from a desire to relieve pain his action may be virtuous, but if its result is death many will say it is wrong. Slote's view can endorse this judgment if the formation

---

13. Slote, *From Morality to Virtue*, pp. 113, 127–29, 135; Swanton, "Satisficing and Virtue"; and Oakley, "Varieties of Virtue Ethics," pp. 143–44.
14. Slote, "Agent-Based Virtue Ethics," p. 254.

of the person's false belief involved thoughtlessness or some other vice of inattention, but if his error was innocent, as when he reasoned soundly from misleading evidence, it can deem even a horribly harmful action right. This may not disturb those who think rightness must be characterized subjectively, in a way that is relativized to the agent's beliefs or evidence. But the more common view is that rightness is at least partly objective, so it depends partly on an action's actual properties. This is the assumption behind the widespread belief that even innocently motivated killing can be wrong, and it is excluded by Slote's view.

Slote's view can be amended to avoid this implication. It can say that to be right an action must be done not only from virtuous motives, but also with all relevant true beliefs, where the second condition is objective. Or, to tie the new condition to virtue, the view can say that right actions must both be done from virtuous motives and conform to those motives, in the sense of actually having the properties for which they are chosen. If a person acts from a desire to produce good, his action must in fact produce good; if he acts from a desire not to mislead others, he must in fact not mislead. As so amended, Slote's view can allow actions to be morally good but wrong. They will be so when they meet the first condition of originating in a virtuous motive but not the second of conforming to that motive.

But no amendments can make Slote's view allow the converse case of action that is morally evil but right. This type of case is illustrated by an example of Sidgwick's in which a prosecutor tries to convict a guilty defendant but does so from malice.[15] If the prosecutor secures a deserved conviction, many will say he has acted rightly even though he has done so from a vicious motive. But Slote's view, by requiring actual virtuous motives, must deem the prosecutor's action wrong. Not only is this claim counterintuitive, but in making it the view can violate the widely accepted principle that "ought" implies "can," or that what is right for a person must be something he is capable of doing. Though people can control their actions, they cannot directly control their motives or produce virtuous desires in themselves from one moment to the next. If what is right for the prosecutor is to prosecute from a reasonably intense desire for justice or the social good, and he lacks those motives, then he cannot act as Slote's view says is right. Slote recognizes the possibility of this

---

15. Sidgwick, *The Methods of Ethics*, pp. 202–3.

objection and tries to answer it, saying a person with an evil motive can always refrain from acting on it.[16] But it is not enough, for someone to act rightly by Slote's lights, that she avoid acting on a particular forbidden motive; she must also act on a required one. This might always be possible if Slote's view required action only from some motive other than a supremely vicious one; it might usually be possible if it required only some motive above the neutral point on the scale of value. But the most attractive version of Slote's view requires motives higher up the scale, ones that are at least reasonably virtuous, and many people have no such motives available. For these people, the view's claims violate "'ought' implies 'can.'" Slote in effect acknowledges this difficulty in his discussion of Sidgwick's prosecutor. He says that if the prosecutor cannot prosecute from any motive other than malice, he acts wrongly if he prosecutes. But he adds that the prosecutor also acts wrongly if he does not prosecute, since he then acts from indifference to justice and the social good.[17] Whatever the prosecutor does he acts wrongly, and the action the satisficing version of Slote's view says is right—prosecuting from a desire for justice—is beyond his power. The principle that "ought" implies "can" is widely held to be essential to the theory of right action, and Slote's discussion suggests that he agrees. But any view that identifies rightness in terms of the absolute value of a person's actual motives, if stated in its most attractive form, violates the principle massively.

The second view, defended by Martineau, likewise considers an action's actual motives, but looks to their comparative rather than their absolute value. More specifically, it identifies right actions as those done from the most virtuous motives a person has available, whatever those motives are. Martineau himself combines this view with a rigid hierarchy of thirteen types of motive, running from vindictiveness and love of sensual pleasure at the bottom to compassion (second from the top) and reverence.[18] But it is surely possible for action from a motive of one of Martineau's lower types to be better than action from a motive of one of his higher types.[19] Thus, it can be better to pursue an immense pleasure for oneself than to re-

---

16. Slote, "Agent-Based Virtue Ethics," p. 244; see also Baron, Pettit, and Slote, *Three Methods of Ethics*, pp. 214–15.

17. Slote, "Agent-Based Virtue Ethics," p. 242.

18. Martineau, *Types of Ethical Theory*, vol. 2, p. 266.

19. Sidgwick, *The Methods of Ethics*, pp. 369–72, and *Lectures on the Ethics of T. H. Green, Mr. Herbert Spencer, and J. Martineau*, pp. 356–61.

lieve, from compassion, another's minor pain. So we should imagine a more flexible version of this view than Martineau's own, one evaluating motives or combinations of them individually rather than by types and identifying right actions as those done from the best such motives a person can act from.

This second view avoids the difficulty Slote's view faces about "'ought' implies 'can.'" If, as both Slote and Martineau assume, a person can always choose not to act on a given motive, she can always act on her best available motive and so act as Martineau's view deems right. But Martineau's view is like Slote's in denying the possibility of pure conscientiousness for people with only true beliefs and in directing the attention of those who want to act rightly inward at their own motives. More seriously, the view is like the first version of Slote's in being unacceptably undemanding. It, too, holds that an action that causes significant avoidable harm and is done from significant malice can be right; this will be so whenever the agent's other available motives were worse than significant malice. And this difficulty is only compounded by the possibility of false belief. To allow that a person who kills from an innocently false belief that a lethal drug will only relieve pain acts wrongly, Martineau's view may want to hold, as we imagined Slote's doing, that right actions must not only be done from certain motives but also conform to those motives. But then consider a person who acts on the least vicious of his many vicious motives, a desire to cause another significant harm. If his action actually causes harm it will be right, whereas if because of a false belief it does not, it will be wrong. Surely that is absurd. Martineau's view satisfies "'ought' implies 'can'" because it evaluates motives by a comparative rather than an absolute standard, but that very feature gives it other highly counterintuitive implications, such as that a significantly vicious action causing significant avoidable harm can be morally right.

The third virtue-ethical view identifies right actions not by reference to their actual motives, but hypothetically. As formulated by Hursthouse, it says that right actions are those that would issue from virtuous motives, or that a virtuous person would perform in the circumstances.[20] But "would" here is too strong, implying that there is always one action a virtuous person will prefer to all others. Especially if virtue ethics goes with a satisficing approach, it is more plau-

20. Hursthouse, "Virtue Theory and Abortion," p. 219, and "Normative Virtue Ethics," p. 22.

sible to allow for a plurality of right actions by identifying these as ones that *might* be done from virtuous motives or *might* be done by a virtuous person.[21]

One version of this view invokes an antitheoretical strand of virtue ethics, to be discussed in greater detail later. It says that right actions cannot be described any further than as those a virtuous person might perform, since the way this person chooses actions cannot be codified, involving as it does his entirely particularized perceptions of morally salient features of situations. This version will attract a common criticism of virtue ethics: that it cannot give practical guidance to people who are not virtuous.[22] Such people are given no rules or principles to follow; they are told only to act as a virtuous person might. This could be of some use if there were a virtuous person present of whom to ask advice, but often there is not. And even if a virtuous person is present, how can they recognize her? They cannot do so by seeing that she regularly acts rightly, since they have no independent grasp of what is right. When deciding how to act, the non-virtuous are left entirely at sea.

This objection does not apply to a second version of the view, which does describe right actions further. It gives a list of virtuous motives, such as justice, kindness, and charity, and says right actions are those that might issue from these motives. If the motives in question involve desires for actions with certain properties, the view's implications for action can be worked out by the non-virtuous. Hursthouse's view takes this form. She sometimes identifies virtuous desires using concepts like Anscombe's, so that people with the relevant virtues want to act justly, kindly, and charitably. At other times she connects these desires to certain ends, so that charity involves a concern for others' good. But whichever line she takes, her view can give practical guidance to the non-virtuous. It is in effect a hypothetical version of Slote's view. Like Slote's, Hursthouse's view starts with a list of virtues, and the lists can in principle be the same. Like Slote's, too, her view is most plausible if it identifies right actions by a relation to reasonably virtuous motives. The only difference is that whereas for Slote right action requires an actual relation to these motives, for Hursthouse it requires only a hypothetical relation.

Because it does not require actual virtuous motives, Hursthouse's view satisfies " 'ought' implies 'can' " and allows actions to be right

---

21. Zagzebski, *Virtues of the Mind,* pp. 233–35; and Kagan, *Normative Ethics,* p. 209.
22. Louden, "On Some Vices of Virtue Ethics"; and Schneewind, "The Misfortunes of Virtue."

but viciously motivated. It also allows pure conscientiousness on the part of the non-virtuous and does not direct the attention of those who want to act rightly self-indulgently inward. But the switch from actual to merely possible motives that brings these advantages creates other difficulties, starting with one about false belief.

Motives do not issue in actions by themselves; they need to be accompanied by beliefs, and they can lead to vastly different actions given different beliefs. So to have determinate implications, Hursthouse's view must specify not just the motives but also the beliefs from which its hypothetical actions spring. One possibility is that what is right for an agent is what a person with virtuous motives and that agent's beliefs might do in the situation, but this will not be attractive if the agent has false beliefs due to thoughtlessness or inattention. Another possibility is that the relevant beliefs are those a virtuous person would have in the situation, but two equally virtuous people can have very different beliefs. In addition, if a situation contains misleading evidence—for example, that a lethal drug will only relieve pain—the resulting view can count extremely harmful actions as right. The natural stipulation, it seems, is that actions are right when they might issue from virtuous motives and all relevant true beliefs, or, in the language used above, when they might issue from virtuous motives and conform to them. This seems to yield the best formulation of Hursthouse's view, one with determinate implications and no claim that seriously harmful actions can be right.

But this formulation raises a serious question about whether Hursthouse's view still gives a distinctively virtue-ethical account of rightness. Once the conformity condition is introduced, the original reference to virtuous motives plays no substantive role and can be dropped: that an action might be done from virtuous motives and would conform to them is true just in case the action would conform to those motives. So how does Hursthouse's view differ from one that evaluates actions just by their properties as actions, with no reference to motives? If one of Hursthouse's virtues involves a desire to produce good, then an action conforms to this virtue if it does produce good; if another involves a desire not to mislead, an action conforms if it does not mislead. So how is Hursthouse's view different from a standard deontology that counts actions as right when they simply produce good, do not mislead, and so on? Her view does give a distinctive grounding for its claims, identifying the right-making properties of actions by reference to virtuous motives, and I will discuss this grounding later. But its substantive judgments about action are identical to those of a theory that makes no reference to virtue. Note that this difficulty does not arise for Slote's and Martineau's views. Since they require actual motives of a certain kind, their judgments about actions, even given a conformity condition, remain distinctive. But when the virtuous motives used to identify rightness are only hypothetical, then a requirement of true belief, which is needed for acceptable implications, ends up doing all the work.

In addition, Hursthouse's view is ill suited for one of the main tasks facing her theory, which is to explain why people have reason to act rightly. Recall the general argument she shares with Anscombe: all of a person's reasons for action derive from his own flourishing, but since right actions relate to virtue, which is needed for flourishing, he has reason to act rightly. This argument might establish its conclusion if right actions required actual virtuous motives, but how can it do so if they require only hypothetical motives? How can the fact that an action might be done from motives a person does not have make it relevant to his flourishing or something he has any reason to do? Many writers distinguish between actions that are merely in accordance with virtue and actions that are genuinely virtuous, where the latter must be done from a virtuous motive and issue from a stable disposition.[23] Only given these further features do actions contribute to a person's flourishing. But this distinction raises very sharply the difficulty for Hursthouse's view. Often a non-virtuous person can act in accordance with virtue but cannot do so virtuously, since he lacks the requisite motives or dispositions. Hursthouse's view can describe his action as right, but what reason can it give him to perform it? If the action will not help him flourish, why should he care at all about it? Essentially the same difficulty arises for rationality theories, like Anscombe's, that use virtue only in their account of reasons. They, too, can say that an action by a non-virtuous person would be right, but if the action will not be virtuous and will not contribute to his flourishing, what reason can they give him to perform it?

An answer sometimes given is that although a non-virtuous person's acting rightly cannot help him flourish now, it can promote his flourishing in the future. Since the virtues are acquired by habituation, the best way for him to become virtuous is to start acting

---

23. For the original of these conditions, see Aristotle, *Nicomachean Ethics*, 1105a31–34.

now in ways that would express virtue and then develop the requisite motives through that pattern of action.[24] But often virtuous motives will not result from a person's acting rightly now. His character may be so set in vicious lines that no virtuous reform of it is possible. What reason do Hursthouse's and Anscombe's views then give him to act rightly? And even if reform of one's character is always in principle possible, a person may lack the requisite time. Imagine that it takes a year of habituation in the relevant actions for a given virtuous motive to appear and another year for that motive to settle into a stable disposition. A person may have a disease that will kill him in eighteen or even six months. So why should he act rightly now?

Nor does this difficulty arise only within theories that connect the virtues to the agent's flourishing. Consider the different version of virtue ethics that identifies the virtues as character traits with an aretaic property of admirability.[25] It can give agents reason to perform right actions if those actions are connected to the virtues in a way that makes them, too, admirable. But how can it do this if right actions are merely ones that might be done from virtuous motives? How can a relation to non-actual admirable motives make an action actually admirable? It is therefore no surprise that Slote, the principal defender of this version of virtue ethics, identifies right actions as ones actually done from virtuous motives, since then actions can inherit admirability from their motives. But the feature of his view that brings this advantage creates the different difficulty of violating "'ought' implies 'can.'"[26]

There are three ways of deriving rightness from virtue, but each faces serious difficulties. Slote's view violates "'ought' implies 'can,'" Martineau's can make seriously harmful actions right, and Hursthouse's gives non-virtuous agents no reason to act rightly. And the last difficulty arises equally for rationality theories that do not derive rightness from virtue: they, too, cannot connect right actions to the reason-giving force of virtue when the actions will not be virtuous.

---

24. See, e.g., Annas, *The Morality of Happiness,* pp. 56–57.
25. Slote, *From Morality to Virtue.*
26. Both Hursthouse's and Slote's views can give non-virtuous persons some reason to choose among available actions, by analogy with Martineau's view. They can say that if acting from some motives will leave a person less far from flourishing or be less deplorable (Slote's opposite of "admirable"), he has reason to prefer acting from these motives. But this reason is detached from the views' claims about rightness and does not allow the preferred actions to be called right.

2. Accounts of Virtue

Alongside its account of moral rightness, a virtue-ethical theory must give an account of what virtue is. Rationality theorists define the virtues in part as dispositions to act rightly, but morality theorists cannot follow this line. They need an account of virtue that is independent of rightness, so that rightness can be derived from virtue. The two principal accounts they defend have already been mentioned: one defines the virtues by reference to flourishing, the other by an aretaic property of admirability.

The first, or *flourishing*, account, defended most explicitly by Hursthouse, defines the virtues as those traits a person needs to flourish or live well and the vices as traits destructive of flourishing.[27] This account is usually combined with a virtue-ethical view of rightness of the kind just discussed, in which case it presupposes an egoistic theory of normative reasons whereby all a person's reasons for action derive from his flourishing. The resulting virtue-ethical theory need not be egoistic in its substantive claims about action; it can tell people to promote others' pleasure and knowledge even at the expense of their own. Nor need it be egoistic about motivation: it can say that to act virtuously, they must care about others' pleasure or knowledge for its own sake. But it is what I will call foundationally egoistic, insisting that their reasons to act and be motivated in these ways derive ultimately from their own flourishing. This foundational egoism is not implicit just in the claim that the virtues contribute to the agent's good; the recursive account also makes this claim. But it seems presupposed in the combination of a virtue-ethical view of rightness and the strong claim that the virtues are *needed for* or *essential to* flourishing. Without this claim, a foundationally egoistic theory could not hold that people always have most reason to act rightly. Though acting rightly might most promote their virtue, which is one element of their flourishing, its doing so could be outweighed by effects on other elements of their flourishing. But if the virtues alone are necessary for flourishing and in that sense have priority over other elements, right action will always most promote the agent's good. Since its wording so clearly fits the needs of an egoistic theory, I will associate the flourishing account with foundational egoism.[28]

27. Hursthouse, "Virtue Theory and Abortion," p. 219.
28. In *The Morality of Happiness*, Annas denies that theories focused on a final good of flourishing or happiness should be called egoistic, since they are not "self-centred in their content" (pp. 225–26). But she allows that they are "formally self-

Despite its prominence in the virtue ethics literature, the flourishing account does not yield a moral theory where virtue is the central property. Virtue may have explanatory priority over rightness, but it is itself explained in terms of flourishing. This raises the question of how distinctively virtue-ethical a theory is whose central explanatory property is in fact flourishing. The answer depends on how the theory understands flourishing and the way the virtues contribute to it.

One possibility is that a flourishing life is just an intrinsically good life in the consequentialist sense, one that is desirable apart from its consequences. Since this understanding makes a flourishing-based virtue ethics share its central property with consequentialism, I suspect many defenders of the flourishing account will reject it. They will say a person's flourishing is not just a good state of affairs but good *for her*, constituting her benefit or what some call her well-being.[29] But I do not see how this proposal makes a substantial difference. A person's achieving what is good for her can also be good in the consequentialist sense, and surely is so in this case. Recall the views of Brentano, Sidgwick, and Kagan, which analyze the good as what it is appropriate for a person to desire or pursue, or what she has reason to desire and pursue (see chapter 1, section 1). Surely the property of flourishing that defines the virtues meets these conditions. If so, a flourishing-based virtue ethics is not distinctive in its central property.[30]

This ethics would not be at all distinctive if it took the virtues to contribute causally to flourishing, as productive means to a separately existing state of flourishing.[31] But this is not the usual view.

---

centered," which I take to mean that they connect all of a person's reasons for action to his own flourishing. Assuming his flourishing is a state of him, this makes the theories egoistic in my foundational sense.

29. For a recent discussion of well-being, see Sumner, *Welfare, Happiness, and Ethics.*

30. To distinguish flourishing-based virtue ethics from consequentialism, Gary Watson proposes that it identify the virtues not by reference to a good human life or, indeed, to any state of affairs, but as those traits necessary for someone to be a good human being ("On the Primacy of Character"). But why does being a good human being have this moral importance while being a good mammal or a good robber does not? Surely it is because someone's being a good human being is a good state of affairs, while his being a good mammal or robber is not. But then we are back with the consequentialist property of goodness.

31. This causal relation has to be intended when the virtues are said to contribute to the good not just of the agent, but either of him or of other people (Foot, "Virtues and Vices," pp. 164–65; and Wallace, *Virtues and Vices,* p. 10). But

Most versions of the flourishing account hold that the virtues contribute to flourishing as constituents, or by instantiating it in particular facets of a person's life; rather than produce flourishing, they embody it in themselves. And this does lead to a reasonably distinctive moral view. Though the virtues are defined by relation to something good, the relation is very different from that in the recursive account, and right actions also relate differently to goodness. Rather than having goodness in their outcome, they embody it by expressing the virtues that themselves embody flourishing. If the virtues instantiate a person's good, they do have a distinctively important if not quite foundational role.

Since both flourishing and virtue admit of degrees, the flourishing account can be formulated in weaker and stronger ways. A very weak version says that to flourish to the highest degree, a person need only be virtuous to some minimal degree—say, any degree above zero; a very strong version says that to flourish even minimally, he must be virtuous to the highest degree. But I think most defenders of the account intend a formulation intermediate between these two: to flourish to a reasonable degree, which is not the highest but sufficient for a person to count simply as flourishing, he must be virtuous to a reasonable degree. This formulation builds satisficing ideas into the flourishing account and connects it to a satisficing view of moral reasons. If what a person has strong or mandatory reason to pursue is just a reasonable level of flourishing—and if not, why use that level to define the virtues?—then what he has mandatory reason to perform are only actions that express reasonable virtue. Once he is acting reasonably justly or courageously, he is not required to act more justly or courageously. At the same time, I will assume that what is needed for reasonable flourishing is a reasonable exercise of each virtue rather than, more weakly, just some reasonable number of them. The latter formulation would imply that someone who is already exercising enough other virtues is not required to act even minimally justly or courageously. Since I assume virtue ethicists want to require some exercise of each virtue, I will assume they require each for reasonable flourishing.

An important distinction is between versions of the account with

---

then the resulting theory looks very much like an indirect version of consequentialism or some other familiar theory. A causal relation also seems intended in MacIntyre's definition of the virtues as traits that enable us to achieve "goods internal to practices" *(After Virtue,* p. 178).

substantive conceptions of flourishing and those with merely formal ones. A *substantive* conception equates flourishing with some determinate state *F* of people or their lives, where both the nature and the goodness of *F* are understood independently of the virtues. In saying the virtues are necessary for flourishing, the resulting account says they are necessary for *F* and, more specifically, instantiate it; the account first gives content to flourishing and then uses that content to define virtue. A merely *formal* conception, by contrast, does not equate flourishing with any independent good *F* but only with the general idea of the human good, whatever its content. Here the resulting account does not say that the virtues instantiate some more fundamental good, but only that they are constituents of a good life, or in themselves and underivatively good: it uses virtue to give content to flourishing. A merely formal account must still understand flourishing as constituting the agent's own good, as making his life go well regardless of its effects on others. It cannot so empty the concept of content that it consists just in a person's acting on all the reasons that apply to him, among which are underivative reasons to benefit others; his flourishing must still be an intrinsically desirable state of him.[32] Subject to this constraint, however, a merely formal conception builds no substantive content into its initial concept of flourishing.

Of these two versions of the account, the substantive one is more philosophically ambitious, because it attempts more of the explanatory tasks we expect of an account of virtue. If it can be successfully worked out, it will use its one fundamental good *F* to explain simultaneously what unifies the virtues, what makes them good, and what distinguishes them from other goods that are not virtues. But there are formidable obstacles facing this account. It must find some independently good state *F* that is instantiated by an intuitively plausible list of individual virtues, including benevolence, courage, and so on, and is instantiated by them as virtues, or for the properties that make them such. If benevolent actions aim at another's good, for example, they must instantiate *F* as having that aim and not for some other property. The account must also yield plausible judgments about degrees of virtue. Virtue ethicists who deny the unity of the virtues hold that when virtues conflict, what is right is what issues from or conforms to the most virtuous motive. Thus, if saving someone's life means forgoing some healthy exercise, benevolence

---

32. McKerlie, "Aristotle and Egoism," pp. 532–33.

takes priority over temperance and the saving is right. To yield this conclusion, the flourishing account must show that in this case, acting benevolently instantiates F to a higher degree than acting temperately, and likewise in all similar conflicts. Finally, the account must justify the priority it gives virtue over other elements of flourishing by showing that F is not instantiated by other states of persons or is instantiated by them only in a secondary way.

I find it most unlikely that there is any state F that meets all these conditions. To show this decisively would require an examination of all possible substantive views of flourishing, which is not possible here. But we can assess one view that has been prominent in the virtue-ethics literature, based on one interpretation of Aristotle's famous "function argument."[33] This view says that human flourishing consists at bottom in the development of properties fundamental to human nature. More specifically, it says that since rationality is fundamental to human nature, flourishing consists in the development of rationality and includes the virtues because they instantiate rationality. The virtues exercise practical reason in different domains of action and are therefore essential to a flourishing life.

This view certainly has the right structure for a substantive flourishing account, since its fundamental goods of rationality and developing human nature can be both grasped independently of virtue and instantiated by virtue. But if the view is serious about appealing to human nature, it must be serious about the constraints this project involves.

On the most plausible view, the properties fundamental to human nature are those essential to human beings or some subset thereof, such as the properties essential to human beings and conditioned on their being living things.[34] And essential properties are in part ones that play a central role in the explanation of humans' other properties. This requires a certain generality of these properties. Even if a given essential property does not explain all human behaviour, it must explain at least a large portion of that behaviour. It cannot be just an arbitrarily restricted version of some more generally explanatory property.

By these criteria rationality is a strong candidate for a human essential property, since it is central to any explanation of why a per-

---

33. Aristotle, *Nicomachean Ethics,* 1097b23–1098a17.
34. The discussion of the human-nature view that follows draws on my *Perfectionism,* chaps. 1–4.

son has a belief or performs an intentional action. But then rationality must be understood in a suitably general way, one that enables it to explain beliefs about all subject matters and actions with all types of goals. This raises an immediate difficulty for the substantive account. Virtuous actions comprise only a subset of human actions, distinguished, as morally neutral and vicious actions are, by a particular type of goal. And why should a property that explains all actions be uniquely or even specially present in this subset?

It is not that an attractive account of rationality as a human essential property cannot be developed. It can, using formal criteria such as those used in chapter 1 to specify knowledge and achievement as base-level goods. The resulting account says that beliefs instantiate theoretical rationality to a higher degree when they are better justified by evidence, have contents that extend further across times and persons, and are arranged in more complex explanatory hierarchies. It likewise says that actions express practical rationality to a higher degree when they involve better-justified beliefs that they will achieve their goals and when their goals are more extended and arranged in more complex means-end hierarchies. Something like these criteria are used in some versions of the substantive flourishing account. Thus, T. H. Irwin both ascribes to Aristotle and defends a human-nature view focused on practical rationality as an essential property of human beings, and he connects this rationality to other-regarding virtues such as friendship and justice by saying they "extend" a person's exercise of practical rationality and, in particular, extend "his practical reason and deliberation beyond his own life and activities."[35] But formal criteria such as extent, however attractive in other respects, do not have the tight connection to virtue required by the flourishing account.

First, even when these criteria do value virtuous actions, they do not value them as virtuous. Perhaps actions aimed at another's good always extend the agent's rationality, but valuing them for the second property is not the same as valuing them for the first.[36] Second, the criteria do not successfully distinguish virtuous actions from neutral and even vicious ones; playing chess and torturing can also extend a person's goals and involve complex means-end reasoning. Because of this, the criteria do not come close to yielding the claims

35. Irwin, *Aristotle's First Principles*, p. 401; see also pp. 394–95, 405–6, 409–10, 415, 431, 433.
36. McKerlie, "Aristotle and Egoism," p. 539.

about degrees and priority that the flourishing account needs. Imagine that a person can either save another's life or continue with a theoretical activity such as scientific research. Given only formal criteria of rationality, why should the practical rationality involved in saving a life always contribute more to her flourishing than the theoretical rationality of the research? Or imagine that saving a life will distract her from some other complex and challenging but not virtuous practical activity such as chess or torturing. Why should the rationality of the saving always be greater? These difficulties seem insuperable if the rationality the virtues are supposed to instantiate has to explain all beliefs and actions. The generality required for the second task precludes any special relation to virtue.

It may be objected that the concept of practical rationality used in the substantive account is not a purely formal one but involves reasoning about, identifying, and successfully pursuing what is good.[37] As truth is the proper aim of belief, so goodness is the proper aim of desire, and practical rationality is directed to this aim. As so directed, it is instantiated especially by virtue.

This proposal in effect abandons the appeal to human nature implicit in much talk of flourishing, since it is not true that reasoning about the good figures in all human action. (As I argued in chapter 6, not all desires are for objects thought of as good.) The proposal also does nothing to show why virtuous actions always contribute more to the agent's flourishing than exercises of theoretical rationality such as research, and it creates new difficulties with its reference to independent goods that practical rationality reasons about.

A first question is whose goods these are—just the agent's, or all people's? If a flourishing-based virtue ethics is foundationally egoistic, it seems natural to assume that the practical rationality it invokes reasons only about goods in the agent's own life. But then the account cannot justify other-regarding virtues such as benevolence and justice, which aim at other people's goods. (It will not do to say that among the goods in his own life that an agent reasons about are benevolence and justice, since that abandons the attempt to derive the virtues from rationality.) So perhaps the goods a person reasons about include the goods of others. But then a second question arises, of why these goods do not themselves generate reasons for action. If an action will save another's life, why does that not by itself

---

37. Irwin might press this alternative understanding of practical rationality; see *Aristotle's First Principles,* chap. 15.

give a person reason to perform it, without needing to be supplemented by the fact that the action will involve correct practical reasoning on his part and so contribute to his flourishing? If it allowed these other reasons, a flourishing-based theory would have a structure very like that of a consequentialism including the recursive account. It would identify the virtues by a relation to the good—now that of reasoning correctly about rather than having appropriate attitudes to it—and it would likewise derive reasons for action from the good. It would contain parallel derivations of virtue and of moral reasons, but no derivation giving virtue pride of place. This parallel structure seems most appropriate given the clearly secondary role reasoning plays in the proposed theory. Imagine that a person can give either a small good to one person or a great good to another. If his practical reasoning tells him to prefer the second good, it is because that good is greater; the claim about the good determines the content of correct reasoning rather than vice versa. And if that is so, it seems best to derive moral reasons directly from the good, with the value of a person's practical reasoning giving him at most an additional reason to perform an action that is already on other grounds best (see chapter 2, section 2). To summarize: the substantive flourishing account offers to derive virtue and moral reasons from an ideal of rationality as part of a flourishing life. But if the rationality it appeals to involves reasoning about other goods, then there are goods independent of rationality, and those goods inevitably determine the content of reasons to act. Even if an acceptable theory can be built around the account, it is not one focused distinctively on virtue.

These difficulties for the substantive account suggest that the defensible version of the flourishing account is the merely formal one. It equates flourishing only with the general idea of a good life, so in saying the virtues are constituents of flourishing, it means only that they are in themselves and underivatively good.[38] Unlike the substantive account, this formal one can easily yield a plausible list of individual virtues. It can simply state that benevolence, courage, and the like are in themselves good, and good for what makes them virtues. It can likewise simply state the desired claims about degrees, for example, that benevolently saving a life is better than temper-

---

38. The clearest statement that the central concept in flourishing-based virtue ethics is merely formal is that of Annas *(The Morality of Happiness,* pp. 9, 44–46, 71, 129, 322–23, 331, 426, 453). But she does not use this concept to define the virtues, preferring a theory with a rationality structure like Anscombe's.

ately exercising, and that the virtues have priority over other goods. But these advantages come at the cost of entirely abandoning the substantive account's explanatory ambitions. To the question of what unifies the virtues, a merely formal account gives no answer; they are simply the items on a list of underivative goods. The account likewise says nothing about what makes the virtues good or gives them priority. Its claims on all these topics are presented as underivative ones for which no deeper explanation is possible.

These explanatory failings are not a decisive objection to the formal account, since every moral theory must make some underivative claims. But it is not it very plausible for these claims to concern the individual virtues. The immediacy with which we recognize traits such as benevolence and courage as virtues suggests that they share some unifying feature; the popularity of substantive accounts of flourishing also attests to this fact. The formal account's failings are especially troubling when there are successful explanations of virtue available, namely those given by the recursive account. This account unifies the virtues as involving attitudes to other goods and evils and shows how, in a recursive structure, that both makes them good and distinguishes them from other goods. When there is a theory that completes these explanatory tasks, the formal account's refusal even to attempt them is a serious mark against it.

There is an even graver difficulty facing this account. It is at least making a plausible claim when it states that benevolence, courage, and so on are good, but it must also give these virtues priority over other goods, by stating that they are uniquely necessary for flourishing. Theorists who connect the virtues to flourishing usually recognize such other goods. They allow that if a virtuous person enjoys pleasure and has knowledge, that makes his life better; if he suffers pain, that makes it worse. But they insist that the contribution these states make to flourishing is secondary to that of virtue. As Anscombe puts it, even if a person "flourishes less, or not at all, in inessentials by avoiding injustice, his life is spoiled in essentials by not avoiding injustice."[39] Any flourishing account, whether formal or substantive, needs this type of priority claim if it is to distinguish the virtues from other goods and also to yield the right claims about reasons. If a foundationally egoistic theory including the account is to imply that a person always has most reason to act rightly, even when doing so will cost him other goods such as pleasure, it must

39. Anscombe, "Modern Moral Philosophy," p. 43.

say that virtue always contributes more to his flourishing. The claim is needed for the same reason in a rationality theory such as Anscombe's that connects the virtues to flourishing only in its account of reasons. A further difficulty for all these theories is that the priority claim they require seems obviously false.

On the simplest reading, this claim gives virtue lexical priority over other goods, so that virtue is infinitely more valuable than pleasure, knowledge, and other secondary constituents of flourishing.[40] As we saw in chapter 5, however, this lexical view has utterly implausible consequences. It implies that a virtuous person who suffers excruciating agony has an overwhelmingly good life, one with only an infinitesimally small element of evil, and that if he were slightly less virtuous but enjoyed ecstasy his life would be overwhelmingly worse. This last implication may not follow in all cases if what has infinite priority is only the reasonable virtue needed for reasonable flourishing. But imagine one life just above the reasonable level but filled with agony and another life just below but ecstatic; the lexical view says the first life is better. And of any two lives below the reasonable level, it says the more virtuous is the better, no matter how little they differ in virtue and how vastly in pleasure or pain. If these claims are read as they must be, as claims about what makes a person's own life best, they are utterly unacceptable.

There is another reading of the priority claim that avoids some of these implications. It allows that when a person both is virtuous and has pleasure or knowledge, the pleasure or knowledge may contribute more to his flourishing. But it still gives virtue priority over other goods because it makes virtue a condition of those goods' having worth. Only when a person is reasonably virtuous, this view says, do states such as pleasure contribute to his flourishing; otherwise they do not. Virtue therefore contributes in two ways to his flourishing: as a constituent and as a condition of other states' being constituents. This implies, as desired, that a person can never have reason to pursue other states at the expense of reasonable virtue. If he does prefer those states, they will not be goods in him.[41]

This conditionality view does not claim only that vicious states such as malicious pleasures lack value as pleasures. It holds that innocent and even virtuous pleasures lack value as pleasures if they

---

40. Annas discusses a view that, though not quite lexical, is close to being so in *The Morality of Happiness*, pp. 122–23, 393–94.

41. This conditionality view is attributed to Aristotle by Broadie in "Aristotle's Elusive *Summum Bonum.*"

are not those of a reasonably virtuous person, as do innocent knowledge and achievement. These claims may seem plausible when applied to vicious people, since in their lives pleasure and knowledge are the opposite of deserved, but even here there is a difficulty. As several philosophers point out, it is hard to explain what is objectionable about a vicious person's enjoying pleasure if that pleasure is not good or a benefit to him.[42] And there are even greater difficulties in the view's claims about virtuous people. If a person who is somewhat but not quite reasonably virtuous enjoys an innocent pleasure such as suntanning or a virtuous one such as pleasure in another's pleasure, the conditionality view says his pleasure is valueless as pleasure. But this is highly counterintuitive. The person himself is virtuous; in the second case his pleasure, too, is virtuous. Why, then, is his pleasure not good as pleasure? The conditionality view could avoid these implications by setting the level of reasonable virtue sufficiently low, so that even a somewhat virtuous person exceeds it. But here the view faces a dilemma. It is needed in part to explain why, given foundational egoism, people have more reason to act rightly than to pursue other goods such as pleasure. It can plausibly allow that when people are sufficiently virtuous this priority lapses, so they are no longer required to act more virtuously. But the lapse must occur at a fairly high level of virtue if the resulting theory is to affirm sufficiently strong moral reasons. And then the level of reasonable virtue is set too high for the conditionality view to be plausible as a view about each person's good.[43]

This is, in fact, just one instance of a general dilemma for any theory that connects the virtues to flourishing, whether it understands flourishing substantively or formally and whether it takes a morality or a rationality form. To give people sufficiently strong reason to act rightly, the theory must make claims about the centrality

---

42. Lemos, *Intrinsic Value,* pp. 43–44; Slote, "The Virtue in Self-Interest," pp. 273–74; and Audi, "Intrinsic Value and Moral Obligation," p. 140.

43. In "The Virtue in Self-Interest," Slote defends a weaker conditionality view, one saying that states other than virtue are good only when accompanied by a particular virtue appropriate to them. Thus, pleasure is good only when accompanied by moderation, knowledge only when accompanied by courage, and so on (pp. 274–83). This weaker view still seems to me exaggerated. Pleasure without moderation may be less good than pleasure with moderation, but surely it is still good to some degree. More important, Slote's view is too weak to serve the flourishing account's needs. As he notes (p. 275), it allows that a pleasure in an overwhelmingly vicious person's life can be good so long as it is accompanied by the one virtue of moderation. The view therefore by no means guarantees that a person always has more reason to act rightly than to pursue his own pleasure.

of virtue in each person's good that are not plausible as claims about his good. As we saw in chapter 5, the plausible view is that virtue is a lesser good, with always less value than its object. And the dilemma is even more pressing if the theory understands a person's flourishing not just as good but as good *for him*, or as constituting his well-being. However implausible it is that a life of virtue and intense pain is intrinsically good, it is even more implausible that it is good *for* the person who lives it.[44] To have a distinctive central property, a flourishing-based virtue ethics must understand flourishing as constituting a person's own good, rather than just the state in which he acts on all the reasons that apply to him. But then it can make plausible claims about those reasons only by making implausible claims about the place of virtue in his flourishing.

The various difficulties facing the flourishing account all stem from its association with foundational egoism, but there appears to be no such association in the second main virtue-ethical account of virtue. Defended primarily by Slote, this second account identifies the virtues as those traits of character with an *aretaic* property of admirability and the vices as traits with a contrary trait of deplorability. Benevolence, courage, and the like are admirable, and to call them virtues just is to call them admirable.[45] According to Slote, a trait's being admirable does not mean the state of affairs of a person's having it is intrinsically good; he says his virtue ethics dispenses with claims about good states of affairs.[46] Nor does it mean the state is good for the person or contributes to his well-being. Slote retains the property of well-being but distinguishes it from admirability: what is most admirable in a person need not be best for him, and what is best for him need not be admirable. An aretaic theory can in principle unite the two properties, for example, by accepting the Stoic view that virtue is the only element in well-being. But Slote finds this view implausible for the same reason we found the lexical view implausible: a virtuous person who suffers intense pain is not well off but very badly off. His virtue contributes to his well-being, but not enough to outweigh his pain.[47]

Given these claims, a virtue ethics including the aretaic account is

44. See Sher, "Knowing about Virtue," p. 113 n. 7; and Sumner, "Is Virtue Its Own Reward?"

45. Slote, *From Morality to Virtue*, pp. 93–94; see also Zagzebski, *Virtues of the Mind*, pp. 78–83.

46. Slote, *From Morality to Virtue*, pp. 193–94.

47. Slote, *From Morality to Virtue*, pp. 211–17.

both more radical and less contentious than a flourishing-based theory. On the one side, the aretaic theory does make virtue its central property rather than deriving it from some more fundamental property such as flourishing. (In Slote's terminology, this makes it "agent-based" rather than merely "agent-focused.") On the other side, the aretaic theory does not claim that virtue has priority over other elements of a person's good. Since it does not assume egoism, it can allow that acting rightly sometimes involves sacrifice by the agent.

In other respects, however, the aretaic account shares features with a formal flourishing account. It, too, can easily yield a plausible list of individual virtues, stating that benevolence, courage, and the like are admirable, and can also make the desired claims about degrees—for example, that benevolently saving another's life is more admirable than temperately exercising. But these advantages come, again, at the cost of abandoning explanation. The aretaic account in Slote's *From Morality to Virtue* denies that there is any unifying feature that makes the virtues virtues; they are just the plural items on a list of admirable traits.[48] This is unsatisfying when a unifying explanation both seems called for intuitively and is provided by the recursive account. In later work, Slote explores versions of the aretaic account that do unify the virtues, by reducing them all to a single master virtue such as inner strength, universal benevolence, or particularistic caring.[49] But this approach, which seems to be the only one available to Slote, does not seem promising. How can the full range of virtues, including love of knowledge, control of anger, and justice, be included under the heading of, say, caring, without so stretching the latter that it loses its distinctive identity?

The aretaic account also has difficulty distinguishing the virtues from other goods. Slote says their being admirable distinguishes the virtues from states such as pleasure that contribute to well-being but are not admirable, but he does not claim that only the virtues are admirable. Personality traits such as wit and charm are not virtues but are admirable,[50] as, I would add, are knowledge and achievement. So how do the virtues differ from these other admirable states? Slote says the virtues are character traits, whereas wit and

---

48. Slote, *From Morality to Virtue*, pp. 130–33, 228, 230, 249.

49. See, e.g., Slote, "Agent-Based Virtue Ethics," pp. 246–58; and Baron, Pettit, and Slote, *Three Methods of Ethics*, pp. 216–29.

50. Slote, *From Morality to Virtue*, pp. 139–40, 198, 202, 256.

charm are personality traits. But what is the difference between the two, and why does it matter? (It will not do to say that character traits involve attitudes to other goods and evils, since that moves away from the aretaic and toward something like the recursive account.) And this difficulty leads to a further one about reasons for action. Slote claims that admirability is an intuitively higher property than pleasure,[51] which may imply that people have more reason to act virtuously than to pursue pleasure. But imagine that a person can tell a witty but malicious joke, and that it would be most virtuous not to tell the joke. If Slote's theory includes his virtue-ethical view of rightness, it will say it is right for her not to tell the joke. But what gives her most reason not to tell the joke? Why should she prefer most expressing admirable benevolence to most expressing admirable wit? Why, likewise, should she prefer most expressing admirable virtue to pursuing admirable knowledge? Slote may say that acting most virtuously is always more admirable than any alternative, but that claim needs defence. Without being strictly egoistic, it parallels the flourishing account's priority claim in holding that the state of a person who acts most virtuously is always preferable just as a state of him. And that type of claim, as in the flourishing account, is highly contentious.

One can even question whether admirability is a distinct moral property in the way the aretaic account assumes. I have proposed understanding moral goodness not as distinct from intrinsic goodness, but as the same property when had by certain objects, namely, attitudes evaluated in relation to their objects (see chapter 2, section 2). One can likewise hold that admirability is just ordinary goodness when had by objective or perfectionist states such as knowledge, achievement, and virtue. (Well-being can then be goodness when had by subjective states such as pleasure and desire fulfillment.) On this reductive view, to call the virtues admirable is not to distinguish them more than verbally from other goods; this makes the aretaic account essentially equivalent to a formal flourishing one and open to equivalent objections. But even if the reductive view is false and admirability is a distinct property, the aretaic account is in important respects similar to a formal flourishing one and faces similar objections about its explanatory failings and the claims it needs to yield strong enough reasons to act rightly.

---

51. Slote, *From Morality to Virtue*, p. 202.

3. *Virtue and Reasons*

The preceding two sections have raised two main difficulties for virtue-ethical theories that try to derive reasons to act rightly from virtue. These theories cannot give non-virtuous people any reason to act rightly; in addition, they can give virtuous people sufficiently strong reason to do so only by making implausible claims about the value of their virtue just as a state of them. But further difficulties would arise even if these first ones were overcome and the theories could complete their derivations. These difficulties, which apply equally to morality and rationality versions of virtue ethics, concern their claims, first, about the virtuous person's motivation and, second, about the ultimate source of his reasons.

A flourishing-based theory, to begin with that, says a person has reason to act rightly only or ultimately because doing so will contribute to her own flourishing. If she believes this theory and is motivated by its claims about the source of her reasons, her primary impetus for acting rightly will be a desire for her own flourishing. But this egoistic motivation is inconsistent with genuine virtue, which is not focused primarily on the self. Even an aretaic theory says a person has reason to act rightly only because doing so will express virtue on her part. But it is again not virtuous—it is morally self-indulgent—to act primarily from concern for one's own virtue. Someone motivated by the theory's claims about reasons will therefore be motivated not virtuously but in an unattractively self-indulgent way.

This is not in itself an objection to these theories. They can say that to flourish or express virtue, a person must act from genuinely virtuous motives, such as a desire for another's pleasure for its own sake. If she instead aims at her own flourishing or virtue, she does not act from the required motives and so does not achieve the flourishing or virtue that is her goal.[52] This requires the theories to be what Parfit calls *self-effacing*, telling agents not to be motivated by or even to think of their claims about the source of their reasons.[53] Self-effacingness is most commonly associated with consequentialist theories, which can tell people not to aim directly at the best outcomes because if they do they will not produce them. But it must likewise be a feature of virtue-ethical theories if they are not to encourage egoistic or self-indulgent motivation. Perhaps these theo-

---

52. See, e.g., Annas, *The Morality of Happiness*, pp. 118, 127–28, 224.
53. Parfit, *Reasons and Persons*, p. 24.

ries can allow people to reflect on their foundational claims about reasons "in a cool hour," when they are not acting; but when people do act, they must banish those claims from their mind.

There is a certain irony here. Some partisans of virtue ethics have been vocal critics of the self-effacingness of consequentialist theories and the "schizophrenia" it allegedly introduces into the moral agent's psychology. But their own theories have the same feature, if anything in a more disturbing way.[54] In consequentialist theories, the source of self-effacingness is a contingent psychological fact: that if people try to produce the best outcomes, they will not succeed. But a virtue-ethical theory must be non-contingently self-effacing. To avoid encouraging self-indulgence, it must say that being motivated by its claims about the source of one's reasons is in itself and necessarily objectionable. Is it not odd for a theory to so directly condemn its own practical influence?

Even apart from this difficulty, a virtue-ethical theory cannot explain why self-indulgence is objectionable; it simply states that it is, with no deeper explanation for this claim. This is characteristic of virtue ethics, which in its merely formal flourishing and aretaic versions simply states that certain traits are virtues, but it is again unsatisfying when an explanation is given by the recursive account. If that account includes the comparative principle defended in chapter 5, it says that a self-indulgent person cares more about the lesser good of his own virtue than about the greater good that is that virtue's object, which is disproportionate and a failing in virtue. This connects the critique of self-indulgence to wider claims about proportionality and gives it the deeper rationale that virtue ethics cannot.

And the position of virtue ethics is even worse: to even state that self-indulgence is a failing, it must deny the compelling claim that it is best to care more about what has greater value or rational importance. Imagine that one person is contemplating giving another person pleasure. According to the theories we have examined, the fact that the second person will enjoy pleasure is not itself of fundamental significance from the first person's point of view. Since it is not a state of her, it cannot contribute to her flourishing or be some-

---

54. For virtue-ethical critiques of self-effacingness, see Stocker, "The Schizophrenia of Modern Ethical Theories"; and Annas, *The Morality of Happiness*, pp. 234–35, 240–42, 299–301, 342. That Stocker's view is self-effacing is pointed out by Slote in *Morals from Motives*, chap. 2. That Annas's has the same feature is noted in Swanton, "Virtue Ethics and the Problem of Indirection," pp. 168–70; and McKerlie, "Aristotle and Egoism," pp. 534–35.

thing admirable in her. (This is clearest when the second person's pleasure is independent of the first's activity, but it is true even when it results from that person's activity.) What can have this significance is only her virtuously acting from a desire for the second person's pleasure, or at best her virtuously producing it (see chapter 4, section 3). In telling her to care more about the other's pleasure, therefore, a virtue-ethical theory tells her to care more about what by its lights has less significance, thereby denying what in chapter 3 I called the minimal claim about division. This claim says it is best to care more about what has greater value and, as I said there, seems intuitively undeniable. Yet to condemn self-indulgence, a virtue-ethical theory must deny the claim. Not only can this theory not explain why self-indulgence is a failing; to even state that it is, the theory must contradict an overwhelmingly plausible claim about the best divisions of virtuous concern.

A related difficulty concerns the *philosophical ground* virtue ethics gives for people's reasons to act rightly. If a person has most reason to benefit another, say, by giving her pleasure, what is the ultimate explanation of his having this reason? A flourishing-based theory says the explanation is self-regarding: that the action will make his own life better or more flourishing. But this is not, intuitively, the right explanation. The right explanation is that the action will make the other's life better. An aretaic theory likewise gives a self-regarding explanation, that the action will be something admirable on the agent's part, and this is, again, not the right explanation. Because they focus so centrally on the agent's virtue, virtue-ethical theories find the ultimate source of his reasons in himself, in what virtuous actions will mean for his flourishing or admirability. But, intuitively, many of his most important moral reasons come from outside him, from the good of others and how his actions will affect their lives. Annas seems to address this objection when she says that flourishing-based virtue ethics "does not imply that its forming part of my good is the *reason why* I should care about the good of others. I care about others for their own sake. Their good is part of my own final good. The second thought does not undermine the first."[55] But her

---

55. Annas, "The Good Life and the Good Lives of Others," p. 137; see also *The Morality of Happiness*, pp. 127–28, 224. Part of Annas's claim is that the good of others is "part of" the agent's good, but this is hard to understand if the agent's good must be a state of her, involving her activity. An agent's virtuously seeking another's pleasure can be part of her good, as can her successfully achieving it. But the other's pleasure itself, especially if it comes about independently of the agent's efforts, cannot.

response concerns only the virtuous person's motivations and not what is currently at issue: the philosophical source of his reasons for action. We are now granting that, if it is self-effacing, a virtue-ethical theory can require a person not to be motivated primarily by thoughts of his own virtue. Granting that, we are asking about the explanation the theory gives of his having reason to benefit others. The explanation is, in the end, that this will make his life better or more admirable, but that is, intuitively, not the right explanation. The right explanation is that it will make the other's life better. Of course, any reasons a person has must be his reasons and concern his actions. But this is a matter of the subject of his reasons and not their source, which is often, intuitively, something outside him. Virtue ethicists tacitly recognize this when they condemn moral self-indulgence and say the truly virtuous person is focused primarily on others' good. But they abandon this recognition when they ground his reasons for action in his own virtue or flourishing. This leads them to their contortions with self-effacingness and to denying that it is best to care most about what matters most. But none of these difficulties arise for the recursive account and moral theories containing it. Because these theories contain parallel derivations of virtue and rightness, they can, given the right comparative principle, hold that virtue is intrinsically good but not the primary source of a person's reasons. That source is the goods his virtue is directed at, goods whose status is independent of his virtue and that give that virtue its content. These theories can give the right explanation of his reasons to act rightly—that doing so will make others' lives better—and can condemn self-indulgence without being self-effacing. They can, in short, do what virtue ethics should do but cannot.

4. *Particularism and Anti-Theory*

To this point, I have examined virtue ethics as a moral theory, with the same systematic ambitions as consequentialist and deontological theories. It starts with foundational claims about flourishing or virtue and uses them to explain derivative claims about how people should act, all within an articulated moral structure. This fits the approach of many virtue ethicists, but there is a contrasting strand in the virtue-ethics literature that is non- and even anti-theoretical. Some writers emphasize the role in a virtuous person's thought of *moral perception*, an awareness of morally salient features of particular situations that they claim is not given due weight in theories that analyze moral reasoning solely in terms of general principles. More radically, some virtue ethicists reject the project of moral theory outright, holding that the moral life is entirely a matter of these particularized perceptions, with nothing systematic to be said either about the content of the virtuous person's thought or about what makes it virtuous. Let us consider these two views in turn.

The less radical view, ably defended by Lawrence Blum, holds that moral perception is needed at least as a supplement to reasoning about principles.[56] A person who accepts a principle condemning, say, any hurtful treatment of one person by another must be able to recognize both when a situation contains hurtful treatment— something that can be far from obvious—and what response to it would be most effective. Both these abilities require a sensitivity to the details of the situation that is not given just by his acceptance of the principle; he can know in the abstract that hurtfulness is wrong but be obtuse about when it is occurring or what might prevent it. It may seem that any theory containing general principles will mandate this type of perception, precisely because it is needed for morally right action. But the mandate, Blum and others say, is in two respects unsatisfactory. It makes moral perception only instrumentally good, or good as a means to right action, when it is in fact intrinsically good; and it restricts that perception's domain to action rather than granting it value even when it informs only feelings that cannot issue in action.[57]

This kind of perception is an undeniably important element in moral thought; if its role could be explained only by virtue-ethical views, that would be a significant advantage for them. But the importance of perception can also be explained by consequentialist and deontological theories that make claims about the intrinsic goodness of virtue, especially if those claims follow from the recursive account.

This account, first, assigns intrinsic value to many attitudes to particular features of situations. Imagine that a person wants to prevent a particular treatment of another because he sees that, in the situation, it will cause her pain. His hating this particular instrumental evil as a means is good not only instrumentally but also, given one of the instrumental principles discussed in chapter 1, intrinsically. A

---

56. Blum, "Moral Perception and Particularity."
57. Blum, "Moral Perception and Particularity," pp. 43, 54. See also Sherman, *The Fabric of Character,* pp. 28, 45–46; and Nussbaum, "The Discernment of Perception," pp. 92–93.

similar point holds if he hates something non-instrumentally related to her pain. Perhaps the treatment that causes her pain has another feature that, while not contributing to its hurtfulness, is regularly associated with it. If so, his hating this feature for that association is, by another relational principle, intrinsically good, as is his hating a particular effect of her pain, such as the particular grimace it causes on her face. The particularity of a situation consists in the particular elements it contains and the relations between them. Given its various relational principles, the recursive account assigns intrinsic value to many attitudes to these elements, and it does so not just when they issue in action but also when they cannot.

Second, the account explains the value of the moral perception that underlies all these attitudes. Someone who genuinely loves a good or hates an evil does not show his attitude only in his reactions when he notices the object is present; he does so also by looking actively for the object and for factors that bear on its presence. If he genuinely wants to prevent pain, for example, he is on the lookout for instances of pain and threats that may cause it, and he notices other features associated with pain, such as a suffering person's particular grimace. His interest in pain alerts him both to particular pains and to whatever is related to them. This is why, in chapter 4, cognitive states such as thoughtfulness, sensitivity, and prudence were counted as expressions of virtue and contrary states such as thoughtlessness as expressions of vice. If someone does not watch out for features of situations that bear on a given good, he shows that he is essentially indifferent to it. His indifference may not be as serious a vice as the callousness of someone who knows an action will destroy a good but performs it anyway, but it is still vicious to some degree. Many writers on moral perception claim that in it the emotions play a cognitive role, leading to and, more grandly, constituting particularized forms of knowledge.[58] The recursive account explains what is plausible in these claims in a non-mysterious way. Emotions and desires lead to knowledge because they make people want and try to learn morally significant facts; they focus their attention on the emotions' objects, which promotes knowledge both of those objects' instances and of factors related to them.

Finally, the account values moral perception not only when it is used to apply moral principles, but also when it is not. If the account

---

58. Sherman, *The Fabric of Character*, pp. 44–50; Nussbaum, "The Discernment of Perception," pp. 75–82; and Stocker, *Valuing Emotions*.

252 Virtue, Vice, and Value

values simple emotional attitudes as well as intellectualized ones (see chapter 6, section 2), it values particularized perception even when it does not involve thoughts about what is good or right. If someone has a simple emotional aversion to another's pain and because of that notices its particular causes and effects, she has the valuable form of moral perception even though the interest behind it is not explicitly moralized. So long as that interest is in some way virtuous, the awareness it leads to is virtuous as well.[59]

This is an attractive account of moral perception, but it stays within the bounds of moral theory. If it values someone's awareness of a particular feature of a situation, it is always because that feature is, or is related to, an instance of a more general value such as pain. Precisely this feature of the account will make it unacceptable to those who defend the more radical view about moral perception. They will say the objects of the virtuous person's awareness cannot be related to more general values or analyzed in any way; they consist in entirely particularized features of situations that can be identified only by virtuous people or as those such people are sensitive to.

This *anti-theoretical* view is sometimes combined with the promotion of "thick" moral concepts, such as Anscombe's concepts of the untruthful and the unjust. Unlike the "thin" concept of rightness, these have descriptive as well as evaluative criteria of application, so each applies only to some of the actions that are morally required. But some anti-theorists say the two aspects of their meaning cannot be prised apart; one cannot identify the descriptive criteria for, say, injustice without grasping that concept's evaluative point.[60] On this view, the point where theory breaks down is where the two halves of a thick concept meet. But an anti-theoretical view can equally well be formulated using just the thin concept of rightness, so that what a virtuous person perceives is always how the descriptive features of a situation combine to make some action right. The latter view is suggested by John McDowell, who, while insisting that the virtuous person's awareness cannot be codified, allows that it may always be expressed in the simple judgment that some action is "the thing to do."[61]

---

59. That moral perception can be independent of moral principles is emphasized in Blum, "Moral Perception and Particularity," p. 42.

60. See, e.g., Williams, *Ethics and the Limits of Philosophy*, pp. 129, 140–45. Anscombe makes some anti-theoretical claims about these concepts in "Modern Moral Philosophy," p. 41.

61. McDowell, "Virtue and Reason," p. 142.

Especially as formulated by McDowell, this anti-theoretical view is crucially different from the versions of virtue ethics discussed in previous sections. It does not derive a person's reasons to act rightly from his own virtue; on the contrary, it locates their source in features of his external situation that impose requirements on him, requirements that his virtue recognizes but does not give their force.[62] In this respect, the view is similar to the recursive account, which likewise equates virtue with a responsiveness to external factors that are the primary source of a person's reasons. But in other respects, the two views are diametrically opposed. McDowell claims that the objects of virtuous awareness cannot be identified independently of that awareness, but only as those a virtuous person perceives. By contrast, the recursive account is built on assuming that independence. Its basic structure assumes that we can identify pleasure, knowledge, and other base-level states as good independently of virtue and only then define the virtues as certain attitudes to them. What McDowell's view denies, therefore, the recursive account fundamentally assumes. More generally, for any anti-theoretical view, an account of virtue that uses recursive principles and (of all things) graphs will seem as misguided as it is possible to be.

What are the arguments for the anti-theoretical view? Some anti-theorists point to particular moral phenomena they say a theoretical approach cannot capture. For example, they note that in love and friendship we care about people's historical properties, such as their having been the unique individual who shared certain experiences with us,[63] or argue that certain pleasures, such as pleasures in fox hunting or in public executions, are not good but entirely evil.[64] But these examples do not at all undercut moral theory, since they involve instances of more general properties that can be shared across people or pleasures and that a sophisticated moral theory can give weight. If the theory contains agent-relativities, it can say that everyone should care especially about people who have participated with them in a certain kind of history, which I have suggested is one of jointly doing good or suffering evil; if the theory allows conditionalities, it can say that all pleasures with a certain kind of object— a pain or, more generally, an evil—lack value as pleasures. And these

---

62. McDowell, "Are Moral Requirements Hypothetical Imperatives?" p. 14.
63. Nussbaum, "The Discernment of Perception," p. 72.
64. Dancy, *Moral Reasons*, p. 61.

more general claims are illuminating. Far from telling against moral theory, the examples only underscore its necessity and explanatory power.

This leaves more abstract anti-theoretical arguments such as McDowell's that the objects of virtuous awareness cannot be identified independently of that awareness. There are many particular objections to this argument. It seems to imply that people cannot successfully counterfeit virtuous behaviour, as hypocrites and con artists regularly do. It also, like Aristotle's doctrine of the mean, excludes the possibility of the worst vices—those pure vices such as malice that involve contrary attitudes to the very same objects as the virtues. If vicious people do not perceive the same objects as virtuous ones, how can they have opposed attitudes to them? And the argument seems obviously mistaken about some examples. If a virtuous person prevents a painful injury to a stranger, of whose particular characteristics he knows nothing, how can he be responding to anything in the situation other than the general fact of pain, and why can that fact not be equally well detected by a non-virtuous person? But the most persuasive answer to an abstract anti-theoretical argument such as McDowell's is the successful construction of a theory. For this reason, this book's main response to the anti-theoretical strand in virtue ethics is its positive development of a recursive account of virtue and vice. This account acknowledges the plurality of moral considerations and of virtuous responses to them that anti-theorists are right to start by insisting on. But it is not passive in the face of this plurality; it penetrates beneath it to find an underlying unity, especially on the side of virtue, and in so doing counters the claim that no such unity exists. It makes the separation McDowell says is impossible and uses it to give more illuminating analyses of the individual virtues than an anti-theoretical view can. Consider the virtue of courage. The recursive account analyzes this virtue as involving a willingness to risk one's safety or comfort for another, greater good, either because one prefers this good from the start or because one makes oneself do so by self-control. And the account uses this analysis to contrast courage both with cowardice, which involves preferring one's safety to a much greater good, and with foolhardiness, which involves sacrificing it for a lesser good that does not merit this treatment. But an anti-theoretical view can give no comparable analysis. It can say only that if a courageous person risks his safety, it is because he perceives in an ineffable way that doing so is in his situation required; if his behaviour differs from foolhardiness, it is only in a way that cannot be described apart from his particularized perceptions. The anti-theoretical view here fails to explain something that can and should be explained, but this only becomes fully evident when we have a completed theoretical account, like the recursive account, from which the relevant explanation follows.

A point analogous to this one about the anti-theoretical view applies to virtue ethics as a whole. This book's main response to virtue ethics is not the particular difficulties raised in this chapter, but the whole development of a superior account of virtue in chapters 1 through 7. As I have argued, this account does a better job than virtue ethics of unifying the virtues and explaining what makes them virtues. It also does a better job of explaining the place of virtue in moral thought, making it at once intrinsically but only derivatively good and not the primary source of a person's reasons. His primary reason to help others is not that this will make his own life better or more admirable, but that it will improve theirs. Finally, the account achieves these aims within a familiar moral structure. Much recent writing has assumed that the importance of virtue cannot be captured in a consequentialist or deontological framework and therefore calls for a "third method of ethics." This is the type of claim philosophers like to make: that previous work not only has neglected some phenomenon but has been totally misguided in its approach. The claim is often overblown, however, and I have tried to show that it is so in this case. It is not true that virtue cannot be properly understood within a traditional moral structure; it can. And it can be better understood there than if virtue is somehow made the centre of moral thought.

Bibliography

Adams, Robert M. "Involuntary Sins." *Philosophical Review* 94 (1985): 3–31.

Annas, Julia. "The Good Life and the Good Lives of Others." *Social Philosophy and Policy* 9, no. 2 (1992): 133–48.

———. *The Morality of Happiness*. New York: Oxford University Press, 1993.

Anscombe, G. E. M. *Intention*. 2d ed. Oxford: Basil Blackwell, 1976.

———. "Modern Moral Philosophy." In *Virtue Ethics,* edited by Roger Crisp and Michael Slote. Oxford: Oxford University Press, 1997.

Aquinas, St. Thomas. *Summa Theologica*. Translated by the Fathers of the English Dominican Province. 4 vols. Westminster, Md.: Christian Classics, 1981.

Arendt, Hannah. *Eichmann in Jerusalem*. Harmondsworth: Penguin, 1963.

Aristotle. *Metaphysics*. Translated by W. D. Ross. In *The Complete Works of Aristotle,* edited by Jonathan Barnes. 2 vols. Princeton, N.J.: Princeton University Press, 1984.

———. *Nicomachean Ethics*. Translated by W. D. Ross and J. O. Urmson. In *The Complete Works of Aristotle,* edited by Jonathan Barnes. 2 vols. Princeton, N.J.: Princeton University Press, 1984.

———. *Politics*. Translated by B. Jowett. In *The Complete Works of Aristotle,* edited by Jonathan Barnes. 2 vols. Princeton, N.J.: Princeton University Press, 1984.

Audi, Robert. "Intrinsic Value and Moral Obligation." *Southern Journal of Philosophy* 35 (1997): 135–54.

Austen, Jane. *Pride and Prejudice*. Oxford: Oxford University Press, n.d.

Baier, Annette C. "Moralism and Cruelty." *Ethics* 103 (1993): 436–57.

Baron, Marcia. "The Alleged Moral Repugnance of Acting from Duty." *Journal of Philosophy* 81 (1984): 197–220.

———. "Remorse and Agent-Regret." In *Midwest Studies in Philosophy,* vol. 13, *Ethical Theory: Character and Virtue,* edited by Peter A. French, Theodore E. Uehling, Jr., and Howard K. Wettstein. Notre Dame, Ind.: University of Notre Dame Press, 1988.

Baron, Marcia W., Philip Pettit, and Michael Slote. *Three Methods of Ethics*. Oxford: Blackwell, 1997.

Beardsley, Elizabeth L. "Moral Worth and Moral Credit." *Philosophical Review* 66 (1957): 304–28.

Bennett, Jonathan. "The Conscience of Huckleberry Finn." *Philosophy* 49 (1974): 123–34.

Bentham, Jeremy. *Introduction to the Principles of Morals and Legislation.* Edited by J. H. Burns and H. L. A. Hart. London: Methuen, 1970.

Blum, Lawrence A. "Compassion." In *Moral Perception and Particularity.* Cambridge: Cambridge University Press, 1994.

———. *Friendship, Altruism, and Morality.* London: Routledge & Kegan Paul, 1980.

———. "Moral Perception and Particularity." In *Moral Perception and Particularity.* Cambridge: Cambridge University Press, 1994.

Brandt, R. B. *Ethical Theory.* Englewood Cliffs, N.J.: Prentice-Hall, 1959.

Brentano, Franz. *The Origin of Our Knowledge of Right and Wrong.* Translated by Roderick M. Chisholm and Elizabeth Schneewind. London: Routledge & Kegan Paul, 1969.

Brink, David O. *Moral Realism and the Foundations of Ethics.* Cambridge: Cambridge University Press, 1989.

Broad, C. D. *Five Types of Ethical Theory.* London: Routledge & Kegan Paul, 1930.

Broadie, Sarah. "Aristotle's Elusive *Summum Bonum.*" *Social Philosophy and Policy* 16, no. 1 (Winter 1999): 233–51.

Brody, Baruch. "The Role of Private Philanthropy in a Free and Democratic State." *Social Philosophy and Policy* 4, no. 2 (1987): 79–92.

Burke, Edmund. *Reflections on the Revolution in France.* Edited by J. G. A. Pocock. Indianapolis: Hackett, 1987.

Campbell, John. "Can Philosophical Accounts of Altruism Accommodate Experimental Data on Helping Behaviour?" *Australasian Journal of Philosophy* 77 (1999): 26–45.

Carson, Thomas L. "Happiness, Contentment, and the Good Life." *Pacific Philosophical Quarterly* 62 (1981): 378-92.

Cartlege, Sue, and Joanne Ryan, eds. *Sensual Uncertainty in Sex and Love: New Thoughts on Old Contradictions.* London: Women's Press, 1983.

Cherry, Christopher. "The Inward and the Outward: Fantasy, Reality and Satisfaction." *Canadian Journal of Philosophy, Supplementary Volume 11: New Essays in Philosophy of Mind,* series 2 (1985): 175–93.

Chisholm, Roderick M. *Brentano and Intrinsic Value.* Cambridge: Cambridge University Press, 1986.

———. "Brentano's Theory of Correct and Incorrect Emotion." *Revue interationale de philosophie* 20 (1966): 395–415.

———. "The Defeat of Good and Evil." *Proceedings of the American Philosophical Association* 42 (1968–69): 21–38.

Crisp, Roger. "Modern Moral Philosophy and the Virtues." In *How Should One Live? Essays on the Virtues,* edited by Roger Crisp. Oxford: Clarendon Press, 1996.

Dancy, Jonathan. *Moral Reasons.* Oxford: Blackwell, 1993.

Davis, Nancy. "Abortion and Self-Defense." *Philosophy and Public Affairs* 13 (1984): 175–207.

Descartes, René. *The Passions of the Soul.* Translated by E. S. Haldane and G. R. T. Ross. In *The Philosophical Works of Descartes.* 2 vols. Cambridge: Cambridge University Press, 1911.

de Sousa, Ronald. "The Good and the True." *Mind* 83 (1974): 534-51.

———. *The Rationality of Emotion.* Cambridge, Mass.: MIT Press, 1990.

Driver, Julia. "The Virtues and Human Nature." In *How Should One Live? Essays on the Virtues,* edited by Roger Crisp. Oxford: Clarendon Press, 1996.

———. "The Virtues of Ignorance." *Journal of Philosophy* 86 (1989): 373–84.

Dworkin, Ronald. "Foundations of Liberal Equality." In *Equal Freedom*, edited by Stephen Darwall. Ann Arbor, Mich.: University of Michigan Press, 1995.

Ewing, A. C. *Value and Reality*. London: George Allen & Unwin, 1973.

Feldman, Fred. *Doing the Best We Can*. Dordrecht: Reidel, 1986.

Flanagan, Owen. "Virtue and Ignorance." *Journal of Philosophy* 87 (1990): 420–28.

Fletcher, George P. *Loyalty: An Essay on the Morality of Relationships*. New York: Oxford University Press, 1993.

Foot, Philippa. "Virtues and Vices." In *Virtue Ethics*, edited by Roger Crisp and Michael Slote. Oxford: Oxford University Press, 1997.

Frankena, William K. *Ethics*. 2d ed. Englewood Cliffs, N.J.: Prentice-Hall, 1973.

Friedman, Milton, and Rose Friedman. *Free to Choose*. Harmondsworth: Penguin, 1980.

Garcia, J. L. A. "Goods and Evils." *Philosophy and Phenomenological Research* 47 (1987): 385–412.

———. "The Primacy of the Virtuous." *Philosophia* 20 (1990): 69–91.

Gauthier, David. *Morals by Agreement*. Oxford: Clarendon Press, 1986.

Greenspan, Patricia S. *Emotions and Reasons: An Inquiry into Emotional Justification*. New York: Routledge, 1988.

Griffin, James. *Well-Being: Its Meaning, Measurement, and Moral Importance*. Oxford: Clarendon Press, 1986.

Grisez, Germain. *The Way of the Lord Jesus: A Summary of Catholic Moral Theology*. 3 vols. Chicago: Franciscan Herald Press, 1983.

Harman, Gilbert. "Moral Philosophy Meets Social Psychology: Virtue Ethics and the Fundamental Attribution Error." *Proceedings of the Aristotelian Society* 99 (1999): 315–31.

———. "Practical Reasoning." *Review of Metaphysics* 29 (1976): 431–63.

Henson, Richard G. "What Kant Might Have Said: Moral Worth and the Overdetermination of Dutiful Action." *Philosophical Review* 88 (1979): 304–28.

Herman, Barbara. "On the Value of Acting from the Motive of Duty." *Philosophical Review* 90 (1981): 359–82.

Hick, John. *Evil and the God of Love*. 2d ed. London: Macmillan, 1977.

Hume, David. *An Enquiry Concerning the Principle of Morals*. In *Enquiries Concerning the Human Understanding and Concerning the Principles of Morals*. 2d ed., edited by L. A. Selby-Bigge. Oxford: Clarendon Press, 1962.

Hurka, Thomas. "The Justification of National Partiality." In *The Morality of Nationalism*, edited by Robert McKim and Jeff McMahan. New York: Oxford University Press, 1997.

———. "Monism, Pluralism, and Rational Regret." *Ethics* 106 (1996): 555–75.

———. *Perfectionism*. New York: Oxford University Press, 1993.

———. "Two Kinds of Organic Unity." *Journal of Ethics* 2 (1998): 299–320.

Hursthouse, Rosalind. "Normative Virtue Ethics." In *How Should One Live? Essays on the Virtues*, edited by Roger Crisp. Oxford: Clarendon Press, 1996.

———. "Virtue Theory and Abortion." In *Virtue Ethics*, edited by Roger Crisp and Michael Slote. Oxford: Oxford University Press, 1997.

Ignatieff, Michael. *The Needs of Strangers*. London: Chatto & Windus, 1984.

Irwin, T. H. *Aristotle's First Principles*. Oxford: Clarendon Press, 1988.

———. "Generosity and Property in Aristotle's *Politics*." *Social Philosophy and Policy* 4, no. 2 (1987): 37–54.

Kagan, Shelly. "Equality and Desert." In *What Do We Deserve? A Reader on Justice and*

Desert, edited by Louis P. Pojman and Owen McLeod. New York: Oxford University Press, 1999.

———. *The Limits of Morality.* Oxford: Clarendon Press, 1989.

———. "The Limits of Well-Being." *Social Philosophy and Policy* 9, no. 2 (1992): 169–89.

———. *Normative Ethics.* Boulder, Colo.: Westview Press, 1998.

———. "Rethinking Intrinsic Value." *Journal of Ethics* 2 (1998): 277–97.

Kahneman, Daniel, and Dale T. Miller. "Norm Theory: Comparing Reality to Its Alternatives." *Psychological Review* 93 (1986): 136–53.

Kahneman, Daniel, and Amos Tversky. "The Psychology of Preferences." *Scientific American* 246 (1982): 160–73.

Kamm, F. M. "The Noble Warrior: Feminism, Contractarianism, and Self in the Light of Hampton." *Philosophical Studies* 89 (1998): 237–58.

Kant, Immanuel. *Foundations of the Metaphysics of Morals.* Translated by Lewis White Beck. Indianapolis: Bobbs-Merrill, 1959.

Kekes, John. "Cruelty and Liberalism." *Ethics* 106 (1996): 834–44.

———. *Facing Evil.* Princeton, N.J.: Princeton University Press, 1990.

———. *The Morality of Pluralism.* Princeton, N.J.: Princeton University Press, 1993.

Korsgaard, Christine M. "Two Distinctions in Goodness." *Philosophical Review* 92 (1983): 169–95.

Kundera, Milan. *The Unbearable Lightness of Being.* Translated by Michael Henry Heim. New York: Harper & Row, 1984.

Kupperman, Joel J. *Character.* New York: Oxford University Press, 1991.

Kymlicka, Will. *Contemporary Political Philosophy.* Oxford: Clarendon Press, 1990.

Landman, Janet. *Regret: The Persistence of the Possible.* New York: Oxford University Press, 1993.

Lemos, Noah M. "High-Minded Egoism and the Problem of Priggishness." *Mind* 93 (1984): 542–58.

———. *Intrinsic Value: Concept and Warrant.* Cambridge: Cambridge University Press, 1994.

Leopold, Aldo. *A Sand County Almanac.* Oxford: Oxford University Press, 1968.

Lewis, David. *Counterfactuals.* Oxford: Blackwell, 1973.

Lomasky, Loren E. *Persons, Rights, and the Moral Community.* New York: Oxford University Press, 1987.

Louden, Robert B. "On Some Vices of Virtue Ethics." In *Virtue Ethics,* edited by Roger Crisp and Michael Slote. Oxford: Oxford University Press, 1997.

MacIntyre, Alasdair. *After Virtue: A Study in Moral Theory.* London: Duckworth, 1981.

Maclagan, W. G. "How Important Is Moral Goodness?" *Mind* 64 (1955): 213–25.

Martin, Mike W. *Virtuous Giving: Philanthropy, Voluntary Service, and Caring.* Bloomington: Indiana University Press, 1994.

Martineau, James. *Types of Ethical Theory.* 3d ed. 2 vols. Oxford: Clarendon Press, 1889.

Mayerfeld, Jamie. "The Moral Asymmetry of Happiness and Suffering." *Southern Journal of Philosophy* 34 (1996): 317–38.

McDowell, John. "Are Moral Requirements Hypothetical Imperatives?" *Proceedings of the Aristotelian Society,* supp. vol. 52 (1978): 13–29.

———. "The Role of *Eudaimonia* in Aristotle's Ethics." In *Essays on Aristotle's Ethics,* edited by A. O. Rorty. Berkeley: University of California Press, 1980.

————. "Virtue and Reason." In *Virtue Ethics,* edited by Roger Crisp and Michael Slote. Oxford: Oxford University Press, 1997.

McKerlie, Dennis. "Aristotle and Egoism." *Southern Journal of Philosophy* 36 (1998): 531–55.

McKinnon, Christine. *Character, Virtue Theories, and the Vices.* Peterborough, Ont.: Broadview Press, 1999.

McNaughton, David. *Moral Vision.* Oxford: Blackwell, 1988.

McTaggart, J. M. E. The *Nature of Existence.* 2 vols. Cambridge: Cambridge University Press, 1921.

Midgley, Mary. *Wickedness: A Philosophical Essay.* London: Routledge & Kegan Paul, 1983.

Mill, John Stuart. "Sedgwick's Discourse." In *Essays on Ethics, Religion, and Society,* edited by J. M. Robson. Vol. 10 of *Collected Works of John Stuart Mill.* Toronto: University of Toronto Press, 1969.

————. *Utilitarianism.* In *Essays on Ethics, Religion, and Society,* edited by J. M. Robson. Vol. 10 of *Collected Works of John Stuart Mill.* Toronto: University of Toronto Press, 1969.

Milo, Ronald D. *Immorality.* Princeton, N.J.: Princeton University Press, 1984.

Montmarquet, James A. "An Asymmetry Concerning Virtue and Vice." *Canadian Journal of Philosophy* 28 (1998): 149–59.

Moore, G. E. "The Conception of Intrinsic Value." In *Philosophical Studies.* London: Routledge & Kegan Paul, 1922.

————. *Ethics.* London: Oxford University Press, 1912.

————. *Principia Ethica.* Cambridge: Cambridge University Press, 1903.

Nagel, Thomas. *The View from Nowhere.* New York: Oxford University Press, 1986.

Newman, John Henry. *Certain Difficulties Felt by Anglicans in Catholic Teaching.* 2 vols. London: Longmans, 1900.

Noddings, Nel. *Caring: A Feminine Approach to Ethics and Moral Education.* Berkeley: University of California Press, 1984.

Nowell-Smith, P. H. *Ethics.* Harmondsworth: Penguin, 1954.

Nozick, Robert. *Anarchy, State, and Utopia.* Basic Books, 1974.

————. *The Examined Life.* New York: Simon and Schuster, 1989.

————. *Philosophical Explanations.* Cambridge, Mass.: Harvard University Press, 1981.

Nussbaum, Martha C. "The Discernment of Perception: An Aristotelian Conception of Private and Public Rationality." In *Love's Knowledge: Essays on Philosophy and Literature.* New York: Oxford University Press, 1990.

————. *The Fragility of Goodness.* Cambridge: Cambridge University Press, 1984.

Oakley, Justin. Morality and the Emotions. London: Routledge, 1992.

————. "Varieties of Virtue Ethics." *Ratio* 9 (1996): 128–52.

Oldenquist, Andrew. "Loyalties." *Journal of Philosophy* 49 (1982): 173–94.

Parfit, Derek. *Reasons and Persons.* Oxford: Clarendon Press, 1984.

Plato. *Protagoras.* Translated by W. K. C. Guthrie. In *The Collected Dialogues of Plato,* edited by Edith Hamilton and Huntington Cairns. Princeton, N.J.: Bollinger, 1961.

————. *Republic.* Translated by G. M. A. Grube. Indianapolis: Hackett, 1974.

Rashdall, Hastings. "Professor Sidgwick's Utilitarianism." *Mind,* o.s. 10 (1885): 200–226.

————. *The Theory of Good and Evil.* 2 vols. London: Oxford University Press, 1907.

Regan, Donald H. "Against Evaluator Relativity: A Response to Sen." *Philosophy and Public Affairs* 12 (1983): 93–112.

Richards, Norvin. "Is Humility a Virtue?" *American Philosophical Quarterly* 25 (1988): 253–60.

Roberts, Robert C. "Will Power and the Virtues." *Philosophical Review* 93 (1984): 227–47.

Rorty, Richard. *Contingency, Irony, and Solidarity.* Cambridge: Cambridge University Press, 1989.

Ross, Lee, and Richard E. Nisbett. *The Person and the Situation: Perspectives of Social Psychology.* New York: McGraw-Hill, 1991.

Ross, W. D. *Aristotle.* London: Methuen, 1949.

————. *The Foundations of Ethics.* Oxford: Clarendon Press, 1939.

————. *The Right and the Good.* Oxford: Clarendon Press, 1930.

Rothbard, Murray. *Power and Market: Government and the Economy.* Menlo Park, Calif.: Institute for Humane Studies, 1970.

Sankowski, Edward. "Responsibility of Persons for Their Emotions." *Canadian Journal of Philosophy* 7 (1977): 829–40.

Scheffler, Samuel. *The Rejection of Consequentialism: A Philosophical Examination of the Considerations Underlying Rival Moral Conceptions.* Oxford: Clarendon Press, 1982.

Schneewind, Jerome B. "The Misfortunes of Virtue." In *Virtue Ethics,* edited by Roger Crisp and Michael Slote. Oxford: Oxford University Press, 1997.

Schopenhauer, Arthur. *On the Basis of Morality.* Translated by E. J. Payne. Providence, R.I.: Berghahn, 1995.

Schueler, G. F. "Why Modesty Is a Virtue." *Ethics* 107 (1997): 467–85.

Searle, John R. *Intentionality: An Essay in the Philosophy of Mind.* Cambridge: Cambridge University Press, 1983.

Sen, Amartya. "Rights and Agency." *Philosophy and Public Affairs* 11 (1982): 93–112.

Sher, George. "Knowing about Virtue." In *NOMOS 34: Virtue,* edited by John W. Chapman and William A. Galston. New York: New York University Press, 1992.

Sherman, Nancy. "Common Sense and Uncommon Virtue." In *Midwest Studies in Philosophy,* vol. 12, *Ethical Theory: Character and Virtue,* edited by Peter A. French, Theodore E. Uehling, Jr., and Howard K. Wettstein. Notre Dame, Ind.: University of Notre Dame Press, 1988.

————. *The Fabric of Character: Aristotle's Theory of Virtue.* Oxford: Clarendon Press, 1989.

————. *Making a Necessity of Virtue: Aristotle and Kant on Virtue.* Cambridge: Cambridge University Press, 1997.

Shklar, Judith N. "The Liberalism of Fear." In *Liberalism and the Moral Life,* edited by Nancy L. Rosenblum. Cambridge, Mass.: Harvard University Press, 1989.

————. *Ordinary Vices.* Cambridge, Mass.: Harvard University Press, 1984.

Sidgwick, Henry. *Lectures on the Ethics of T. H. Green, Mr. Herbert Spencer, and J. Martineau.* London: Macmillan, 1902.

————. *The Methods of Ethics.* 7th ed. London: Macmillan, 1907.

Slote, Michael. "Agent-Based Virtue Ethics." In *Virtue Ethics,* edited by Roger Crisp and Michael Slote. Oxford: Oxford University Press, 1997.

————. *Common-Sense Morality and Consequentialism.* London: Routledge & Kegan Paul, 1985.

————. *From Morality to Virtue.* New York: Oxford University Press, 1992.

————. *Morals from Motives*. New York: Oxford University Press, forthcoming.

————. "The Virtue in Self-Interest." *Social Philosophy and Policy* 14, no. 1 (Winter 1997): 264–85.

Smith, Holly M. "Varieties of Moral Worth and Moral Credit." *Ethics* 101 (1991): 279–303.

Solomon, Robert C. "The Virtues of a Passionate Life: Erotic Love and 'the Will to Power.'" *Social Philosophy and Policy* 15, no. 2 (1998): 91–118.

Stocker, Michael. "Agent and Other: Against Ethical Univeralism." *Australasian Journal of Philosophy* 54 (1976): 206–20.

————. "Emotional Thoughts." *American Philosophical Quarterly* 24 (1987): 59–69.

————. *Plural and Conflicting Values*. Oxford: Clarendon Press, 1990.

————. "The Schizophrenia of Modern Ethical Theories." In *Virtue Ethics*, edited by Roger Crisp and Michael Slote. Oxford: Oxford University Press, 1997.

Stocker, Michael (with Elizabeth Hegeman). *Valuing Emotions*. Cambridge: Cambridge University Press, 1996.

Suits, Bernard. *The Grasshopper: Games, Life, and Utopia*. Toronto: University of Toronto Press, 1978.

Sumner, L. W. "Is Virtue Its Own Reward?" *Social Philosophy and Policy* 15, no. 1 (1998): 18–36.

————. *Welfare, Happiness, and Ethics*. Oxford: Clarendon Press, 1996.

Swanton, Christine. "Profiles of the Virtues." *Pacific Philosophical Quarterly* 76 (1995): 47–72.

————. "Satisficing and Virtue." *Journal of Philosophy* 90 (1993): 33–48.

————. "Virtue Ethics and the Problem of Indirection: A Pluralistic Value-Centred Approach." *Utilitas* 9 (1997): 167–81.

Tawney, R. H. *Equality*. London: George Allen & Unwin, 1964.

Taylor, Charles. *Multiculturalism and "The Politics of Recognition."* Edited by Amy Gutmann. Princeton, N.J.: Princeton University Press, 1992.

Taylor, Gabriele. "Envy and Jealousy: Emotions and Vices." In *Midwest Studies in Philosophy*, vol. 13, *Ethical Theory: Character and Virtue*, edited by Peter A. French, Theodore E. Uehling, Jr., and Howard K. Wettstein. Notre Dame, Ind.: University of Notre Dame Press, 1988.

————. *Pride, Shame, and Guilt: Emotions of Self-Assessment*. Oxford: Clarendon Press, 1985.

Thomson, Judith Jarvis. "On Some Ways in Which a Thing Can Be Good." *Social Philosophy and Policy* 9, no. 2 (1992): 96–117.

Titmuss, Richard M. *The Gift Relationship: From Human Blood to Social Policy*. New York: Vintage, 1972.

Trianosky, Gregory W. "Rightly Ordered Appetites: How to Live Morally and Live Well." *American Philosophical Quarterly* 25 (1988): 1–12.

Tyler, Anne. *Breathing Lessons*. New York: Knopf, 1988.

Wallace, James D. *Virtues and Vices*. Ithaca, N.Y.: Cornell University Press, 1978.

Watson, Gary. "On the Primacy of Character." In *Identity, Character, and Morality: Essays in Moral Psychology*, edited by Owen Flanagan and Amelie Oksenberg. Cambridge, Mass.: MIT Press, 1990.

Wiggins, David. "Weakness of Will, Commensurability, and the Objects of Deliberation and Desire." In *Essays on Aristotle's Ethics*, edited by A. O. Rorty. Berkeley: University of California Press, 1980.

Williams, Bernard. "Ethical Consistency." In *Problems of the Self.* Cambridge: Cambridge University Press, 1973.

——. *Ethics and the Limits of Philosophy.* Cambridge, Mass.: Harvard University Press, 1985.

——. "Imagination and the Self." In *Problems of the Self.* Cambridge: Cambridge University Press, 1973.

——. "Justice as a Virtue." In *Essays on Aristotle's Ethics,* edited by A. O. Rorty. Berkeley: University of California Press, 1980.

——. "Moral Luck." In *Moral Luck.* Cambridge: Cambridge University Press, 1981.

——. "Persons, Character, and Morality." In *Moral Luck.* Cambridge: Cambridge University Press, 1981.

——. *Shame and Necessity.* Berkeley: University of California Press, 1993.

——. "Utilitarianism and Moral Self-Indulgence." In *Moral Luck.* Cambridge: Cambridge University Press, 1981.

Wolf, Susan. "Happiness and Meaning: Two Aspects of the Good Life." *Social Philosophy and Policy* 14, no. 1 (1997): 207–25.

Wollheim, Richard. *The Thread of Life.* Cambridge: Cambridge University Press, 1984.

Zagzebski, Linda Trinkaus. *Virtues of the Mind: An Inquiry into the Nature of Virtue and the Ethical Foundations of Knowledge.* Cambridge: Cambridge University Press, 1996.

Zimmerman, Michael J. "On the Intrinsic Value of States of Pleasure." *Philosophy and Phenomenological Research* 41 (1980–81): 26–45.

Index